Northern Ireland
A Triumph of Politics

Interviews and Analysis 1988–2008

FRANK MILLAR

IRISH ACADEMIC PRESS
DUBLIN • PORTLAND, OR

First published in 2009 by Irish Academic Press

44 Northumberland Road,
Ballsbridge,
Dublin 4, Ireland

920 NE 58th Avenue, Suite 300
Portland, Oregon,
97213-3786, USA

www.iap.ie

British Library Cataloguing in Publication Data
An entry can be found on request

978 0 7165 3001 5 (cloth)
978 0 7165 3002 2 (paper)

Library of Congress Cataloging-in-Publication Data
An entry can be found on request

Printed by Biddles Ltd., King's Lynn, Norfolk

Contents

Acknowledgements and Author's Note

It was Marigold Johnson, the dynamic organising force behind the British Irish Association, who first suggested that some of the original series of *Irish Times* interviews featured here would make a book. Old friends such as Paul (Lord) Bew and Ambassador Sean O hUiginn also encouraged the view that such a publication would make a useful tool for future students of a truly remarkable period in Northern Ireland politics. I had some reservations about the journalist recycling previously published work. However, any doubts were dispelled by the commitment and enthusiasm of my editor at Irish Academic Press, the excellent Lisa Hyde. Moreover, the journalism featured here is of the kind I most enjoy, the set-piece interview allowing the subject to be heard – while hopefully discovering and learning, and informing the public debate in the process.

I will always be grateful to the editor of *The Irish Times*, Geraldine Kennedy, and to her predecessor Conor Brady, for giving me the opportunity to do so. It is salutary to recall that Conor's original idea back in 1988 was to have the newspaper fill a 'political vacuum' already of such duration as to convince many that Northern Ireland was a problem beyond solution. During Geraldine's editorship, likewise, there were periods of intransigence and gloom when hope and the suggestion that a breakthrough was still possible struck many as positively perverse. Both of them were driven by the strong personal conviction that this unresolved 'national question' could not be ignored; by the desire to reach out, increase understanding and encourage dialogue where there was none; and by the uncompromising belief that future generations in Northern Ireland demanded and deserved release from a violent and divided past. However, while they may have made *The Irish Times* 'the house journal' of the talks process, neither Geraldine nor Conor did so under any illusion that this was a story that sold newspapers. That, I think, only adds to their great credit.

The road travelled here begins with a drive to Pat and John Hume's Donegal retreat a couple of days after Christmas 1988, and an incident that spoke volumes in its own way for the challenge facing all the North's politicians. Stopping at the police road-check outside Derry I asked the armed RUC officer for directions once I had crossed the border. 'I can't help you, I'm afraid,' he replied cheerfully. 'I've never been over there.' I could hardly have imagined that the interview conducted that day would so inform a book twenty years later which, courtesy of the Belfast and St Andrews Agreements, would celebrate a triumph of politics and a dynamic new set of relationships within Northern Ireland, between Northern Ireland and the Republic and between the Irish and British peoples of these islands.

My warm thanks then to all the politicians – plus the Churchman and the diplomat – who went on-the-record, and specifically to those featured in this necessarily limited selection: Gerry Adams, Bertie Ahern, Dermot Ahern, Tony Blair, Peter Brooke, Cardinal Cahal Daly, Jeffrey Donaldson, Peter Hain, John Hume, Seamus Mallon, Ian Paisley, Chris Patten, Ambassador Mitchell Reiss, Peter Robinson, John Taylor and David Trimble.

I have been helped and sustained over the years by many political and official sources and by the camaraderie of journalistic colleagues too many to mention here. Most in any event would probably wish to remain anonymous – but they know who they are and they have my gratitude and respect. In the context of this work, however, I must thank some of those who have been crucial in making things happen. I always enjoy dealing with Richard McAuley, Gerry Adams' key aide, even when he has officially (or even unofficially) nothing to say. Richard is invariably cheerful and welcoming, and I am always grateful to him for stretching already hectic schedules and timetables to help me keep mine. Likewise Ian Paisley Jnr, though a politician in his own right, was always available and enthusiastic and true to his word in all his dealings with me on his father's behalf. Even after he graduated from the Northern Ireland Office to become Tony Blair's official spokesman, Tom Kelly was always generous with his time and delivered for me big time, and on more than one occasion. The same must be said of Dermot Gallagher, the Secretary General of the Department of Foreign Affairs in Dublin, who has done me many favours and kindnesses over long years of friendship. While many can now justifiably claim their share of the credit for the new dispensation, our mutual friend the late Harold McCusker would gladly have testified that Dermot was one of the earliest modernisers.

Thanks are due to Aonghus Meaney, copy editor, for making the process so painless, to the staff of *The Irish Times* library, and to my daughter Catherine who is a whizz on the keyboard and whose interventions prevented meltdown at several critical moments. However, it is no exaggeration to say that this work might never have materialised – and certainly that its production would have been infinitely more difficult, time consuming and challenging – without the assistance of the brilliant Mick Crowley from *The Irish Times* editorial systems department in Dublin. Mick initially volunteered to retrieve some of the older articles and promptly found himself landed with the role of unpaid researcher, working particular magic to transform some of the early archive material into digital form. I am hugely in his debt.

My thanks, too, to Dr Steven King, Jonathan Caine, Bernard Purcell and Peter Smith QC for reading the manuscript, for their wise advice, and most especially for their friendship. And finally, and above all, to my family – to Liz and the girls, Sarah, Sophie and Catherine – for all their love and support.

This book does not purport to provide a definitive account of the end of the troubles. For how could any? Myriad friends, colleagues and others have already published or are planning their own analyses of this complex, multi-dimensional story, with its national and international dimensions, plots, sub-plots and intrigues set alongside conflicting hopes, interpretations and perceptions.

What I have set out to do is chart, hopefully in an accessible way, the progress from a state of no consensus to one where 'consent' provides the basis for constitutional stability in Northern Ireland and dictates the exclusively peaceful and democratic rules of engagement for those committed to future constitutional change. In cutting through the fog I have also ignored a tremendous amount of detailed argument and political engagement along the way. Yet here in essence is the triumph of John Hume's constant assertion that 'majoritarianism' could not work in a divided society; unionism's slow and often painful acceptance of equality, 'parity of esteem' and 'the three sets of relationships' indispensable to a stable settlement; and, equally, nationalist and republican Ireland's reluctant recognition of the price – in terms of the principle of consent, the withdrawal of the Republic's territorial claim, support for policing and acceptance of the legitimacy of the British state in Northern Ireland – necessary to secure unionist acceptance of power-sharing and 'the Irish dimension'.

The book also comes with the warning that we can, and should, take nothing for granted – this reflected in the decision to change the title from 'the triumph …' to 'a triumph of politics'. It seemed entirely appropriate to conclude with interview and analysis of the Taoiseach and Prime Minister on whose watch the historic breakthrough finally occurred. From Bertie Ahern there is the reminder, spelt out in his historic address to both houses of the British parliament in May 2006, that this tender plant will require the continuing highest priority in Dublin and London. The acknowledgement that Tony Blair really did make history in Ireland is also attended by the observation that 'even he … could not have thought to end it'.

It is neither insulting nor impertinent to observe that questions remain about the character and temperament of Northern Ireland's new political elite: 'Having seized power, will the DUP and Sinn Féin prove capable of genuinely "sharing" it for the common good? Can commitments to justice and equality have meaning without a shared commitment to reconciliation between communities still living a segregated "apartheid" existence behind so-called "peace walls"?'

In that context I am delighted to report that Jigsaw and the Northern Ireland Community Relations Council have made funds available to Irish Academic Press to enable the release of copies of this book to various schools, inter-faith and cross-community groups and through the Northern Ireland Council for Integrated Education. This book, finally, is dedicated to those communities on both sides still awaiting their 'peace dividend', and to the next generations who have the opportunity now to make Northern Ireland the still-better place it can and deserves to be.

Frank Millar,
London, September 2008

The publishers make grateful acknowledgement to *The Irish Times* for permission to reproduce Frank Millar's interviews in this book.

The publishers also gratefully acknowledge permission to reproduce an extract from *Blair's Britain, 1997–2007*, ed. Anthony Seldon (Cambridge University Press, 2007), pp.509-529, © Cambridge University Press, and acknowledge the reproduction of an extract from *David Trimble: The Price of Peace* by Frank Millar (Liffey Press, 2004, 2008).

1

Defining the Problem – John Hume
1988–1989

'When they come to write the history this will be regarded as a seminal piece.' That was John Hume's confident prediction when we concluded this interview at his Donegal retreat just days after Christmas 1988. I was somewhat taken aback and looked at him quizzically – but the then SDLP leader plainly wasn't joking.

Even without listening to the tape, I knew there was significant, potentially ground-breaking material here. That was why I had made the journey from London in the first place. That Hume would get a planned *Irish Times* series off to a cracking start was never in doubt. Yet I could be forgiven for not knowing he had actually just defined the architecture of what, ten long years later, would become the historic Belfast Agreement.

The series after all was devised to fill a political vacuum so stubbornly enduring as to convince many people that Northern Ireland was a problem beyond resolution. Incredible though it may seem now, many, probably most, unionists at the time saw Hume himself as a major part of 'the problem'. The unionist political class were certainly more than just sceptical about his repeatedly declared willingness to talk 'any time, any place, anywhere' about 'the problem of relationships' and 'the accommodation of difference and diversity' on the island of Ireland. As I put it to him, they regarded his talk of 'an agreed Ireland' as code for a coercive agenda and 'a united Ireland or nothing'. The prevailing proof of that, from the unionist perspective, had been the 1985 Anglo-Irish Agreement (AIA) concluded by Prime Minister Margaret Thatcher and Taoiseach Garret FitzGerald. While purporting to uphold 'the principle of consent' this agreement for the first time formally recognised the right of the Irish government to be consulted about Northern Ireland. Inevitably, not least given their exclusion from the process leading to it, unionists saw the AIA as a denial of their basic entitlements as citizens of the United Kingdom and a practical advance of the Irish Republic's constitutional claim to the territory of Northern Ireland. Widely held to be John Hume's finest hour, they saw it too as proof of a nationalist preference for a British–Irish framework by which to bypass 'the people of Northern Ireland' and, specifically, to over-ride 'the unionist veto'.

Not least courtesy of my long-standing friendship with then SDLP deputy leader Seamus Mallon, I understood that the North's 'constitutional nationalists' had a very different take on their role – standing, as they would have it, on the ramparts defending the integrity of the political process itself against the ravages of republican and loyalist violence and the deeply-ingrained sectarianism of which they considered the unionist leadership a prisoner.

Yet just as Hume was lauded in parts of Westminster and revered in Europe and Irish America as a statesman, the unionist complaint was that he and his party enjoyed disproportionate attention and political leverage precisely because of the turmoil and instability generated by the Provisional IRA's campaign to force a British withdrawal from Northern Ireland. In the wake of the eventual IRA ceasefires in 1994 and 1997, unionists, likewise, would detect a readiness on the part of 'nationalist Ireland' as a whole to try and extract a price for peace hardly consistent with the principle of consent. Nor could it always be said that their fears and misgivings were wholly unfounded. Hume might excel at 'the vision thing' but not even he had done all of what Tony Blair might later describe as the 'joined-up thinking'. Hume himself at one stage produced an extraordinary proposal that would have put the EU and the Irish alongside the British in a joint administration or council of ministers that would have effectively reduced unionists to a minority shareholding in their own government in Northern Ireland. When British Prime Minister John Major concluded the Joint Declaration for Peace with Taoiseach Albert Reynolds in 1993 – and the subsequent Downing Street Declaration with Taoiseach John Bruton in February 1995 – nationalists and republicans appeared to anticipate at least an emergent embryonic all-Ireland institution with what then Irish Foreign Affairs Minister David Andrews suggested would be powers 'not unlike a government'. Unionist anxieties about the underlying nature and purpose of the emergent peace process were also fuelled by Sinn Féin's initial demand – supported in one leaked Irish government paper – that the British government should in turn become 'a persuader for Irish unity'.

Such grandiose schemes were never going to survive an actual engagement with Ulster's unionists. But here was the rub. For probably as wounding and discomfiting as any was the recurring nationalist charge that the unionists lacked the confidence to define themselves and negotiate on their own behalf. To add insult to injury, the mocking charge wholly disregarded the unionist fear – born of the nationalist and republican hope – that when they did finally enter into negotiations unionist politicians would find it impossible to resist change far beyond that to which they would ever freely consent.

Taoiseach Albert Reynolds, who would later play a critical role in bringing Sinn Féin president Gerry Adams' internal republican initiative to fruition, once famously asked 'who could be afraid of peace?' By that stage people had only to look at a 'pan-nationalist' pact stretching from the Office of the Taoiseach to the Clinton White House to find their answer.

Yet, incredibly, when then Ulster Unionist Party leader David Trimble found the courage for them in 1997/98, he was able to set unionism's limits within the parameters outlined by John Hume back in 1988: the elevation of people over territory, an entirely new concept of Irish 'unity', and a crucial re-definition of 'self-determination' for the divided peoples of Ireland by way of the unprecedented dual referendums held in Northern Ireland and the Republic to ratify the Good Friday accord in May 1998.

The result would be stability and the constitutional status quo, albeit with a radically re-ordered 'union' of Great Britain and Northern Ireland centred on the principles of partnership, power-sharing and 'parity of esteem', and with its devolved government operating also within a wider context of North–South and British–Irish ministerial councils. And, of course, Nobel peace prizes for Trimble and for Hume, the grand designer.

FROM *THE IRISH TIMES*, 13 JANUARY 1989

I first put it to John Hume that the Anglo-Irish Agreement was designed, among other things, to improve Catholic confidence in the police and in the judiciary. Did he consider that in the three years since there has been a qualitative change and improvement in the standard of justice available to the Catholic community?

HUME: There is a large number of reasons why the Anglo-Irish Agreement was created. The essential reason was to create, first of all, a framework within which a solution could be pursued, and in that sense the framework of the solution has to be the framework of the problem. For the very first time we have a framework which is addressing all the relationships which go to the heart of this problem. One of the reasons why we disagree so often with the unionists in our treatment of the problem is that we disagree about what the problem is. I will state very clearly that the problem is the failure to resolve relationships, a number of them, the central relationship being that of the unionists and the rest of the island, and then the relations between Ireland and Britain, and within the North. So that essentially is what the Anglo-Irish Agreement is about, it's about treating the disease. Now while the disease remains to be cured, which is the politics of it, the symptoms keep recurring. One of the symptoms being the administration of justice, the relationships between the Catholic community and the security forces. I think that most people would accept that since the Anglo-Irish Agreement was signed, there has been, for example, a distinct improvement in one area which gave grave offence to the Catholic community and that was the handling of parades, and Orange parades in particular. Because we could never see the reason why such provocative parades – by provocative I mean triumphalist marching through Catholic areas – were allowed. I have no objection whatsoever to the Orange tradition being celebrated in Ireland, it's part of our tradition. But it should be done in a manner that is neither triumphalist nor provocative. It should be done in a genuinely celebratory manner. I believe in that area there certainly has been an improvement. On the question of the administration of justice itself, I think there are many people who would argue that you are more likely to get a fair trial now in Northern Ireland than you would get in Britain if you are an Irish person being tried for an offence concerned with violence. They would argue that one of the reasons for that is the existence of juries in Britain for such trials, because of their emotional nature. We would accept the reason why, in Northern Ireland, it was necessary to remove juries, because of intimidation and so forth, which is self-evident. But that being so, we would have argued that the responsibility therefore should not be left on the shoulder of one person, and that is why we would argue for three-judge courts rather than one-judge courts.

MILLAR: I want to put two things to you. Firstly, the very fact that you cite as one of the major improvements post the agreement the handling by the RUC of Orange marches appears to many unionists to be saying: 'When the RUC is beating Protestants over the heads at Orange demonstrations in Portadown or wherever, we approve.' And there appears to be in that situation an enthusiasm for the RUC discharging their duty which, to many unionists, is not apparent in other circumstances.

HUME: It's not an enthusiasm, it's a welcome that they are moving to a more impartial situation in handling parades of that nature, which is what a police force should be doing. I mean the vast majority of the work done by the RUC is not complained about at all by the SDLP. There are a lot of people who have been brought to trial in Northern

Ireland for many different kinds of offences and there hasn't been a word of complaint by the SDLP, nor by the people that they represent.

MILLAR: There have been plenty of complaints from the SDLP about RUC attempts to police Provisional IRA funerals which have been stage-managed, in the view of the authorities and the majority community, as triumphalist exercises. Are you happy that you are entirely even-handed when it comes to apportioning blame and credits to the RUC?

HUME: When you tell me about policing IRA funerals and policing Orange parades – the problem in the past was that they didn't police Orange parades at all. They simply let them march freely through Catholic areas in a very provocative fashion. In terms of policing IRA funerals I think the police themselves have now learned from their experience that their original handling of those funerals gave enormous propaganda, television coverage in particular, to the IRA, which isn't supposed to be the purpose of policing such funerals, and that much more sensitive policing was the proper way to handle them. I think the RUC themselves would now admit that our original criticisms were correct. They seem to have admitted it by accepting them.

MILLAR: The second point that I want to put to you is a point put to me by people from within your community. If I were a member of the Provisional IRA, or a supporter, I would be tempted to say to you: forget about your theories about the process which you embarked on three years ago; in practice, the RUC and the courts behave much as they did before the Agreement, encouraged perhaps by the political environment created by Mrs Thatcher's fairly loud, public exchanges with her opposite numbers in the Irish Republic. What are you saying to Catholics in west Belfast or in the Bogside in Derry and elsewhere who say to you we are at the coalface and, in terms of day-to-day experiences of the police force and the UDR, we don't see any change?

HUME: Well, of course, it's in the interests of people like Sinn Féin and their supporters to keep on saying we don't see any change. In fact, there is an identity of interest between the IRA and the unionist opponents of the Anglo-Irish Agreement. I mean every time the IRA commits an atrocity the unionists use it as a reason for saying that the Anglo-Irish Agreement has failed. In other words they are, if you like to use an old phrase, living off the backs of the IRA. First of all the Anglo-Irish Agreement wasn't signed, we made clear – and I made very clear in particular – as a solution to the problem: therefore, don't expect that you are going to see an overnight change in everything. It works at two levels, as I have said often, the level of the symptoms and the level of the disease. The symptoms will always be there in one form or another until the disease is cured, the symptoms being the sort of things that you are talking about – relationships between people and police and so forth. Until the underlying problem is solved, those will recur in different forms. In the meantime attempts have to be made to improve them, and attempts are being made to improve them. Where the real change has occurred is at the deeper level of the problem itself. Going to the heart of the problem is the relationship between the unionist people and the rest of the people of the island. The unionist people made a choice to hold all power in their own hands, to protect their tradition. Every time that was challenged by a British government they threatened the Orange card and of course the British governments always backed down. And that meant that leadership of the unionist community was confirmed in the hands of those who argued for living apart rather than living together, and it also gave justification and strength to the IRA argument that the only thing the British understood is force. While that vicious circle continues we are never going to solve anything. I am saying that for the first time since 1920 that vicious circle is being broken because the British have not backed down. A new fluidity has been created in the political arena which must be taken advantage of. And if it is taken advantage of and developed, then we will move towards a political solution that will eradicate all these other grievances which are symptoms of the problem. It is the function and duty of politicians like myself to keep their eye on the problem and on ways of solving it. In the meantime everybody does their best to try and restore and cure the symptoms that keep arising. But it is only reasonable to suggest that if the disease persists the symptoms will persist in different forms.

MILLAR: I have no difficulty understanding all that. Can I put it back to you that unionists believe that you have lived, and your party have lived, off the backs of the IRA since the beginning of the troubles. Unionists believe that there would never have been an Anglo-Irish Agreement but for the ferment and the chaos created and generated by the IRA campaign. I mean do you, standing apart from it, taking as objective a view as possible for one who has been a principal player for the last 20 years, do you give the IRA credit for any changes that have been made, and that have occurred in the last 20 years?

HUME: Yes, there are a lot of changes in the landscape, in towns and cities that they have blown to bits; there are a lot of people in their graves. If it's credit they want for that, they can have it. They have also made the problem much more difficult to solve in that they have deepened the divide between the two sections of the community in terms of positive ways forward. The IRA are against the Anglo-Irish Agreement although I hear them sometimes saying that they are responsible for the advances. Those sort of contradictions I don't have much time for. Basically the IRA existed in the 1920s, the 1930s, the 1940s and the 1950s. They had campaigns in all those periods and they all failed miserably, and the only time any change started to emerge in Northern Ireland was in the non-violence of the civil rights movement, which challenged and asked a very simple question of the unionists: can you give us justice? And can you survive with the answer 'yes'? It was a completely new approach. We started the process of change in Northern Ireland, which is working, and the IRA came in on the back of that. They have prolonged the process and they have made a solution much more difficult to find. Now it suits the unionists, of course, to make those sort of charges, but in fact the real allies in Northern Ireland have always been the unionists and the IRA. I come back to my theory, as you call it: unionists made a choice in order to protect themselves, to hold all power in their own hands, and every time the British government moved to change that they threatened, and the British government backed down. That was the unionists' fault and the British government's fault. But that also gave sustenance to those in the nationalist community who said that the only thing that the British understand is force. So that is a vicious circle – the unionists and the IRA – they would have paralysed all political progress that would take place in a normal democratic society without violence and without people trying to all hold power in their own hands. Therefore, they are natural allies, and they are natural allies in trying to bring down the Anglo-Irish Agreement because any peaceful person must accept that, in a society where you have a conflict of identity, the best possible way of dealing with that problem is for the two governments that represent the identities to work as closely as possible together to resolve it.

MILLAR: Can I put it to you that your statement sounds remarkably triumphalist and has sounded triumphalist in unionist ears since November 15th, 1985. Because when unionists hear you talk in terms of the veto that they held, the threat that they posed, the cowardice of successive British governments in the face of it, but this time being different – translated, that means to unionists that the Agreement, in fact, was an exercise in facing down the unionists. And indeed I don't know, off the top of my head, whether you ever coined the phrase, it's a phrase that has been attributed to you. Was the Agreement in part an exercise in facing down the unionists, albeit from your perspective a necessary part?

HUME: I would not dispute that there was a necessity to face down a certain type of unionist entirely because that, in my view, goes to the heart of the problem. No section of the community should be able to hold all power in its own hands and should be able to blackmail governments of the day from changing that society. And if that goes to the heart of the problem, then it has to be done, it has to be faced up to, and facing up to that is not triumphalist. In fact the traditional unionist approach has done no favour to the unionist people because they are no happier than the rest of the community in Northern Ireland. The lack of peace affects everybody and the violence affects everybody and, therefore, I believe that, in the long term, as I said in my recent speech, what Mrs Thatcher and the Anglo-Irish Agreement have done for unionism is what President Kennedy did for the whites in Alabama. They knew that something had to be done, they knew they couldn't do it for themselves but, once it was done, in their own heart of hearts they were glad it was done and to go on from there. Now, where to 'go on from there' is what is important because if we were really triumphalist then where we would go on from there would be that we would be seeking to walk over the top of unionists. But there is no way that I believe that we can solve our problem by doing that – what I want to see is, on the basis of equality, that we stand together on an equal footing and resolve our differences, which we have never done. You can't resolve those differences if one section has its hands on all the power or if it has a veto on what a British government is going to do, and I think now that we are on an equal footing, that the next stage is the development of a solution. But why do people want a solution? I mean there are some people who don't want a solution. There are some people who simply want to hold all power in their own hands. They have shown no sign of wanting to address our relationship.

MILLAR: Those people would contend, unionists would contend generally that to go on talking about them holding all power in their own hands is a bit absurd. Unionists haven't held power in Northern Ireland, in fact, since 1972. That's a pretty long time without power to continue to be held responsible for the state of play in Northern Ireland. And they might feel with some sense of grievance that the criticism, if there is criticism to be made, should be left with the British.

HUME: What they have done is they have spent all that period seeking to get the power back into their own hands and, on one occasion, when the power was shared, they used blackmail to bring it down. When they get to the stage of realising that the alternative way of protecting their interests, which is the way that is used in every democracy in the world, is by coming to terms and accommodating the differences that live in the society without anybody being triumphalist, then I think we are on the road. Now, in that sense, as I have said before, the unionists hold the key to peace in Ireland. Do they want to choose a road which protects their distinctiveness by holding all power in their own hands and continuing to seek that or a return to that, or do they want to go down the road where they sit down with their fellow citizens who share an island and work out in their own interests and to their own satisfaction with the rest of the people of this island how we share the island? Those are the two routes. The second route is the route that most democracies in the world have used and has resulted in very diverse societies indeed, but very stable societies.

MILLAR: I want to come to the route, but I want to put to you one further unionist point. There are unionists who say yes you have been trimphalist and in fact left to your own devices would continue to be triumphalist and that for all the fine words you, John Hume, and your party might proceed to walk over them, but for one enormous change. The change in terms of a clear deterioration in relationships between the British and Irish governments. I mean, for all your commitment to it and for all your obvious reasons to preserve public faith in it, do you not start the New Year with an uneasy feeling about the beginning of a new cold war between London and Dublin?

HUME: No, if you read what I have said about the Anglo-Irish relationship from the beginning – I have said it is not the Agreement that will go down or up, it's the behaviour of governments. Different governments will behave differently: but the strength of it is that each government that comes into office, whether in London or Dublin, can make its own contribution, whatever it is, to the building process that's necessary to solve this problem. In other words, it is not going to be solved in a week or a fortnight. Some governments will do very little, some may even do nothing, others may do a lot.

MILLAR: So, it's a process that could actually be put on ice? It's a process capable of being virtually frozen over for a period?

HUME: Well, you could get a government that might want to do that. But in fact there's another government sitting there going to try and prevent that happening, obviously. So it's the behaviour of governments that you are talking about, you are not talking about the Agreement in itself. And also, to go back to your actual question about unionists saying that we would still be triumphalist – all you have to do and all they have to do is something that they have never done, actually – to read what we say; read what we say to our electorate and our election manifestos; read what we say to our party at our annual conference about our analysis of the problem and about our proposals for solving it. I am interested in accommodation of difference. That's what I am interested in. I'm interested in a recognition that the problem is that we have differences on this island, that differences are very normal in human societies everywhere. The stable united societies are stable and united precisely because they accept difference and diversity. They accommodate them to the mutual satisfaction of the different people. That's a task that has never been set about on this island. What the outcome of that task would be, if we set about it in a genuine fashion, I'm not even prepared to predict. As long as it is an outcome with the accommodation of differences acceptable to the different traditions – that'll suit me.

MILLAR: Let me put it to you directly, then, there are unionists in positions of leadership within the two unionist parties who actually think there is no point talking to you; who say in private and, indeed, in fairness to them, in public, the nature of the division in Irish politics is quite clear: we want union with Britain and for John Hume, because it is a policy that has been identified more with John Hume than with anybody else over the last ten to fifteen years, for John Hume it's a united Ireland or nothing. The positions are irreconcilable. And there is no point in talking. Is it, for John Hume, a united Ireland or nothing?

HUME: It depends what you mean by unity. What I am concerned about isn't concepts, I am concerned about the fact that Ireland has for too long concerned itself with territorial attitudes rather than the fact that there are people who live on an island and that the people who live on that island are divided. One is a Protestant tradition which feels that its only protection can be within a particular context. The other is the Irish Catholic nationalist republican tradition which feels that its only protection can be within a particular context. That's the essence of the division and that division has led to terrible tragedies in the island for both sections. It also leads to hurts and to folk memories which keep recurring in successive generations, each side genuinely believing what the other has done to it. And how do you deal with it is the question; not how you perpetuate it – not how you perpetuate the ethos of your own side. And I am saying what we should do, and try to do. There are societies in the world where the differences are far deeper than ours, but yet they live together in perfect peace and harmony because they know how to accommodate their differences. All I am saying is what unity for me means – it means agreement on how we share the island. That is what unity actually means. Unity without agreement isn't unity at all, it's conquest and you are back to that. And what I am saying is that it is time for the representatives of the different traditions in this island to sit down together and decide how they're going to share this island, how they are going to protect their traditions in a manner that is satisfactory to both sides. Now, that could be a hell of a long process of search, but that is the real search and that's the search we have got to be engaged in. It's easy to indulge in name calling, to say: 'Well I don't trust you.' The unionists don't trust me – fair enough, maybe I don't trust them. I don't have to trust them and they don't have to trust me. What I have to do is trust myself and what they have to do is trust themselves to represent their own people, anywhere, with anybody else and come to a settlement that protects their own people. And I have to do precisely the same thing; whether I trust Ian Paisley or not is irrelevant. What is important is whether I trust myself to be able to deal with him and produce solutions that are acceptable to the people I represent, and he has to do the same thing.

MILLAR: But what I am talking about is unionist politicians who trust themselves, in terms of protecting the interests of their people, just as much as you trust yourself in terms of protecting the interests of yours, who believe that a united Ireland or nothing is the sum total, is the embodiment of John Hume's view, that that is the solution you hanker after and that you will continue to hang out until you get it.

HUME: Well, even if I had said that, in when was it, in 1972, have they not read anything that I have said in the intervening years? I mean I could list, if I was interested in that sort of politics, a whole series of remarks, quotations and what-have-you from the Ian Paisleys of this world, from the Peter Robinsons of this world, from James Molyneaux, from the lot of them. But that's easy stuff. It's point-scoring politics. What I am saying is let's concentrate on the problem and how we resolve it. And let's recognise before we start that there are differences.

MILLAR: And the fundamental difference is between a nationalist aspiration for the unification of this island and the unionist aspiration to retain the British connection. Well what you appear to be saying, let me put it back to you so that I am clear, what you appear to be saying is that for you as a nationalist that your definition of self-determination for the Irish people is the agreement of all the people on this island on some basis on which to share the territory?

HUME: Oh, absolutely. My definition of self-determination is self-evident, it is that the people of the island as a whole should sit down – first of all. There's a lot of people say the Irish people have a right to self-determination. Nobody disputes that, but what they seem to ignore is that the Irish people, if one defines the Irish people as the people who live on the island of Ireland, are divided on how they exercise that right. That division goes very deep. That division goes back beyond partition. It goes back a very long way. Therefore, if we are going to exercise self-determination then the people of the island as a whole have got to agree, have got to reach agreement. That is, those who are divided have got to reach agreement. But when they do reach agreement on how they are going to share the island, then I believe you have the basis for real unity because you have got agreement and the essence of unity is agreement. You can't have unity between divided parties unless they agree.

MILLAR: But as I understand and interpret your definition of self-determination, it could be a unity based on an agreement by the people on both sides of the island to continue to live apart.

HUME: Well, the people of the island if they are given a choice – you see one of the problems is that throughout this century the people of the island as a whole, either North or South, have never been given an opportunity to speak on how they are to be governed, apart from elections, which is choosing their government. They have never been allowed to actually speak on the system of government for the island as a whole or in the relationships within the island as a whole. And therefore what would be the outcome of discussions between representatives of both parts of the island, I couldn't forecast. I wouldn't attempt to forecast because if I am quite genuine in saying that I want the different representatives to come to the table and discuss the shape of the future island, then I must leave them to be free to put on that table whatever they wished to put on that table. To prejudge the outcome would be wholly wrong and politically foolish.

MILLAR: But let me put it to you, you are nothing if not a political realist. And you know that the unionist community in Northern Ireland are not going to freely, of their own accord, vote themselves into a unitary Irish state. Are you therefore accepting that this process that you wish to see the leaders of the two traditions embark upon would inevitably lead to some settlement short of a unitary Irish State which has heretofore been regarded as your objective?

HUME: Well, in the first place what I am saying is what I want to see is the representatives of the divided people of this island reaching an agreement on how they share the island. As to how they share the island would have to emerge from that conference table. That means that whoever goes to that table to represent the different sections of the people must be free to put on that table any proposal they wish. I think that there has been an absence of face-to-face dialogue among the people of the island as to why they are what they are. That face-to-face dialogue may well produce quite an amount of realism on all sides as to what the real problem is. Up till now I think it's not unfair to say that each tradition in Ireland, both unionist and nationalist, has sought to persuade the British as to what was in the best interests of the people of Ireland, rather than face one another. I am asking them to face one another and I am saying that I accept, before we start, that any outcome of that must have the agreement of both and that in order to assure them of that, before they do go to that table, they should devise a mechanism to ensure that the people on each side have a means of expressing their view on whatever agreement is reached.

MILLAR: Would it be fair to take that to mean that you would envisage at the end of this process, however long it might take, the emergence of an agreement which would be put to the people in Northern Ireland and simultaneously to the people of the Republic?

HUME: That's precisely what I am proposing.

MILLAR: Say you reach an agreement as to the basis on which you think the two parts of the island should co-exist, and you put it to the people of Northern Ireland and they buy it, and it's put to the people of the Irish Republic and it's rejected. Surely the effect would be to enhance the position of militant republicans who would cite the rejection of the settlement by the people on the other side of the border as a national mandate?

HUME: Yes, well let's not look at the negatives. You're looking at the worst possible scenario and you are assuming the people sitting around a table do reach agreement on how we share the island, and I am assuming that that's going to take a while. They are not going to come out with, nor are they going to reach, agreements that they can't deliver. I don't think that's the sort of thing that's likely to happen. For example, I think the first thing that would happen if such discussions started would be that it would transform the atmosphere in the island as a whole. The goodwill would be quite enormous. And a lot of the old prejudices might quickly be eroded because of the new atmosphere of goodwill. And we should also understand that that new atmosphere existed inside a wider world context and a wider European context, that both parts of Ireland have already committed themselves to. They have committed decision-making out of our hands altogether and what I am proposing is that it is time we got back into the decision-making processes about how we relate to one another in the island. I don't have any doubt that if that process took place either agreement would be reached or it wouldn't. If it wasn't, then there would be nothing to be put to any people, but if agreement was reached I would have no doubt that it would have the approval of both sections.

MILLAR: This by necessity would be an agreement reached between the unionists and you, on the one hand, and between you and the unionists and the Republic, on the other.

HUME: The real relationship that has never been faced up to is a relationship between the unionist people and the rest of the island. I would like to see the unionists taking the bull by the horns and going to Dublin and sitting down and saying: right, we're here, you tell us our agreement is required as to how we share this island. We want that before we start talking, we want the mechanism for approving that agreement settled, and having settled that we will sit down with you for however long it takes to work out with you how we share this island, and having done so to build the common institutions to which we will all give our loyalty in both parts of the island. Then we have the basis for peace and stability.

MILLAR: You say to me it's not the most profitable thing to look at the negatives though I would have thought that anybody entering negotiation would be prudent to try and gauge the worst scenario by way of an outcome. And while it's also valid for you to say that it's wrong to attempt to prejudge the outcome of negotiations, it seems to me inevitable, unless we are talking pie in the sky, you have got to be talking about a new political settlement which would leave Northern Ireland in some continuing relationship with Britain because there is no basis to suppose that a majority in Northern Ireland is prepared to depart from that.

HUME: I am certainly talking about a new settlement. I am talking about a new settlement which addresses the central relationship that goes to the heart of our problem – the relationship between the unionist people and the rest of the people in the island. What I am saying is that that relationship should be settled to the mutual satisfaction of both. I would be very foolish, and so would they and so would anybody, before going to seek such a settlement at a table to spell out in detail what the eventual outcome should be because that's not very good politics. What we should state are the objectives – that we want to reach agreement on how we share this island to our mutual satisfaction and having done so to ask the approval of the people who sent us to the table in the first place. What the details are of how we share the island must be details that emerge from such discussions. And it must also, of course, and I have always made clear and I think this is self-evident, that the relationships, that is the central relationship is that between the unionists and the rest of this island. There are other relationships as well that have to be addressed, that's become known as the totality of relationships. They've got to be addressed as well and they've got to be resolved to mutual satisfaction but the central one, the one that has never been addressed, is the unionists and the rest of the island sitting down together. In the past they have always tried to use the British to settle the relationships for them and, I would put it mildly, not very successfully by either.

MILLAR: Notwithstanding your lack of desire to anticipate the outcome or, naturally, to reveal anything of your hand before you would enter negotiation, can I put it to you that the kind of settlement you are talking about in theoretical, broad terms carries enormous implications for the existing Constitution of the Irish Republic?

HUME: The one thing that is absolutely certain is there's no chance whatsoever of any government in the Irish Republic changing the Constitution or proposing a change in the Constitution to the people of the Republic of Ireland in advance of any settlement. That would be regarded as not being politically very wise either. But what has been accepted always by all parties in the Republic is that any new settlement which involves the unionists and themselves would mean their willingness to look at the possibility of an entirely new Constitution. Most political leaders in the Republic have said time out of number that in the event of a settlement between themselves and the unionists they would not object at all to considering a new Constitution. I think that that's self-evident.

MILLAR: Would you accept that solution, based as it has to be, as you have always made clear, on the consent, freely given, of the majority of the people in Northern Ireland?

HUME: Yes.

MILLAR: That you say is their ultimate guarantee in going into any negotiation?

HUME: Yes.

MILLAR: Could any settlement work, have a ghost of a chance of standing, if the Republic were thereafter to continue to retain the territorial claim to the six counties?

HUME: Well, you are into the ifs again, and let me put an if in reply. If the unionist people and the representatives of the people of the Republic reach agreement on how we share the island and that is approved by the people in both parts of the island, then, I think, we will worry about the ifs. I think that such an agreement, to use an old phrase of mine, would transcend in importance any previous agreement ever made because it would be the first time ever that the divided people of the island as a whole had reached agreement on how they were going to live together. And I think that such an agreement would lead to, in the future, an evolution of relationships that would have been unthinkable ten years ago, twenty years ago, or whatever.

MILLAR: And on the subject of relationships can I ask you bluntly: is your relationship with the present Taoiseach such that you are confident that this is an enterprise that he would enthusiastically join?

HUME: Well, I would never put myself in the position of speaking for the Taoiseach [Charles Haughey] or indeed for any Taoiseach or government who must, and do, speak for themselves. What I do know, from my discussions with him and from his public utterances, is that he would be very, very swift indeed to take up any opportunity of dialogue with the unionist people that could lead to a settlement of relationships between the unionist people and the rest of the people of this island. I know that. And I know that he is very willing to do that. What would emerge from the details of those discussions must be left to such discussions.

MILLAR: Moving on to the achievement of the process, the unionists have said that they won't enter negotiation about a new agreement without some sort of suspension of the existing Agreement. Would you care to comment on the existing state or non-state of dialogue or non-dialogue between yourselves and the unionist parties?

HUME: Well, I am very keen to get into dialogue with them. What I would propose to them, of course, would be that we would make clear in advance that we are having our discussions outside the framework of the Anglo-Irish Agreement. That means that there would be no sacrifice of principle by any of the parties involved in their attitudes to the Anglo-Irish Agreement. Our objective would be to seek an agreement and find an agreement that would transcend in importance any previous agreement ever made. I think that's a clear straight way to do it and I think that the unionists don't abandon their mandated position by so doing.

MILLAR: Does the period of the review of the work of the Agreement afford any possible opening whereby you could meet the unionists half way?

HUME: Well, I think if we are going to talk in terms of talking completely outside the framework then the review is part of the framework. I think we are searching after moonbeams to try and go down that road and I don't think it's a very honest road to go down anyway because I think it would mean that one side or the other would be trying to explain things away to the constituents. I think it's cleaner, more honest to say we are having a discussion completely outside the framework of the existing Agreement, that it means no sacrifice of principle by any party and all parties accept that. We accept that the unionists are not sacrificing their principled view of the Anglo-Irish Agreement. We both accept that we are going to try to seek an agreement which transcends in importance any previous agreement. I think that that is a fairly rational and reasonable way of opening up the dialogue.

MILLAR: But is there any possibility, for example, that a formula could be devised whereby meetings of the Intergovernmental Conference, and presumably by implication the Maryfield Secretariat, would be interrupted for a stated period for the purpose of facilitating this alternative discussion?

HUME: Well, you could go about it two ways. You could go about it that way, the way you are suggesting or you could go about it the way that I am suggesting which is a complete, clean break and saying that you are outside of the framework. This is the clean way to do it. I think that once you get into trying to produce word-formulas within the existing Agreement, that's all you are doing. You are only producing word-formulas. And that is going to lead to controversy on each side and I don't think it's worth that. I think it's cleaner and more honest to simply say: Look, we are talking outside the framework of that Agreement. All sides accept that nobody has given up any principles in this matter and all sides accept that if we reach agreement that it would transcend in importance any other agreement we have ever had. That's our approach to it and I also accept at the moment that unionist leaders want to have dialogue. I also accept they want to have it in keeping with the principles that they have stated and with the mandates that they have received. I would be anxious to try and facilitate that.

MILLAR: What are the consequences of failure?

HUME: Well the consequences of failure are very obvious to everybody. The tragedies of the last twenty years have been terrible, not just in the terrible loss of life that has taken place and the destruction, but in the absence of hope for young people, not just in the North, throughout the island as a whole. People tend to forget, particularly people like Mrs Thatcher, that the South has paid a terrible price for the troubles in the North, economically if no other way. Costs in security, costs in jobs, cost in lost revenue, lost investment, lost tourism. Massive costs leading to lack of hope for our young people, North and South. The price is too high to think about and I would have thought the price of failure or the price of continuing the deadlock might force political leaders into examining ways of getting together.

MILLAR: Is there one other possible consequence of failure? Do you ever worry, as some unionists have suggested might happen and fear it might happen, that Britain, if not this government, some future British government, might tire of dealing with people like you and might on the advice of civil servants or whatever decide to go direct to the people who cause them the pain, namely the IRA? Do you think it's conceivable that Britain would ever tire of the search for a political way forward?

HUME: I suppose everything is conceivable but they should remember that the IRA don't speak for the people of Ireland, either North or South, and therefore while they might lay down their guns I don't think they could make an agreement stick in that sense. Such an agreement would hardly be acceptable to the people of Ireland as a whole. Secondly, I don't see, frankly, a British government doing that and undermining the existence of an existing Irish government, because that's what they would be doing. And thirdly, there is another element today which didn't exist in the past and it is called international terrorism. We saw it in the terrible tragedy of the Pan-Am jet. There is no Western government today who can afford for any reason whatsoever to surrender to that sort of blackmail. That is one reason, and one very powerful reason, now today, because of the international implications of all of this that in fact no British government in my view will go down that road.

MILLAR: That's a pretty forthright declaration – no civilised Western government can afford to have any truck with terrorists. Does that mean that there is no role therefore in this search for agreement for Sinn Féin?

HUME: There is a role in the search for agreement for every section of the Irish people that has got an elected mandate provided they come to the search on the same terms as everybody else, armed only with their own convictions and their own ability to persuade but not with guns or bombs.

MILLAR: So for as long as Sinn Féin remains linked/married whatever the nature of their relationship to the IRA …

HUME: You can't expect anyone to sit around a table with somebody who reserves the right to pull a gun if he doesn't get his own way.

MILLAR: That's clear enough.

'RULE OF LAW REQUIRES CONSENSUS ON FORM OF GOVERNMENT'
FROM *THE IRISH TIMES*, 13 JANUARY 1989

MILLAR: What do you feel about the levels of security that are available to the community in Northern Ireland? Should people be reasonably satisfied or is there anything in unionist complaints about security that you identify with?

HUME: I identify completely with unionist concerns and anger at the number of lives that are being lost, injuries that are being carried out, and damage done, and I think that that concern is shared right across the community. But unionists treat it purely as a security problem – if the security problem were resolved everything would be all right. Our view – and I think this is a view that would be pretty widespread in most democracies – is that security and law and order are based on consensus. If the society is agreed on how it is governed then policing, courts and everything else, as a matter of form, are fully regarded by the community as a whole as 'our police' and 'our courts'. Where there is a division in the society about how it is governed, and where there is a deep division and bitterness, as there has been in the North, particularly since 1920, then there is always going to be a problem about security, attitudes to security forces and to the institutions of law and order; one side is going to see them as 'ours' and the other side is going to see them as 'theirs'. The best that one can do in those circumstances, if you are in my position and the position of my party – and it is the best – is to do what we have done because of our concern about the killing, the destruction, and the need to bring people to justice! We fully and unequivocally support the police force in impartially upholding the rule of law and in bringing to justice anybody who commits a crime. That is a very major position for us and I know it's a position that is sneered at by quite a few of our opponents, but if you actually think about the realities of the North, then most people would recognise that for what it is. But I believe that we are only ever going to really have a secure position on all of these matters when there is agreement between the different sections of our community as to how we live together and as to how we govern one another.

MILLAR: But the search on which you are engaged for that agreement has taken a pretty long time. There isn't, even to be optimistic, any immediate, obvious prospect that the kind of agreement you envisage is close. In the meantime, people in your community, in the whole community, are being killed. Now politicians have to get on with the business of politics but Mrs Thatcher would certainly say, and many of the people who vote for you presumably would say, in the meantime the state has obligations to act to protect life and property. What many unionists are not clear about is what specifications the state can take to diminish the threat from the IRA with the wholehearted support of the SDLP.

HUME: Well, they will always have our wholehearted support in rigidly upholding the rule of law. What we have always queried is when the state departs from the rule of law and moves into the invasion of what would be regarded as civil liberties in a democracy; we believe they are much more likely to get the full support of the community when they are upholding the rule of law rigidly and thoroughly than, as when internment was introduced, the rule of law is abandoned completely. We have seen that that produced a far worse security situation, far greater violence. It brought the law into disrepute. Now, while saying all that, we are not in a black and white situation and here is where we get down to the real question: do we agree on what the problem is? Many unionists give me the impression that they think it is purely security. We would disagree totally. We think it's a problem of relationships – the fact that sections of the people haven't agreed on how they are going to live together in a manner which is acceptable to both. Once that is done, the institutions of law and order become everybody's institutions, which naturally strengthens one's position against people who wish to stand in the face of the democratic will of the people.

MILLAR: But if I was a Conservative backbench member of the House of Commons who, despite my long-standing association with Ulster unionism, had voted three years ago for the Anglo-Irish Agreement, I would say to you: whatever your problem with the unionists, Mrs Thatcher and the British government have accepted that it isn't exclusively a military problem. They have accepted your framework, despite intense unionist opposition, in which to address the totality of relationships, but still there is a terrorist threat and the government in the state have steps that they must take to curtail it. Now, as a matter of first principle, are you saying unequivocally to members of your community that if they obtained information about terrorist activities – knowledge or information that could assist in the identification of the murderer of a policeman or a UDR man – their obligation is to report that information to the authorities and to cooperate in the pursuit of the guilty men?

HUME: I think it is the obligation of every citizen, if they are in receipt of any information of any description that can save other human lives, to give that information to the appropriate authorities in order to make sure that those lives are saved, and if it's a question of bringing to justice people who have committed serious offences such as murder then I would have no hesitation either in saying that they have the same obligation. We have made our position brutally clear: we fully and unequivocally support the security authorities in upholding the rule of law. The only qualification we put is that they do so impartially. I think that that position has not been given proper credit – we know the people in many districts have the greatest difficulty in dealing with the police force because of the past and the perception that the police force was the unionist party in uniform. That is a political problem that one cannot ignore. We deal with it on two fronts: first, we believe that we will only have total, unequivocal identification with the institutions of law and order when there is agreement among the people as a whole as to how we are governed; secondly, in the meantime everybody must do their best to ensure that justice prevails.

MILLAR: You presumably don't, just for the record, believe the RUC today at the end of 1988 to be the unionist party in uniform?

HUME: No. I don't, no. I believe that the RUC reflect the community from which they come. Any police force, no matter who, in a divided society is going to be, in a sense, the meat in the sandwich. The RUC reflect the community from which they come. They are 97 per cent from the Protestant community and they reflect that community. They have among them some very, very decent men who simply want to do a decent job of policing. They have among them others who have much more bigoted points of view and that emerges from the young people on the street. They undermine the whole notion of policing. They simply reflect the community from which they come. That will never be solved to total satisfaction, I repeat, until we have a situation where the communities identify with the institutions of order.

MILLAR: That's perfectly clear. I want to come to the question of the process by which you can reach that happy state. But if I could delve just a bit further – unionists complain that sentencing policy in Northern Ireland is, if anything, too lenient. Do you have any view about sentencing policy?

HUME: In the early 1970s the sentencing policy was pretty savage because there was a great deal of sectarian violence on the streets and that inevitably led young people from both sections of the community into violent organisations in the belief that that was their duty to the community in which they lived. I obviously didn't agree with that, looking ahead to where violence leads, but at the same time most people in politics on both sides would recognise that in the 1970s those emotions were loose. I wouldn't have the same sympathy for people who join violent organisations today because they are quite clearly making a cold calculated decision that they want to use violence to achieve political ends.

MILLAR: So, people today who join terrorist organisations don't enjoy the benefit, for want of a better description, of the argument that they were caught up in a highly emotional situation where it was easy to get involved?

HUME: No, I don't think they do. I think most people who lived through the early 1970s, particularly in Belfast and in Derry, would recognise that it was an intensely emotional time. Street rioting was regular and a lot of young people got caught up in it. That's a very different situation from those who now coldly, calculatedly decide to join a violent organisation and go out to shoot somebody or to blow them to pieces.

MILLAR: And presumably it follows from that that those who do make that cold calculated decision, when successfully prosecuted, through the courts, should expect the utmost severity from the state?

HUME: They should expect to be sentenced in accordance with the crime they have committed. I think that they probably do expect that.

MILLAR: John, can I ask you about the death penalty? Everybody knows you are against the death penalty and the argument is familiar that you create martyrs and so on. Yet there are many people, relatives of policemen and UDR men who have been killed, relatives of ordinary civilians who have been killed on both sides, who contend that it isn't fair that a person convicted of murder should be eligible for consideration for release after a period of maybe as little as 10 or 11 years. At one end of the spectrum there is a view that a life sentence should mean life. There are other people who say that, at least, life sentences should carry a minimum recommended period. What would the SDLP view be?

HUME: Well, there is no question about our opposition to the death penalty. I think that revenge is no substitute for justice and I think that people found guilty of taking the lives of other human beings should serve the proper sentence which society lays down in the normal democratic manner when a parliament passes laws and judges implement them. I don't think they should be interfered with for political reasons after that. I think that the rule of law should be upheld by those who have the responsibility of doing so. I think, of course, that the emotions of people who are victims of these crimes are emotions that everybody should understand. And I think that even those people would agree that decisions of this nature should not be based on emotions. They should be based on a practical application of what is right and just.

MILLAR: But I put it to you that, while you continue to search for the overall solution, the British government certainly has to grapple with the reality of terrorism and it has recently announced a package of measures. Now the opposition of the SDLP to a number of those measures is clear. Is there anything in that package that you would favour? For example, the increased powers of the police to seize the assets of terrorist organisations and the decision to cut back on the remission available to people convicted of terrorist offences?

HUME: While we are searching for political agreement I think the best that people can do, in the absence of identification of the whole community with the institutions of State, is that we fully and unequivocally give our support to the security forces in impartially upholding the rule of law; and I would like to see them upholding the rule of law – abandoning the rule of law plays into the hands of violent people. In terms of the recent package and going after the assets of violent organisations – particularly violent organisations who are using racketeering in order to increase their resources – I would fully support that and my party would fully support that. And I would throw in a line here which many people probably don't know, but the Mafia began their career as a movement for the liberation of Sicily. They began with many Sicilians genuinely believing that they were a genuine patriotic movement. They ended up as the Mafia. It appears now that there are paramilitary organisations which in the eyes of many people who support them began as movements in a patriotic tradition but seem now to be moving in the direction of the Mafia in a very big way. And I am quite sure that the vast majority of the community would fully support the police or anyone else going after such ill-gotten gains, particularly when such ill-gotten gains are being used as the material for killing other human beings.

2

Catholics and the State: Obligations and Entitlements – Bishop Cahal Daly
1989

Revisiting this interview and the issues discussed almost twenty years after the event, it is startling to find how far this determinedly non-political Bishop was ahead of the game.

When I met him at his Lisbreen residence in north Belfast I was deeply impressed by his quietude, and by his gentle insistence on the equal nobility of unionist and nationalist aspirations.

Bishop (Cardinal) Daly was unapologetic in explaining the 'counter-productive' nature of many of the security policies operational at that time, and in his belief that there could be no 'military solution' to the problem of Northern Ireland. Yet he had no hesitation either in endorsing a decision by members of his Church to join the then Royal Ulster Constabulary, even as he acutely understood the difficulties and dangers faced by those who did. Nor was there anything ambiguous about his view that Sinn Féin and the IRA were 'living in a political past' and had still to 'come to terms with the reality of the thinking of the people of Ireland'.

I put it to him that, if the principle of consent was to have any meaning, that surely must impose an obligation on nationalists to accept their minority status and play their democratic part, even while hoping for eventual constitutional change and Irish unification. The bishop readily concurred: 'Certainly. But with the proviso that they are regarded as fully legitimate citizens retaining their traditional nationalist identity and their nationalist aspirations, their Irish culture, their Irish self-definition. All of that has to be conceded and therefore the institutions of Northern Ireland now and from now on must be pluralist in that sense, that Northern Ireland has to be shared, just as in the familiar nationalist language that Ireland has to be shared ... Northern Ireland has to be shared between the two traditions which must be accepted as fully legitimate and must be allowed full access to responsibility and to power in the operation of the institutions of that pluralist Northern Ireland.'

In his advocacy of a new, pluralist Northern Ireland Bishop Daly, too, was pointing with remarkable prescience to what would become the Good Friday accord. In defining the duty of the good citizen, moreover – and the reciprocal obligations of the state – he might also have been providing a preview of the Patten Commission reform of the RUC and the ensuing debate about policing that would eventually enable the historic post-St Andrews deal between the DUP and Sinn Féin.

FROM *THE IRISH TIMES*, 23 AUGUST 1989

MILLAR: Bishop Daly, can I first of all put to you a view that you will be familiar with, a view that you will certainly have heard articulated on behalf of Northern Protestants: that Home Rule for the island of Ireland would of necessity be Rome Rule. Are you, as a Churchman, disappointed that both the Church and the representatives of the traditional Catholic nationalism have failed significantly to alter that perception within the Protestant community?

Dr DALY: Yes. I think that we have to regret that something they seem to see in the Catholic community and in the Catholic Church seems to them to be a threat and a danger. This has been caused by a number of very complex reasons but it is regrettable. I would have to say that, side by side with that, there is a great deal of contact and a great deal of growing understanding at certain levels in the Churches and in the communities, but not yet nearly enough. That's to some extent negatived by the propagation of crude and anachronistic anti-Roman Catholic propaganda which is deplorable. I have also to say that the fears of Protestants are in practice greatly augmented by the campaign waged by the IRA who are seen, mistakenly, to be somehow representative of the Roman Catholic community and somehow or other latently, secretly, tacitly approved if not sanctioned by the Roman Catholic Church. I have to say, to my very great regret – I don't want to name names – that one leading public figure, one leading representative of the Orange Order, spoke two years ago at the unveiling of an Orange banner and warned Protestants that the Roman Catholic Church is 'mobilising all its forces, religious, political and military,' to subjugate the Protestant community. When I challenged this but said that possibly he had been misquoted, he replied that yes indeed he had been misquoted. He had, he said, unfortunately failed to note on his script 'check against delivery'. He said he had, in fact, altered his text, making additions which he hoped I would find reassuring and he was herewith enclosing the text. The text had one hand-written insertion, which ran as follows: 'With some notable exceptions, both among clergy and laity, the Roman Catholic Church is mobilising all its forces, religious, political and military, against the Protestant community.' In other words, here is an intelligent man, a responsible leader, stating that the IRA are the military arm of the Roman Catholic Church. That is absolutely deplorable. I cannot comprehend how any person could responsibly say that.

MILLAR: Can I take it from your opening remarks that in terms of the issue of the unification of the island, that the Roman Catholic Church is neutral? I mean does it support the campaign for unity or does it regard that as none of its business?

Dr DALY: As a Churchman, I, have to say it is none of my business. In my own Catholic community in which I preach the Gospel, a Gospel of reconciliation, a Gospel of harmony and peace, in which I have to be an instrument and a sign of the power of the Church to make peace and to unite, I dare not, I morally must not, take political sides. In that community there are all shades of opinion, most of them broadly nationalist, certainly as a statistical fact, but I have to have respect for all shades of political opinion.

MILLAR: Would you accept that there may be a significant number of your flock who in fact would favour the continued link between Northern Ireland and Britain?

Dr DALY: I certainly would not be able to put a figure on that. I think that it would be very hard to formulate the question in terms that would produce an unambiguous kind of response. I would assume I have no more authority in this matter than anybody on the street, that the majority of Roman Catholics would be in favour of the eventual reunification in dialogue and mutual respect and peace and through the political process of the island of Ireland. But that's not a matter of their religious conviction and certainly is nothing to do with the teaching of their Church, and I would be grossly failing in my duty as a Christian pastor if I were to adopt any political position.

MILLAR: Would you therefore say that it is wrong for people, whether unionist or nationalist, to represent the issues that have to be addressed and positions that have to be accommodated in any form of political set-up, to represent those issues and interests purely in terms of Protestant and Catholic interests?

Dr DALY: Oh, certainly it would and I think the tendency to speak of, particularly, Catholic paramilitaries and Protestant paramilitaries is totally deplorable. I do have to admit that there has been, historically, a close inter-relationship, a close correlation between people's religious affiliation and their political aspirations, and that this has had wholly negative consequences in the history of Ireland. I think there should be a clear distinction between people's religious faith and their political aspirations.

MILLAR: When you and your fellow bishops went to the New Ireland Forum you said, I think, at one stage in the oral questions, that if any plan for a new Ireland was formulated which challenged or diminished in any way Protestant rights – the rights of the Protestants currently living in Northern Ireland – that the voice of the Catholic Church would be raised most strongly in their defence.

Dr DALY: Indeed.

MILLAR: Can I ask you what sort of rights did you have in mind at that time?

Dr DALY: Their religious freedoms. Their complete freedom of religious practice. Their complete freedom of religious preaching, mission and evangelism. All of this would have to be absolutely guaranteed and those civil rights which obviously are part of any democracy. And in addition, those rights which are frequently called the civil rights of Protestants but which I don't think Protestants would necessarily want to have regarded as their distinctive claims or rights, such as divorce, the right to contraception, and in general legislation affecting sexual morality. Many Protestants would agree in greater or a lesser measure with Catholics in respect of such matters; but in general most Protestants would regard them as matters of private conscience rather than public legislation.

MILLAR: I am sure you are certainly right that Protestants would not wish to have those rights regarded as purely Protestant. I wonder whether in any sense in your mind they appeared as Protestant rights. I mean do you in any sense regard Protestants as having a set of rights or expectations in those areas which should not necessarily extend, or be expected to be extended, to the Catholic community?

Dr DALY: I have always been reluctant to speak of these as Protestant rights. I was interested in an address given recently in Dublin by Archbishop Caird where he protested against the association of such matters with the Protestant faith and affirmed that the Church of Ireland is totally committed to the unity and indissolubility of marriage. And he expressed a fear, if I quote him correctly, that some people were quite prepared to exploit the Protestant community in the interests of something that has nothing to do with the Protestant faith, or indeed the Christian faith in general. Nonetheless, de facto, in popular parlance, the civil rights of Protestants are assumed to include matters of this kind. Now it would seem to me that the Protestant community is divided on these matters. For example on the question of abortion, the Life movement in Northern Ireland was organised by a very committed Protestant clergyman and his wife. Now, sadly, they have been called to mission elsewhere, not in Northern Ireland, but they were totally committed to the same view on the sacredness of human life from the moment of conception as Roman Catholics are. I give that as only one instance and we know very well there is a strong resistance to a change of legislation about abortion here on the lines of British legislation and it comes from Protestants even more vocally than it does from Roman Catholics. So there is an anomaly in speaking about these matters. Nevertheless in popular parlance there is a set of rights and liberties which are regarded as Protestant civil and religious liberties.

MILLAR: I think I understand all of what you outlined about the stresses, the contradictions, the different views that would be held, but you are talking about a set of rights where even if there was some accord with Catholic attitudes and specific issues towards marriage, about contraception, about abortion, the Protestant disposition would be to regard them as conscience issues and not the subject of clerical direction.

Dr DALY: That is correct.

MILLAR: At the Forum, you made clear that it was not your function to draft blueprints for constitutional change. Nonetheless, you were addressing the need for a new political climate, whatever shape the result would take, and the question has often occurred to me, as I have considered the submissions and admissions to the New Ireland Forum, whether you are proposing or hinting that, in the event of great constitutional change, a set of arrangements could be devised for Protestants or whether any set of rights established as part of the new political deal could not be a set of rights purely for Protestants but would be rights available and extended to all the people who would be party to the new political arrangements.

Dr DALY: I think that we would, in any future situation in Ireland, whatever it may be, and it is not for us, as you said, to propose a blueprint for constitutional change, but in any set of political institutions and under any regime in Ireland, we would be proclaiming the same Gospel. In fact, over the past 60 years, when we have had the two jurisdictions in Ireland, we have proclaimed exactly the same values in Northern Ireland and Southern Ireland, touching on all of these matters. We have responded to discussion documents, White Papers and so on in Northern Ireland on proposed changes in legislation regarding abortion, divorce, homosexuality, and we have adopted exactly the same position here as we did in the Republic because we feel that this is the Gospel of Christ as we understand it, and it is our mandate to proclaim it. As we said at the Forum, we do not want any power other than the power to proclaim the Gospel as we have inherited it and as we feel convinced we have received it from Christ. And we depend on the power of the Gospel and on the consciences and convictions of the people who accept that teaching. In matters of this kind, we have also recognised that there is a difference between the moral principle on the one hand and the duty of politicians to enact legislation on the other, and that in the enactment of legislation there are other factors to be taken into account as well as the distinctive moral principles which the Church proclaims. But we insist that the moral values be not left out of account. We have a responsibility to alert the consciences of those who listen to our teaching on the moral consequences and the moral implications of any proposed piece of legislation. We ask them not to neglect these, not to leave these out of account, to take these into the reckoning, to put them, as we said, into the balance, along with other factors, and in 1973, in connection with the first Health and Family Planning Bill introduced in the Republic, we mentioned specifically the need to promote reconciliation on this island of Ireland, and said that must be part of the balance as well. Then we leave it to the consciences of our people to reconcile these values, never neglecting the moral values. We are not telling people how they are to vote, we are talking to them about the moral aspect of the vote which they are to register.

MILLAR: But would you accept that you have been marginally more successful in the persuasive process on the other side of the border than you have here, that your voice is heeded in the Republic perhaps in a way that it is not here? Would you accept that the Protestant view in Northern Ireland would be that you rely a wee bit on something more than the sheer power of the argument, that is that the Church in the Republic does wield, whether directly or indirectly, a considerable amount of influence and it is a question of that influence and the manifestation of that influence that has dominated much of the discussion about the quest for a new Ireland from the beginnings, and indeed was one of the underlying themes of the whole experiment of the New Ireland Forum?

Dr DALY: But that influence to which you refer, which is undeniable – has that any basis other than what I have called the consciences and convictions of the people who freely accept the teaching of the Catholic Church? I doubt that it has as regards direct political influence.

MILLAR: What about the consciences and convictions of people who don't share an affinity with the Catholic Church?

Dr DALY: They freely expressed this in their votes in the two referendums to which I think we are indirectly referring.

MILLAR: And in the last referendum, we had the embodiment of a ban on divorce within the Constitution.

Dr DALY: It was in the Constitution and the referendum was to see whether it should be struck out or not.

MILLAR: The constitutional ban was reinforced by the will of the people, presumably by the will of the Catholic people. Do you at least understand that, as far as Ulster Protestants are concerned, that is the manifestation of the link between Church and state, which you in your submission to the New Ireland Forum disavowed?

Dr DALY: Yes, but we accompanied that disavowal with the assertion that people cannot separate their consciences from their political actions. They cannot leave their consciences outside the polling booth, and we feel an inescapable obligation to try to inform, to enlighten, to alert the consciences of Catholic people to the moral aspects of legislation, and I don't see how we can get away from that.

MILLAR: I can see why you want to do it and I can see that it is rather easier for you to do it in a country where the disposition of the over-whelming majority accords to your attitude and belief. But when you are addressing, as you were at the New Ireland Forum, the question of a wholesale restructuring of the political institutions in this island, the question really is whether the Church would be prepared to see its influence diminished to permit the creation of a framework of social legislation that just might be part of the necessary price for facilitating the kind of political change that the nationalists wish to see. To come back to the question that I was attempting to formulate; when you talked about Protestant rights and the need to protect them, and you defined what those Protestant rights broadly speaking were, did you have in mind that, if all else was equal, and a new Ireland was indeed part of the political agenda, that those Protestant rights which would have to be guaranteed as part of the new political structure would be rights that would be available to all the people in that new political structure, or would they somehow be a set of arrangements for Protestants grafted on to the end of some variety of the existing order?

Dr DALY: Again I would say that it is not for us to draw up constitu-tional blueprints for a new Ireland, a new united Ireland, but what we did say, and what I would strongly reiterate, is that in whatever polit-ical future there would have to be some constitutional legislative framework for it in which the existing historical rights, civil and reli-gious, of Protestants within Northern Ireland would be safeguarded. They are an existing fact, they are an existing legislative reality and that has to be respected whatever be the constitutional future.

MILLAR: Aren't they also, Bishop, a fact for the Catholic community who live in Northern Ireland, whatever the view of the Church about their access to these various things, the framework and social legisla-tion that pertains here? The Protestant community in Northern Ireland doesn't enjoy rights that are not available to the Catholic com-munity as well.

Dr DALY: I don't think that Catholics would identify with institutions of this State to the point of feeling that they enjoy all the rights that others do. All things that are regarded as rights to the consciences of some Protestants are not necessarily rights to be embraced by the con-sciences of Catholics. That is part of our problem here in Northern Ireland, that we have some Protestants, maybe many Protestants, who would see the Republic as a Catholic state for a Catholic people.

Catholics would historically see Northern Ireland as a Protestant state for Protestant people. But I don't see that I, as a Churchman, can go much beyond saying that we would demand, in the interests of reconciliation, in the interests of religious understanding, tolerance and humanism, that there be no infringement of the existing civil and religious liberties of the Protestants in Northern Ireland.

MILLAR: Would you not prefer, if you had the choice, to maintain the existing constitutional arrangements and have a Catholic State by and large for a Catholic people in the Republic than to pay the necessary price to persuade Protestants to take their place in a new Ireland, a price too high?

Dr DALY: I have no right as a Churchman to say whether I want a united Ireland and whether I am prepared to pay a price for that. I don't think we are talking of similar values. We are not trading, surely. We are not surely being asked to trade moral convictions against political gains. The Church has worked in Ireland and works worldwide under very diverse regimes, political and constitutional regimes, and all that we want is the liberty to preach the Gospel. You talk of the influence of the Church. The influence of the Church can wane for a very large number of reasons. That does not make us modify our teaching, or lessen our conviction of the truth of what we are saying. We are not in the business of getting votes but of forming consciences and we depend on the power of the Gospel we preach in order to do that and on the consciences of those who accept our teaching and we want no more power than that.

MILLAR: Do you believe that tinkering with social legislation touches the core of unionist dispositions that if only the Republic could have contraception, abortion, divorce, it would become the attractive place that for generation after generation of unionists it has failed to be?

Dr DALY: I've been a long time around in Northern Ireland, spent all my boyhood, 50 years of my early life here, and I have been hearing the same refrain so often that I have become somewhat blasé about it: if only Ireland had remained in the United Kingdom; if only Ireland had not left the Commonwealth; if only Ireland had not had the 1937 Constitution; if only … I think that we should go on to accept the existing realities and try to go on from there.

MILLAR: Unionists have accused your Church of ambivalence time and time again, of ambivalence on the question of the IRA campaign. Is there any validity to the charge?

Dr DALY: I would feel no, but I have to try to understand the views of those who sincerely think that there is, and I am often puzzled myself as to how they come to do so. I am wondering whether somehow or other it is difficult for some unionists to accept a valid distinction between nationalism – constitutional nationalism – and terrorism. It is often said that there isn't any fundamental difference between those who agree in wishing for a united Ireland. They are, after all, espousing the very same aims as the Provisional IRA claim to be fighting for, so what basically is the difference? They want the same thing, wanting it by different ways. I think that that has something to do with it and then the historical fact that most Catholics are nationalists as most Protestants are unionists and that historically there has been some intermingling and some confusion and some identification between Catholicism and nationalism on the one hand, and between Protestantism and unionism on the other. I think that is part of the explanation, but I would like to reiterate very strongly that it seems to me the campaign of the Provisional IRA is as harmful to nationalism as it is to unionism and is a threat to both of our communities and to the whole island of Ireland. It's a threat to the Republic of Ireland and its institutions as much as it is to Northern Ireland and its institutions.

MILLAR: A threat to the Republic of Ireland as well as the government in Northern Ireland?

Dr DALY: Absolutely, of course it is, because the IRA are ultimately there to subvert the institutions, the democratic institutions of the Republic of Ireland, too, and I think the Republic of Ireland realises that very well and has historically taken a very strong and very effective line against subversion of that kind. They do see it as a serious threat.

MILLAR: Do you think that within the Catholic community and not within the pro-Sinn Féin community there is the same clear understanding that you have just articulated: that the Republic as much as Britain must see the IRA campaign defeated?

Dr DALY: I think that this would be widely held, but permit me please to question the use of the word 'defeated', because that could suggest that there is a military solution, that there is a military defeat, and that I think is not the way forward. That is not the way to overcome that threat, which is very real to democratic institutions in both parts of Ireland. Any effective strategy for overcoming paramilitary violence has to have a very broad spectrum and has to redress the basic underlying social and economic problems which foster violence, which make it possible for violence to continue and to flourish in the deprived communities where it has its particular footholds.

MILLAR: I certainly would not want *The Irish Times* to headline that Bishop Cahal Daly calls for the military defeat of the IRA, unless that was in fact what Bishop Daly was calling for, but do you accept that the military is nonetheless an essential ingredient in the strategy and that there is no purely political way to deal with a terrorist organisation which is as entrenched and as sophisticated and as competent as the IRA has shown itself to be?

Dr DALY: There certainly has to be military protection of the public. There certainly have to be determined efforts to prevent explosions, murders, atrocities, everything that we associate with paramilitary violence. That has to be done in any society that aspires towards a peaceful democratic situation. So my answer is yes. But I would have to qualify that because all of these matters are very complex. I would have to say that certain military strategies and tactics can be counter-productive and can, in fact, have the opposite result to that which is intended. And it seems to me that security force tactics have to be kept under continuous review to make sure that they are not driving people into sympathy, however reluctant, with the IRA. I am convinced that the massive security presence, the constant interrogation, particularly of young people, leads to the almost universal perception in certain areas, particularly in west and north Belfast, that everyone, but everyone in such areas, is a suspect terrorist in the eyes of the security forces until he or she proves that that is not the case. The military operate under extremely difficult circumstances. The police operate in impossible circumstances, that has to be granted, and nevertheless there is a perception that they act as if they are in enemy territory and as if everyone, as I said, were a suspect enemy activist.

MILLAR: Isn't the reality, Bishop Daly, that in many cases they *are* in enemy territory?

Dr DALY: No, that is not the case and that is a fatal misreading of the situation. To treat people as if they were terrorists until they prove to the contrary is in fact to force many people into some kind of reluctant sympathy, if not active support of the IRA. I think that is a very important factor in our present situation and I am convinced, and I say it with sadness, that many of the activities and postures of the security forces are in fact having negative consequences.

MILLAR: What sort of activities of the security forces would you approve of?

Dr DALY: I think there has to be patrolling, but I question the turning of certain sectors, particularly in west and north Belfast, into places put on a war footing with massive concentration of troops in military posture, in combat gear at combat readiness. I find this intimidating. I find it frightening. I wonder just how effective it could be even in a strictly security sense.

MILLAR: The security forces might say the visible presence of their men you and others doubtless find intimidating isn't half as intimidating as the invisible but ever-present force that is sustained within those communities, where they operate, in what you yourself said, in conditions of great difficulty. If saturation of areas with troops is counterproductive, is the logical development of that argument not the withdrawal for all practical purposes of authority and is the consequence of that withdrawal not in fact to cede the territory to the terrorists?

Dr DALY: No, certainly not. What I am talking about is avoiding operations which in fact foster and favour the terrorists and which the terrorists want, which provide them with opportunities of mobilising young people into confrontation with security forces, keeping a constant fever of anger and resentment going on. And they are devilishly clever at scapegoating the security forces and directing the anger and resentment of people in what often is a very hopeless situation of chronic unemployment, chronic deprivation, chronic environmental neglect, diverting all that anger away from themselves, the IRA, and on to the security forces, and that's very easy to do. And they do it with enormous success and it seems to me that there should be a very cold critical look at security policies in order to make absolutely sure that that is not the end result of some of their behaviour.

MILLAR: Do you understand that when people like yourself say much of the security operation is counterproductive, in the minds of many, many unionists throughout Northern Ireland that that is the habitual cry that greets one security initiative after another, and it has formed over the years in the average unionist mind an expectation that almost any initiative taken by the security forces will be deemed by spokesmen from the Catholic community, or the nationalist community, to be counterproductive? So can I ask you again, apart from conceding the need for patrolling, what kind of security policy you would consider necessary and would support?

Dr DALY: You understandably think I am copping out on answers to questions of this kind, but I would have to say that I am not a security expert. But it would seem to me, after 20 years of experience, that a lot more could nave been learnt about how to deal with situations of this kind with sensitivity to community feelings, and that lessons could have been learnt from past experience, and I would sincerely hope that security commanders would look urgently at the experience gleaned over 20 years and decide now that if this kind of patrolling, this kind of activity, this kind of house searching has been counterproductive, then let us reduce this and try other ways. What I am certain of is that certain kinds of security operation are and are continuing to be counterproductive.

MILLAR: Do you accept the necessity of house searching?

Dr DALY: Yes, I think there have to be searches if explosions and murders are to be averted and if arms caches are to be discovered. And primary responsibility for this rests with the IRA, who use houses in which to cache their arms, and the tactics which they use are such that there has to be a very radical kind of search of a house – weapons could be discovered under six feet of concrete and searching for these weapons is necessarily going to be a painful experience. But nevertheless there are ways in which this is done without apparent sensitivity to the feelings and to the upset and the panic caused to children and old people and of course the people who are thereby grossly inconvenienced. Ways have to be found of ensuring that the inconvenience is reduced to a minimum and that alternative accommodation is quickly provided for those people and that every consideration is given to them. A house in which arms are stored is not necessarily a terrorist house.

MILLAR: Do you sense a great deal of disappointment within the Catholic community about the progress since the Anglo-Irish Agreement was entered upon?

Dr DALY: I feel that there has been a beginning of slow progress in certain domains. I think that there is a beginning of a movement towards fairness of employment. For example, statistics published recently about the denominational balance in the Civil Service are a hopeful sign. I think that the initiative called 'Making Belfast Work' is beginning to have some impact in very deprived areas, like west and north Belfast. I have honestly to say that I think it is still too little, that many more resources need to be put into that effort. It needs to be sustained and it needs to be intensified but it is most definitely on the right lines and it is just beginning to give people hope in the long term. The only way to overcome political armed conflict is to prove that other means, peaceful means, can deliver.

MILLAR: Do you think that the nationalist expectation of the Agreement is more to do with that material quality of life – economic prospects – than it is to do with a step-by-step process leading to the unification of the island of Ireland?

Dr DALY: I think that there is a link in most nationalists' minds between the two, because of their feeling of frustration and despair at the impossibility of progress under the old Stormont unionist-dominated regime as they experienced that state, and I do think that there is a very real aspiration towards an eventually reconciled and reunited island of Ireland. I think that's very real and I think it would be misleading to underestimate it or to feel, as was unfortunately said on one occasion, that if you give Catholics jobs and cars and modern conveniences etc they would just behave like Protestants, or unionists.

MILLAR: I don't believe that either, do you?

Dr DALY: I don't think so. But that's an opinion; I'm not speaking as a Churchman when I say that, but I don't believe it. But that's not to say that people either want or would accept an Ireland in which Protestants were subjected to the same kind of discrimination, subjugation, oppression, as Catholics were subjected to in all of Ireland historically in the past and feel they were subjected to and had the experience of being subjected to in Northern Ireland in the more recent past.

MILLAR: It would not, therefore, be a case of the shoe being on the other foot?

Dr DALY: Oh, certainly not. I would like also to say that the revulsion against the IRA which there is in large sections of the Catholic community is very, very strong. I wish unionists realised how strong it is. I ministered for 15 years in the Republic of Ireland; I therefore know the Republic of Ireland well and I know that there is a very, very strong and deep and widespread revulsion, perhaps even more marked in the Republic of Ireland, against the IRA, and I think that one of the greatest weaknesses of the IRA and Sinn Féin is that they are so totally out of touch with even nationalist opinion, throughout the island of Ireland as a whole, that they just simply do not know how utterly peripheral they are to that opinion. They are living in a political past. They are politically yesterday's people. They have not come to terms with the reality of the thinking of the people of Ireland of today.

MILLAR: Yet the Protestant perception, generally, in Northern Ireland is that it is the IRA who have provided the stimulus of the continued movement, bit by bit, towards the unification of the island. Do you give them no credit whatever, Bishop Daly? Did you believe, for example, that there would ever be an Anglo-Irish Agreement?

Dr DALY: The one certain thing which the IRA can claim to have achieved – no, shall I qualify that and say the one thing which, with great plausibility, the IRA can claim to have achieved – is the abolition of Stormont. The abolition of Stormont meant the institution of direct rule by the British Westminster parliament. Now I don't see how that could be regarded by the most committed IRA activist as an Irish republican victory.

MILLAR: Now that's a nice, almost political, argument, Bishop Daly, but it wasn't just the IRA in 1971/72 who decided that Stormont had to go. I think you would have to concede that a variety of people who were either then, or most certainly were to become, influential leaders of what you would term constitutional nationalism also agreed that Stormont had to be removed. What I put to you is that probably in the average Protestant, unionist mind in Northern Ireland, there is little or no doubt that it was more the muscle of the IRA than the persuasive arguments of an assortment of constitutional nationalists that secured that development. Can you see that to unionists and Protestants in Northern Ireland there is a link between a sustained campaign of violence and the period of 20 years which has been marked, dare I say it, by a series of pretty substantial reversals for unionism?

Dr DALY: And what has the role of the IRA been as a stimulus for all that? The 'if onlys' of history are, I suppose, always matters of debate. If only civil rights movements had not been resisted by sectarian mob-fuelled attack and so on. If civil rights had been peacefully conceded ...

MILLAR: But you don't believe that they would have behaved like good unionists anyway?

Dr DALY: I think that some of their more enlightened leaders were trying to point them in a new direction, and I think that people like Terence O'Neill saw very clearly that unionism in its own self-interest had to change, because he was as committed a unionist as any unionist ever was.

MILLAR: No, I meant the nationalists would not have behaved like good unionists, if the civil rights demands had been ...

Dr DALY: They wouldn't have behaved as good unionists, but they certainly would not have given any succour whatever or any kind of support to the IRA. The IRA was non-existent at that time.

MILLAR: And, after 20 years, the prospect of a united Ireland is further away and not closer.

Dr DALY: It has been made more distant and more difficult. The polarisation of the communities has become greater than ever. The suspicion between the communities, I think, is very acute.

MILLAR: Do you think that talk of a united Ireland at this point in time is an absurdity?

Dr DALY: No. I do not. Acceptance of the fact that a majority of nationalists aspire to a peacefully reconciled and reunited Ireland is part of the recognition and respect between the two traditions which is essential to any reconciliation and peace in this society. That is a legitimate aspiration. It has to be recognised as totally legitimate, totally legal, totally morally, legally and constitutionally acceptable, provided that, as it does, it rejects all recourse to violence.

MILLAR: Do you regard nationalism as in some way morally superior to unionism? Do you regard the aspiration for a union with the Republic as somehow more noble than the aspiration for a union with Britain?

Dr DALY: No. I can fully respect and accept the deep convictions which unite Protestants/unionists in Northern Ireland with the UK. I believe that unionists are fully justified in maintaining their political loyalty, identity and convictions. Equally, of course, unionists have to accept the legitimacy of the nationalist aspiration towards a united Ireland, which is a noble aspiration. Nationalism and unionism must be mutually recognised as equally noble.

MILLAR: But given that each accepts the legitimacy of the other's aspiration if they are equally noble, there is nothing invalid or lacking in legitimacy about the union between Northern Ireland and Britain. At the end of the day, doesn't the minority have to accept that, for the moment, they are a minority and the political future of the province has to be subject to the will of the majority?

Dr DALY: As the de facto situation, certainly, yes. And I think a very important and historic political opportunity was missed when the nationalist parties in Northern Ireland abandoned their sterile and negative policies of abstention and came together to form a united nationalist constitutional policy and party and expressed their willingness to enter into and operate through the institutions in Northern Ireland, that is to say to respect and operate within the institutions of Northern Ireland with a view to promoting peacefully and politically their ultimate united Ireland aspiration. I regret the fact that unionists sometimes failed to distinguish between that aspiration and treachery to, or treason against, Northern Ireland. I think somehow they felt that constitutional nationalists were dishonestly availing of the institutions of Northern Ireland in order to wreck them and to destroy them.

MILLAR: Given that there is a clear majority for unionism and that it shows no sign even after 20 years of violence of changing its position, would it be legitimate for the political minority to withhold their consent from the institutions and agencies of the State, and say we shall simply bide our time until the majority effectively changes its mind? Would that be a legitimate stance for the minority to take?

Dr DALY: No, I think, if they are committed to dialogue and to the peaceful political process and, as far as I read their declarations, constitutional nationalists are totally committed to operating the institutions of Northern Ireland and thereby abiding by those institutions in order eventually, with no time-span prescribed, to try to convince unionists that, particularly with the changing political realities in Europe and of the modern world, it will be in the interests of all of us that we come together peacefully in a reconciled Ireland eventually. But nationalists would, it seems to me, from their declarations, fully recognise that reconciliation has to begin here with the de facto situation and work within that situation; because in any kind of future institutional framework for Ireland we have got to have mutual respect and peaceful co-existence and co-operation between the two communities in Northern Ireland. That's where the conflict is, that's where the conflict has assumed such disastrous proportions. That's where solutions must be found. That's where the beginning of reconciliation has to be sought. That's not to go into the semantics of an internal Northern Ireland solution, that's not to agree with those who say that all ambiguity about the future status of Northern Ireland must first be removed. That, it seems to me, is to ask for the impossible. That is, in fact, to ask that nationalists become unionists as a condition of their belonging legitimately to the Northern Ireland State. I would like to say that that, too, is connected with a false identification between people and land, people and territory. On the one hand, you have the simplistic nationalist view that because Ireland is one island, one single land block, one land mass, it is therefore destined by providence to be one united nation. Now that's confusing the aspirations of a majority of the people who live in that land mass with the totality of the territory of the land mass.

MILLAR: All this is not necessarily on the side of the nationalists.

Dr DALY: Certainly not, the same confusion exists on the side of the unionists; because, on the other hand, when people talk about the integrity of the UK and the identity of Northern Ireland as being as British as wherever, they are identifying that part of the land mass of Ireland which is the six counties of Northern Ireland with that part of the population of these counties which is unionist. The simplistic nationalist view that I have spoken about effectively disenfranchises and denationalises, deprives of their national and political identity, 900,000 plus unionists who live here. Because they happen to live in a certain land mass, they are supposed to share the nationalist identity and aspirations of the majority of the inhabitants of that land mass, and this is not by any means the case. Equally, unionists have no right to assume that a condition of living constitutionally and lawfully within Northern Ireland is to accept that that territory is irreversibly part of the UK – for that in effect means to become a unionist.

MILLAR: I have heard various unionist politicians say that if a majority emerged within Northern Ireland in favour of change and leaving the union with Britain, they would accept that. I think there's a caveat, the proviso would be that until and unless that day comes, the political minority within Northern Ireland must accept that it is the minority. It must consent to the institutions of the State and it cannot adopt this spoiling, grudging role which says that until you are prepared to play the game by our rules we are simply not going to play the game. Do you accept as a general proposition that if the principle of consent is not merely a word used as a figure of speech between one kind of nationalist force and the Provisional IRA, if the oft-repeated principle of consent has meaning, that must impose, surely, obligations on the majority, but equally obligations on the political minority to play its part as a political minority, albeit hoping that some day the situation will change?

Dr DALY: Certainly. But with the proviso that they are regarded as fully legitimate citizens retaining their nationalist identity and their nationalist aspirations, their Irish culture, their Irish self-definition – all of that has to be conceded and therefore the institutions of Northern Ireland now and from now on must be pluralist in that sense, that Northern Ireland has to be shared just as in the familiar nationalist language Ireland has to be shared, so Northern Ireland has to be shared between two traditions which must each be accepted as fully legitimate and must be allowed full access to responsibility and to power in the operation of the institutions of that pluralist Northern Ireland.

MILLAR: Pending the point where the power is devolved, and presumably you were presupposing the creation of a new internal form of government in Northern Ireland, there are a set of political arrangements to which constitutional nationalists do consent and they are represented in the form of the structure of the Anglo-Irish Conference. What I am driving at through all of this is to the key question: whether, given that the State, as we have agreed, is legitimate, that the exercise of the majority will to remain within the community of Britain is legitimate, that there is nothing that can justify the campaign by the IRA to override the wish of the majority in Northern Ireland by force. Can it be legitimate in those circumstances then for constitutional nationalists to withhold their support from the security forces?

Dr DALY: I have already talked about some of the activities of the security forces which, it seems to me, are oppressive to innocent nationalists and I cannot withdraw that. I do think that there is a large degree, in practice, of support and cooperation extended to the security forces in nationalist communities. Where the RUC are doing a professional policing job, there is no problem. It is only when their zeal, their understandable zeal, for counter-paramilitary activity makes them be perceived as an oppressive, intrusive, occupying force that there is hostility towards them. That hostility can be reduced. It can be removed. And if the RUC were willing and were able to perform more strictly policing roles, in an area where there has been an acute proliferation of ordinary crime, the acceptability of the RUC would be rapidly enhanced. But this is not easy, in circumstances of IRA activity, when the next culvert or the next vacant block can be a position for a sniper or a bomb.

MILLAR: But you are a Churchman, not a politician, you can't pick and choose. I mean the good citizen isn't greedy. What's the teaching of the Church? Is the good citizen free to pick and choose when to support lawful authority and when to withhold that support?

Dr DALY: The good citizen has a right to protest against injustice by the security forces just as much as against injustice perpetrated by any citizen or agency. We are talking of abuses by security forces which must be resisted.

MILLAR: When it comes to a situation such as obtains in Northern Ireland, isn't it true that 'he who is not for us is against us'?

Dr DALY: If and when security forces are, in fact, abusing their authority, and are creating a situation which is conducive to paramilitary violence, then those who resist and who reject and repudiate paramilitary violence have a right to protest against the security forces' activities. You were asking for unconditional support of security forces. I don't see how any citizen in any democracy can do that.

MILLAR: Does reservation about abuses or excesses by the security forces in any circumstances free the good citizen of his obligations to fully cooperate with the security forces?

Dr DALY: No. It does not relieve the citizen of the obligation, the *prima facie* obligation, to cooperate with the security forces in ending acts of murder and bombing and destruction, and attacks on human life.

MILLAR: Would you consider the decision by a member of your Church to join the RUC a laudable action? Would you endorse it?

Dr DALY: Without qualification, I certainly would endorse a Catholic's decision to join the RUC.

MILLAR: So Catholics should be prepared, in your view, to join the security forces.

Dr DALY: They should, and I think that, if we are to have an acceptable police force, the religious balance within that police force must reflect the balance in the community as a whole.

MILLAR: The fact that the political difficulties, special difficulties, that pertain to all of these matters denies this – the kind of religious balance you would seek – should not this be regarded as justification or an excuse not to join?

Dr DALY: Quite right; but I would have to have great respect and great awareness of the enormous difficulties and dangers faced by Catholics who join the police force. Many of them do. They do so in a real desire for public service. They see policing as a legitimate form of service to the total community. The price of doing so will often be to put their own lives on the line. It almost certainly will mean their leaving certain Catholic areas, for some of these, because of IRA activity, would be out of bounds for a Catholic member of the police force. That's going to be an upheaval, that's going to create all sorts of pressures and difficulties for himself or herself as a person, and for the family. One would have to admire the courage of those who, nevertheless, take the decision to join the police force.

MILLAR: The decision to join is certainly something you would uphold as a Churchman and as a citizen?

Dr DALY: Absolutely.

MILLAR: You've resisted the role of draftsman of political formulae and there is just one particular blueprint that has been put to me in the course of this series of *Irish Times* interviews which I would like to tempt you to consider, and it is the blueprint devised by John Hume. He has redefined, it seems to me, self-determination for the Irish people. He has proposed, though there has been little response yet to it, a process of dialogue which, if successful, would arrive at a point where a set of proposals for the future sharing of this island could be put simultaneously to people in Northern Ireland and in the Republic by way of referendum. And he has said that if a majority were found, on both sides of the border, for such a new arrangement, that would constitute self-determination by the people of the island and therefore the resolution for all time of the ancient quarrel.

Dr DALY: Yes.

MILLAR: Would you see virtue in that fairly radical change in the nationalist disposition?

Dr DALY: Certainly. I would have to say that I have never had discussions with John Hume nor have I ever had discussions with any SDLP politician. I have done that quite deliberately, because I feel that any discussions of this kind could compromise my position as a Churchman and be misunderstood – and I have been called the vicar-general of the SDLP!

MILLAR: You've been called worse.

Dr DALY: I have never had meetings with any SDLP politician or indeed with any politician. Nevertheless I think that any formula for dialogue, any movement towards dialogue, is desirable and urgently needed. I should certainly welcome some response to that proposed context for dialogue being put forward on the unionist side. Some tentative moves seem to have been made or to be likely to be made in that direction, but I think there has to be some public indication by politicians of readiness for dialogue and some spelling out of at least the broad parameters, the broad context in which dialogue should take place. The essential thing is that the dialogue should take place.

MILLAR: If in fact this process of dialogue were to be successful, that the proposals were put to joint referendum, given that the central ingredient of Hume's plan is that, if the majority in Northern Ireland withheld their consent, there would be no agreements; has it occurred to you the end result of such a process offered by John Hume would be a far cry from the unitary Irish State that has been the dream of Irish nationalists all these years?

Dr DALY: All I shall say to that is that there has to be a movement away from the simplistic unitary nationalist point of view which simply ignored the existence of nearly a million people in Northern Ireland who did not share that view, but who are legitimate inhabitants of this island of Ireland, who have been here for many more years than any white person has been in the US or in North America. They have been simply semantically doomed to non-existence, to non-citizenship, to non-identity by that elementary error of identifying land with people. Politics is about people, not about land masses. It's about people. It's about political identity, the national identity of communities of people.

MILLAR: If that reconciliation that you would wish for as an Irishman and as a Churchman is to take place, you presumably accept that it is the unionist/British identity of those people who have been previously disregarded that nationalism has to address.

Dr DALY: Exactly. Just as unionists have to address the nationalist identity of the people who are legitimate inhabitants of that part of Ireland which unionists claim as exclusively British.

MILLAR: A final question. If there isn't a new political development within Northern Ireland in the not too distant future, what do you see as the future of this place?

Dr DALY: Rather grim. Redeemed, however, by the enormous resilience of the people in both communities, and by the great spirit of goodwill which exists at grass roots level in both communities. It is redeemed by the developments which have in fact been slowly and with painful difficulty taking place at the level of reconciliation between the Churches and at the level of distancing of the Churches from the political communities to which their adherents belong. That is a very significant fact, that now there has been a perceptible distancing of all the Churches, all the mainstream Churches, from political unionism on the one hand and political nationalism on the other hand. That is a very hopeful sign for the future. It's slow and painful, but it is beginning to go on. I wouldn't want to see dialogue being promoted solely for the purposes of the overcoming of violence. It's necessary and good and right in itself; political dialogue is something that we must pursue for its own sake, not necessarily holding it out as a panacea for the elimination of violence; it's good and right and necessary in itself, it's a political imperative. Politicians who refuse it are simply refusing to accept their political responsibility.

3

Desperately Seeking an Alternative – John Taylor 1989

John Hume might have been pretty certain about his direction of travel in the late 1980s but there were few if any signs that unionist politicians thought to make the journey with him.

A month after he had outlined it for the *Irish Times* I put the Hume vision to James Molyneaux, then already the long-serving leader of the Ulster Unionist Party (UUP). What did unionists have to lose from his idea of a standing conference and an agreement, if it could be found, to be put to the peoples of Northern Ireland and the Republic in separate or dual referendums? It seemed to me that if a majority could be found for such a settlement in both jurisdictions that could only serve to underpin and reinforce the British unionist position in Northern Ireland. But Mr (Lord) Molyneaux was notoriously hostile to grand schemes and talk of major initiatives – what he liked disparagingly to call 'the high wire act'. 'With great respect to Mr Hume,' he told me, 'I can't understand that philosophy, and I can't see the validity of it.' (*The Irish Times*, 14 February 1989)

In fairness to Molyneaux, he was reflecting the deep-seated unionist view that talk of a political solution itself encouraged IRA violence because of what he perceived as British ambiguity about Northern Ireland's constitutional position. An advocate of modest administrative devolution for the province, he and his parliamentary colleague Enoch Powell had once defined the upper limit of what they thought possible as an arrangement offering participation for all sides 'that would neither endanger the union nor confer contrived privileges on any section of the community'. This was barely-concealed code for their opposition to significant power-sharing, which Molyneaux insisted meant compulsory coalition: 'It's not power-sharing; it's compulsory and permanent. It's permanent, compulsory coalition and that, of course, would not work in any civilised, democratic state.'

Molyneaux could barely have imagined that his eventual successor as UUP leader, David (Lord) Trimble, would broker such an arrangement with the SDLP in 1998. Nor, still less, that his ally in the joint unionist leadership of the time, the Rev. Ian Paisley, would eventually sit as First Minister in a Stormont Executive with Sinn Féin's Martin McGuinness as his co-equal Deputy First Minister.

Sinn Féin, of course, barely featured in anyone's best-case scenario at this point. It would later emerge that the republican transition that would lead to the 1994 and 1997 IRA cessations and Sinn Féin's entry into the political process was at least being contemplated even before the Anglo-Irish Agreement. In 1989, however, it was difficult enough to find unionists ready to cede a role that might prove attractive even to the SDLP.

Molyneaux's veteran UUP colleague John Taylor (Lord Kilclooney)also reflected the general unionist antipathy toward the SDLP. 'It has now become a very green party,' he told me. Taylor likewise baulked at Hume's proposed self-determination by way of dual referendums, which he considered a potentially dangerous and (in terms of republican sentiment in the Republic) inflammatory idea. At the same time Taylor, like many others, also divined opportunity in the 'weakness' of the Anglo-Irish Agreement, namely the exclusion of the unionist community and its representatives. Hume would repeatedly insist there were 'three sets of relationships' to be resolved – those within Northern Ireland, those between Northern Ireland and the Republic and those between both parts of the island of Ireland and Britain. Would Taylor accept that? 'Oh, absolutely,' came the reply. 'And that, of course, underlines the weakness of the Anglo-Irish Agreement – it was only a Dublin–London axis. The most important player in the political scene is Belfast, and Belfast was totally ignored in the Anglo-Irish Agreement. We have got to get Belfast into the political game again, and once access is gained, that's where we have to be fairly positive in what we are offering London, the two communities in Northern Ireland and Dublin.'

John Taylor maintained the Molyneaux/Paisley line that time was on the side of unionists seeking its suspension as the price for entering talks about 'an alternative to and replacement of' the Anglo-Irish Agreement. The architects and supporters of the Agreement could of course counter that getting Belfast back 'into the game' was precisely what it had been designed to achieve.

The then Strangford MP was the great survivor of unionist politics. A junior Home Affairs minister in the old Northern Ireland Parliament, he had survived an assassination attempt by the Official IRA in 1972 shortly before Edward Heath's Conservative Government suspended Stormont. Famously independent-minded, critics and rivals alike respected his unerring instinct for what would pass muster with the unionist community. It is highly unlikely David Trimble would have signed the Belfast Agreement on that famous Good Friday 1998 had his defeated leadership rival-turned-loyal-deputy not been solidly by his side.

Interestingly, too, Taylor appeared to sense a change in Irish policy on Northern Ireland that would prove crucial to eventual agreement but would not become apparent for many years. 'Dublin in many ways has been the South Africa of the Irish island; it has helped destabilise government in Northern Ireland,' he said. 'But that has been counter-productive for Dublin as well because many people now agree that the events of the past 20 years have damaged the economy of the Republic of Ireland. So it's not in the interest of Dublin to destabilise political administration in Northern Ireland and certainly it is not in our interest, as a majority unionist community in Northern Ireland, to have an unfriendly neighbour.'

After Ian Paisley and Martin McGuinness were installed in office in May 2007, former Taoiseach Garret FitzGerald confirmed the change that had occurred and, in his view, the reason for it. Writing in the *Irish Times* that same month, FitzGerald said it was the Provisional IRA's violence that forced a re-think of what he described as 'the counterproductive and provocative anti-Partition policy' to which the parties in the Republic had committed themselves between 1949 and 1969. He went on: 'It also forced a recognition that the security interests of the Irish state required a stabilisation of the Northern Irish polity within the UK.'

Back in 1989 John Taylor could not have known that he and Trimble would be the beneficiaries of that policy change – with all its implications for Articles 2 and 3 of the Irish Constitution, the genuine embrace of the principle of consent and its enabling power to permit a Northern Ireland partnership based on equality. Nor that it would be delivered by a Fianna Fáil Taoiseach called Bertie Ahern.

FROM *THE IRISH TIMES*, 27 SEPTEMBER 1989

Having been around through the advent of the civil rights campaign and the birth of the troubles, I began by asking John Taylor to what extent it might be said unionists had been the authors of their own misfortunes.

TAYLOR: Well, I think in the late 1960s we were authors of our own misfortune in that the leadership of the Unionist Party was making promises and offering more than it could deliver. And that is the worst thing to do in politics. Of course, this made the Irish minority in Northern Ireland anticipate that they were getting more than could be delivered. This led to the civil rights confrontations and the internal rows within the Unionist Party. That was the first fatal mistake – the form of leadership given by Terence O'Neill created a lot of the problems which we have had during the last 20 years.

MILLAR: Do you think, though, in hindsight, that if O'Neill, whatever the deficiencies of his leadership, had been permitted to respond as he wished to respond to the civil rights campaign, you could have prevented, if not the Provisional IRA campaign, certainly a campaign so strongly supported within the Catholic community?

TAYLOR: That's fair comment. But in politics sometimes the logical thing is not necessarily what the people will allow you to do. And in Northern Ireland such are the intense feelings and deep-seated fears that what an outside observer might consider logical is not the kind of thing you can deliver politically. And that we must always take into account.

MILLAR: Do you not think, though, that unionist leaders have been prepared since O'Neill to shelter unduly behind that fear of going too far ahead of their troops? The converse surely is true – the function of leadership is to lead. Do you think there is anything in the complaint that unionist leaders have been too reticent?

TAYLOR: I would consider that to be a very unfair charge against the Ulster Unionist Party. We have one prime example of what happened when a leader did go beyond the troops – Brian Faulkner signing the Sunningdale Agreement – and you saw what happened then. He did not have the political support in the country, the people would not accept the logic or otherwise of the Sunningdale Agreement and he and the power-sharing Executive were torn asunder.

MILLAR: With hindsight do you have any regrets about the demise of the power-sharing Executive?

TAYLOR: None whatsoever. I would be opposed to any imposed system of government and any power-sharing Executive whereby the government was selected by English overlords and not by the free will of the Ulster people. Of course, the power-sharing Executive was overthrown mainly because of the executive powers given to the Council of Ireland. That was the main issue.

MILLAR: So the issue was the relationship between Northern Ireland and the Republic rather than the role of the SDLP within the internal government?

TAYLOR: Yes. English observers misunderstood the situation. We were very embittered that the Council of Ireland, and thereby the Republic of Ireland's government, were given executive powers. In the English press it was presented that we were against Catholics and being governed by the power-sharing government; that wasn't the case. Unionists would accept Catholics in the devolved administration of Northern Ireland but not power-sharing in the way it was structured and enforced by English ministers.

MILLAR: Would you accept that, whatever the justification for the decisions taken, however valid the worries of unionist leaders about going too far ahead of their troops, unionism has been saddled for 20 years with a perception that it is a reactionary, negative, ungenerous force and that it represents a determined and consistent attempt to keep all power in its own hands?

TAYLOR: That has been a very damaging image in Great Britain, Europe and, of course, in the US. And your image is 50 per cent of the battle. If you have a good image you can usually deliver other things. But you must remember that we have been a community under siege for the past 20 years. Politically, London turned against us. Militarily, we have had the IRA against us. And we had an expectation in the Irish minority community, which was a lingering threat in the1960s, '70s and early '80s that in some way the majority would cease to be the majority in Northern Ireland. Three factors – political support, security threats and demographic trends – were running against the Ulster unionists. Luckily, they are beginning to change now; certainly, the demographic one isn't the threat it was 20 years ago.

MILLAR: The civil rights campaign was also marked by the emergence of Ian Paisley as a dominant force within unionism. Do you think Paisley has been good for Northern Ireland's image?

TAYLOR: You could not expect me to say that. I have been a colleague of Ian Paisley in the European Parliament and certainly the image he has portrayed there has been very damaging for the British majority community in Northern Ireland. There is more to politics than continually expressing a distaste for the Pope and regrettably that is the image he presented in Strasbourg. I am glad to say that there was another unionist image presented, hopefully by myself, which was respected by members from all the political groups in that parliament. I think we have got to show that unionism isn't an anti-Catholic force.

I'm certainly no supporter of the Roman Catholic Church – I'm a member of the Presbyterian Church – but Roman Catholics have a part to play in the life of Northern Ireland. I respect their right to their own religion, and as a British majority we must show our Catholic neighbours that they have equal opportunities in this province and we mustn't go out of our way to be distasteful towards them because of their religion.

MILLAR: Ian Paisley's appeal, of course, has been in part to people who perceive the Ulster Unionists as weak in their approach to Northern Ireland's enemies. Would unionism be in a stronger or weaker position today had Paisley not been on the scene?

TAYLOR: He naturally scored because the Protestant community felt under siege, for the three reasons I have given: demographic, IRA and lack of support in London. When you are under siege you run to the strong voice and no-one would deny that Ian Paisley has a strong voice. The trouble was that his actions were in many ways counterproductive and damaging for the British majority in Northern Ireland. It lessened respect for the British people of Northern Ireland, in London or on the Continent, and in some respects it was actually counterproductive because it made London more anti the unionist community than perhaps they would have been.

MILLAR: Do you think your party suffers by its continued association with the DUP?

TAYLOR: No, I think electorally we have actually advanced. Facts show that.

MILLAR: So the pact has worked to the disadvantage of the DUP?

TAYLOR: The pact is very important and I support it. The British community in Northern Ireland must be united in its opposition to the Anglo-Irish Agreement if they are going to have it replaced by another form of agreement. It also encourages the DUP to think in political terms and not in terms of the politics of climbing mountains late at night or capturing Clontibret in the evening and things like that.

MILLAR: Would you not accept that the unionist community has by and large stopped thinking about the Anglo-Irish Agreement? That the Anglo-Irish Agreement is not perceived by unionists to be in any way as threatening as the unionist political establishment decreed it to be three-and-a-half years ago?

TAYLOR: No I don't think so. There is a great underlying bitterness within the Northern Ireland community about the Anglo-Irish Agreement. Public opinion poll after opinion poll confirm that the opposition has actually increased. The elections show that the Ulster Unionist vote is increasing. Their share of the poll is increasing. I think that anyone who believes for one moment that opposition to the Anglo-Irish Agreement has declined is misreading the situation. Certainly there is no boycott of parliament. But then I was always against the boycott of parliament. Certainly, the councillors are back on the councils; I always felt they should never have resigned anyway. But just because people are doing the kind of things they should always have been doing doesn't mean they have weakened in their opposition to the Anglo-Irish Agreement, because I certainly haven't.

MILLAR: There isn't much of a manifestation of unionist opposition to the Anglo-Irish Agreement. I mean those tactics which you have referred to, pursued as part of the campaign against the Agreement, were designed to manifest, weren't they, the abnormal and changed circumstances in which the province had been placed? Now, to all intents and purposes, political life has been resumed ...

TAYLOR: No, it hasn't. The main part of the political life in Northern Ireland has not resumed, and that's the creation of a devolved institution. You see, if you resign from Castlereagh Borough Council, which I would serve on now as a member, it's not going to bring the wheels of government in Northern Ireland to an end. Nor, indeed, is Mrs Thatcher going to do away with the Anglo-Irish Agreement because I suspect she has never heard of Castlereagh Borough Council. So the idea of resigning from councils was ineffective and always would be. Where we (the British majority in Northern Ireland) have the power is to decide what form of devolution, if any, there is going to be. And that was the main objective of the Anglo-Irish Agreement. That is the political way in which we can give leadership in Northern Ireland. And we have stopped devolved government getting off the ground and it will fail to get off the ground until an alternative to the Anglo-Irish Agreement is in place.

MILLAR: So killing devolution is the direct political route for unionism to strangle the Anglo-Irish Agreement?

TAYLOR: Yes, that is it.

MILLAR: And devolution? It remains your view that devolution would be an essential ingredient of the Anglo-Irish process and that for unionists to participate in any devolution within the context of an ongoing agreement would be to facilitate and further extend the authority of the Agreement?

TAYLOR: Absolutely. Anyone who would contribute to the creation of a devolved system of government at Stormont at the moment would simply be underpinning the role of Dublin within Northern Ireland, and the next day there would be a further extension of republican rule in Northern Ireland. So the one way we can stop it, and we have done this for four years, is not to participate in any devolved system whilst the Anglo-Irish Agreement is in place. And that's why the Anglo-Irish Agreement is now seen more and more in London to be a failure. More and more people see that there is total stalemate in Northern Ireland due to the intransigence of Mr Tom King and the Northern Ireland Office in the handling of the various initiatives from the unionists.

MILLAR: Would you not accept, John, that the situation is considerably different from that which pertained at the time of the Agreement? You've got a different government as partner to begin with, and the present Taoiseach has never exhibited any strong disposition for devolution. There does appear to be a strong lobby of criticism within the Republic, from Fine Gael and Peter Barry, at the failure of the government of Charles Haughey to support devolution. Hasn't the ball game altered?

TAYLOR: It's very easy for them to criticise Mr Haughey in this respect, because they know what I said earlier. That the main objective of the Anglo-Irish Agreement was to create a power-sharing devolved system of government at Stormont. Four years later they have failed to achieve that and they have been embittered by the failure of the Anglo-Irish Agreement in its main objective. But it's too simplistic to blame Charles Haughey for this. In many respects he is reading the situation correctly. He knows that you could not tomorrow get agreement in Northern Ireland for devolved government, because he knows the Anglo-Irish Agreement is a barrier and he knows that the idea of Ian Paisley and, for example, Seamus Mallon being in the same cabinet in Northern Ireland is not practical politics. It would not last more than a week.

MILLAR: You have been successful in stopping devolution for the period of the Anglo-Irish Agreement. But you are not in real terms any closer than you ever were to securing the suspension of the Agreement. Do you think that for the unionist leadership to continue to insist on suspension as a prerequisite to negotiation is realistic?

TAYLOR: Yes I do, and we have been partly successful. What one must look at, first, is what has happened in the Republic. Many of those who were adamant that the Anglo-Irish Agreement was the solution are now saying … well, perhaps it could be suspended, perhaps it could be kicked to touch. Even Dick Spring, the leader of the Irish Labour Party, who was one of the signatories at Hillsborough Castle, has now said that perhaps it should be put to the side to allow political progress to take place in Northern Ireland. Even the most adamant supporter of it, Peter Barry, used some phrase like 'it was not written in holy rock' or something like that. They are beginning to see that an alternative is needed and likewise in Great Britain you now find newspapers like *The Independent* or *The Spectator* criticising the lack of progress as a result of the Anglo-Irish Agreement. More and more people recognise that to get political progress in Northern Ireland it would be wise to leave the Anglo-Irish Agreement to the side – to suspend it for a period during which real political negotiations could take place. Of course, this problem in Northern Ireland, this stalemate, can only be resolved by political negotiations in which the Ulster Unionists will have to give the leadership when that time comes.

MILLAR: Suppose the British government remains stubbornly opposed to some form of suspension, why not take or avail of the alternative route offered to Mr Molyneaux by Charles Haughey in one of those smoke signals that he and Mr Molyneaux have exchanged from time to time? He offered talks outside the parameters of the Agreement, about an alternative agreement which could transcend the existing agreement. Is that not a way out of the impasse?

TAYLOR: No, because I think the people in Northern Ireland would see through that as a totally dishonest exercise. It's slightly like the Duisburg operation; you are going to have some kind of statement to be sold to one section of the community saying that the Agreement would be suspended and to the other section of the community saying that it hadn't been suspended. You can't play like that in Northern

Ireland. You must play the bat straight and openly. The clear thing to do is to have a temporary suspension of the Anglo-Irish Agreement to get real political progress here. As I say, there has been some movement in Dublin which I welcome as an Ulster Unionist. That has been brought about partly by the change in government there. You will find the same in London. You must remember we had to suffer four years of the Anglo-Irish Agreement under a Thatcher government with a 100-seat majority. But life does not continue like that forever. There will be some day when Thatcher will go. In fact, it looks sooner rather than later. At the end of the day this is a contest between a government in London and the people of Northern Ireland. But one thing you can guarantee is that the government in London will go before the people in Northern Ireland; and when it goes, we'll still be here. And we still have to be dealt with.

MILLAR: Do you believe that the Agreement leaves Northern Ireland, as Peter Robinson once described it, on the window ledge of the union with England? How important is it to get rid of the Agreement quickly?

TAYLOR: There is no doubt in my mind that the Anglo-Irish Agreement was a skilful operation by the British Conservatives and officials, both within the Foreign Office and the Northern Ireland Office, and indeed the Home Office, to nudge Northern Ireland out of the union of Great Britain and Northern Ireland – out of the United Kingdom – and to give the South of Ireland a foothold in the internal affairs of Northern Ireland. That is why it is essential that we stand firm on this issue of bringing an end to the Anglo-Irish Agreement and get a replacement which will improve relations within this island of Ireland and above all improve relations within Northern Ireland itself.

MILLAR: What would the parameters of an alternative agreement be?

TAYLOR: The first thing is to accept that there are two states in this island – Northern Ireland and the Republic of Ireland. And the main problem in Northern Ireland is to recognise what the realities are within Northern Ireland: first, there is a majority community which looks upon itself as being British and is certainly going to remain British. It has no intention of getting out of Northern Ireland. So, like it or not – and I would like to think that most people like it – there is going to be a majority British community in Northern Ireland for many years to come. And academics in the universities now project that the balance will be 60/40 as far as one can see, right into the 21st century. You may remember that there was a time when the Northern Ireland Office were promoting articles in *The Times* of London and other papers about 10 years ago to say that very shortly there would be an Irish majority in Northern Ireland.

MILLAR: Well, in fairness to the Northern Ireland Office, Terence O'Neill, I think, was the author of the original article.

TAYLOR: Yes, that's right. But they did really promote that idea in the last decade. That has all changed. So Dublin and London have to live with the reality that there is going to be a British majority in Northern Ireland and that British majority in Northern Ireland have to live with the fact that a large number of people are embarrassed by what goes on there: that we have a minority that are unhappy and that we have a neighbour which has continued to destabilise the internal situation in Northern Ireland in political and security ways for the past 20–30 years. Dublin in many ways has been the South Africa of the Irish island; it has helped destabilise government in Northern Ireland. But that has been counterproductive for Dublin as well, because many people now agree that the events of the past 20 years have damaged the economy of the Republic of Ireland. So it's not in the interest of Dublin to destabilise political administration in Northern Ireland and certainly it is not in our interest, as a majority community in Northern Ireland, to have an unfriendly neighbour. So we must try and create conditions where there is better cooperation between North and South. So then what do we do?

MILLAR: John Hume defined three sensible requisites, and Peter Robinson told *The Irish Times* that he accepted that a new agreement would have to address the relationships between the Protestant and Catholic communities within Northern Ireland, between a devolved institution in Northern Ireland and the parliament and government of the Irish Republic, and between both parts of the island of Ireland and Britain. Would you accept that, whatever your intention and whatever your objective in terms of structures and the exact relationships, those are the three sets of relationships that would have to be incorporated in the new agreement?

TAYLOR: Oh, absolutely. And that, of course, underlines the weakness of the Anglo-Irish Agreement – it was only a Dublin–London axis. The most important player in the political scene is Belfast, and

Belfast was totally ignored in the Anglo-Irish Agreement. We have got to get Belfast into the political game again, and once it gets access and Dublin and London face up to the need to get Belfast involved, once access is gained, that's where we have to be fairly positive in what we are offering London, the two communities in Northern Ireland and Dublin. And that's what unionists have to address.

MILLAR: How positive are you going to be with what you have to offer the minority community within Northern Ireland?

TAYLOR: They themselves have to face up to the fact, like it or not, there is going to be a British majority community in Northern Ireland and they have to try to live alongside that community. There is no question of them taking over or becoming the majority, as far as one can see. Once they have accepted that position, we must be generous and magnanimous to them and involve them in the administration of the State within the framework of the United Kingdom and in an increasingly friendly relationship with the Republic of Ireland. Now, how do you do it? There are those who talk about integration, but I'm an Ulsterman first and foremost and I do not like integration in its entirety. Because I have a sneaking suspicion about English politicians and their attitudes towards the Ulster people and I would prefer to see Ulster people, Roman Catholic and Protestant, in the leadership as far as possible in the administration and government of Northern Ireland.

MILLAR: Can we be clear that when you say Protestant and Catholic, that you are talking about unionist and nationalist as well? Presumably, this generosity extends to a role for nationalists in the new administration in Northern Ireland.

TAYLOR: Obviously. No question about it. Nationalists who would like to have a united Ireland eventually but who hopefully accept that there is no likelihood of that in the next 50 years plus. But certainly not united Irelanders who support violence – they would have no role to play in this. But if you get a political settlement, political support for the IRA would begin to wither away.

MILLAR: It's an important point which Bishop Daly raised with me. I was questioning him about the role of the minority and the acceptance of the fact that it is a political minority and the responsibilities that would impose upon them. He acknowledged their role as a minority and he said that acceptance of the majority's rights was conditional on unionists not expecting nationalists in effect to become unionists, not expecting them to forfeit their aspiration to see the island of Ireland united. To permit them, notwithstanding their aspiration for Irish unity, a full part to play in the new political system: you accept that?

TAYLOR: Yes, I've no question about that at all. I would fully support that. You can't expect a nationalist to become a unionist. He's going to be a Roman Catholic. He's going to want a united Ireland. He's going to play Gaelic football. He's going to go to a Catholic school. These are the realities of life in Northern Ireland and we've got to accept them.

MILLAR: So, if it's going to succeed, it's not going to be a few token Catholics?

TAYLOR: Not at all. That's not a credible situation and that is not the kind of solution which would bring about political stability in Northern Ireland. Certainly not the type of solution that would wean support from Sinn Féin, and that must be the ultimate target – to weaken and eventually destroy Sinn Féin in Northern Ireland.

MILLAR: Do you run away from the description of that kind of arrangement as power-sharing?

TAYLOR: It's not power-sharing. Power-sharing is a specific term which is widely misunderstood. Power-sharing was a system of cabinet government where one party, the SDLP, was, as of right, guaranteed positions in that cabinet for evermore in Northern Ireland, and the personalities who would enter that cabinet would be selected by an English Secretary of State. That was power-sharing. But what we want to get is Catholics and Protestants working together, sharing responsibilities for the administration.

MILLAR: Ken Maginnis is fond of that expression. Is that a more acceptable description?

TAYLOR: It is. Because that is not sharing power. You have got to define what the power is. So what is the power? Well, you see I don' t think we can get a devolved government now in Northern Ireland. I was a keen devolutionist. I served as a junior minister and then as a cabinet minister in a devolved government, and, as I said earlier, I am a strong Ulsterman and would like to see as much power here as possible. But I think the realities of the last few years, caused regrettably by the Anglo-Irish Agreement, have created such bitterness and division within this community that the idea of a full-blooded devolved legislature at Stormont is not a political possibility.

MILLAR: Is that because of the depth of unionist hostility to the SDLP? Distrust of the SDLP?

TAYLOR: Yes, I think the personalities that have emerged in the SDLP in recent years have made the divisions worse than they were.

MILLAR: John, let me run that past you again. Is that because of the depth of unionist hostility to the SDLP?

TAYLOR: Yes, it is. These divisions in the community are partly because of that, partly because of the Anglo-Irish Agreement. The image of the SDLP has changed in the last five years. It has now become a very green party, with a very rabid anti-security image, anti-UDR, anti-police, wanting a united Ireland or nothing. The Curries have fled, Paddy Devlin has resigned, Gerry Fitt has disappeared, it has a new image which is not acceptable in sharing government in a legislature. So what do you do? You've got three problems: Who makes the laws? Who administers the laws? And what is the relationship with Dublin? I think that we cannot have a devolved government, for the reasons I have outlined, and I am certainly against any rigged form of devolved government here in Northern Ireland.

MILLAR: So what is the way around it?

TAYLOR: Well the way around it is, if you accept that we cannot have a devolved government, we then have to decide who is going to make the laws. And the obvious answer is, as we are in the United Kingdom, the laws must be made by the national parliament at Westminster. And, strangely enough, laws emanating from Westminster are more widely accepted by both religious communities in Northern Ireland. Catholics feel that they are being treated more fairly by the law-making body in London than they would at Stormont. So you are satisfying one of the built-in fears that the Catholic minority have by having the laws made in Westminster. And they should be made in the normal parliamentary process, by means of bills, with full readings and full rights to debate and amend, which we are all denied at the moment; and there should be a grand committee of Northern Ireland Affairs at Westminster.

MILLAR: So you have the laws being enacted at Westminster. What do you have here?

TAYLOR: You must have a body to administer those laws and this is where you must try to involve Catholic nationalist people as much as the Protestant unionist people. There I would like to draw on my experiences in Strasbourg and the European Parliament, where we have had this committee structure: one for every department, which we would have at Stormont – one for health, agriculture, environment, etc. etc. – and every political party, in this kind of devolved assembly, would be represented on these committees pro rata their strength. That's what we do in Europe, in the European Parliament. You've communists on every committee, even though there are only 40 of them in the parliament out of 520. The chairmanships would also be shared. In other words, not only would the Ulster Unionists and the DUP hold chairmanships, but the Workers Party, the SDLP, the Alliance Party all would hold chairmanships of committees. We could do it on the same kind of proportional representation system as they do in Europe, which is called the d'Hondt system. It gives fair power to all parties in the assembly.

MILLAR: So what would the relationship be between this devolved administration and the government of the Irish Republic?

TAYLOR: Well, we have talked about the British dimension: the laws are made in London, Westminster. There is the Ulster dimension: they are administered by a new assembly at Stormont. And then there is still the Irish dimension and this is the one that unionists cannot run away from. To get a settlement here you've got to involve all three. I keep condemning the Anglo-Irish Agreement, that it only has the British and Irish dimension, and ignored the most important, the Ulster dimension. What I am saying is, yes, we can have the British dimension and the Ulster dimension, but we must also have the Irish dimension.

MILLAR: And what is it?

TAYLOR: It must be the creation of some institution in this island through which there is representation from the Dublin parliament and from the Stormont devolved assembly. It would meet on a regular basis to discuss items of mutual interest between the two parts of Ireland and that's more relevant today than it ever was, because the EC is advancing day by day – not only in 1992, which is a catch-word used by everyone, but in many other things like the common fisheries policy and environmental policy. I found in Strasbourg that I was very often working with the Fine Gael and Fianna Fáil members on fishery matters. I found that Ian Paisley and myself were signing motions with Fianna Fáil or Fine Gael on the Common Agricultural Policy.

MILLAR: As he and Mr Molyneaux have gone with Mr Hume to Downing Street to discuss Harland & Wolff?

TAYLOR: Yes, but that was an internal matter. I'm talking about North–South cooperation. If a nuclear power station blows up on the Welsh coast, its radioactive dust won't stop at the Irish border. We have got to cooperate on a multitude of issues which are now affecting both North and South. Of course, I have always been keen about this, that is why I led the Young Unionists down there to meet Fine Gael in 1963. I have also felt there is room for more cooperation, and I'm convinced of it now more than ever.

MILLAR: Is that not in essence, John, what the two unionist leaders and the working party of 10 represented to Tom King almost two years ago?

TAYLOR: It is. But, of course, I would be very critical of Tom King. I have no time for the man, I can safely say. I think he was an absolute failure in Northern Ireland. He has presided over four years of complete political deadlock and he never seized any opportunities which were presented to him. I think that the document which was submitted to him was the opportunity to get the door opened again and to get political progress, but instead of that he was insulting. He ignored it.

MILLAR: Do you not accept that the reality is that that document, that scenario, has singularly failed to excite attention either in terms of the British government or the Irish government or the SDLP? It just isn't enough.

TAYLOR: They are playing for time. They are hoping that the unionists will weaken and enter into some negotiations without the Anglo-Irish Agreement being suspended. But more and more of them are now realising – you get more and more quotations you can refer to which show that they now recognise – that what they are doing in Dublin and in London is maintaining a stalemate for political progress in Northern Ireland and that something has to be done to get negotiations started. I think more and more of the unionists are showing their willingness to be positive and to negotiate internally here with the other constitutional parties, with London and perhaps even with Dublin, because I think there is a greater opportunity to negotiate with Dublin now than three or four years ago.

MILLAR: I was going to ask you about that. If the Agreement was suspended, could all these relationships be discussed or negotiated under the umbrella of one conference, attended by both parties in Northern Ireland and the governments of Britain and the Republic?

TAYLOR: No, I wouldn't want to get involved in that type of scenario. What we are talking about is the internal administration of Northern Ireland. That would be a matter to be ultimately decided by the British parliament and government – after, of course, the political parties in Northern Ireland had been fully consulted, which they were not at the time of the Anglo-Irish Agreement. We ourselves, within Northern Ireland, would have to have inter-party talks to try and agree the form of the devolved assembly. Yes, we certainly would. In so far as relations with Dublin are concerned, there could be no negotiations with them about the structures of internal government in Northern Ireland; that is strictly a matter for us in Northern Ireland and for the national parliament of Westminster. But the Irish dimension, which I mentioned before, is a matter for negotiation between Northern Ireland and the Republic of Ireland.

MILLAR: After the internal arrangement has been established, or simultaneously?

TAYLOR: Simultaneously. There would be a disagreement in unionist ranks about that. I would say simultaneously, because I think all three things must go at the same time. I think that the British dimension, the Ulster dimension and the Irish dimension must be identified and concluded at the same time. But the negotiations for the Irish dimension would have to be between Dublin and the people of Northern Ireland, because what we are talking about is cooperation and, quite honestly, I think the presence of English politicians might damage those negotiations. Because their knowledge of the situation in

Northern Ireland is always very limited. Only last week we had the Northern Ireland Office saying that 10 per cent of the people in the Twelfth of July parade were Roman Catholics.

MILLAR: Would you not accept that, even if you have a prospect of success, there is a necessity, because that is the way of the world, for something short of negotiation in advance so that you can establish your bona fides to the satisfaction of the other parties? An interim process by which you show evidence of your intent, try to persuade them that there would be virtue in setting the Agreement aside?

TAYLOR: I think unionists have done that following the local government elections in Northern Ireland. We now have eight councils, I think, where they are evenly divided between unionists and nationalists and there we have a system of sharing the administration between the SDLP and the unionists. I think goodwill has been shown on the part of the unionists, and if we promise that there will be goodwill when the Anglo-Irish Agreement is suspended and then fail to honour that promise, why then we as a party would be totally discredited to the outside world as well as in front of our own people in Northern Ireland.

MILLAR: There are some unionists who would take the view that negotiation, given simply suspension of the Agreement, would be negotiation under duress. Would you expect that if you got it suspended, you went in and your bluff was called, if unionists got to the conference table and were incapable of delivering an alternative agreement, would you expect the political consequences to be fairly grave?

TAYLOR: For the people in Northern Ireland it would be very grave. What would happen would simply be the re-establishment of the operation of the Anglo-Irish Agreement, a complete political stalemate. If the London government once again went over our heads and decided to create a devolved institution, the Ulster Unionists would simply fight that election on the basis of being opposed to the Anglo-Irish Agreement and they would win. Such is the reality of the situation in Northern Ireland, whether we walked out of talks or not we would still win that election. This would bring about the collapse of that assembly just as the last assembly collapsed in 1986, six months after the Anglo-Irish Agreement. Simply to threaten that if the unionists don't sign on the dotted line within three months we are going to re-establish the Anglo-Irish Agreement – that is not the way for political progress.

MILLAR: John Hume says that the way around the problem of unionist distrust of the SDLP – the view that the SDLP would be fifth columnists within a devolved parliament – is for unionists to talk directly to Dublin, to secure Dublin's agreement for an internal arrangement for Northern Ireland and, in the knowledge that Dublin had approved and ratified the settlement, the cause of the distrust of the SDLP and its motivation would be removed. Is there not virtue in that approach?

TAYLOR: No. Well, of course, I have no problem in talking to John Hume. I respect John Hume. I have no hesitation in talking to John Hume about the internal administration of Northern Ireland. It may be some of the others in his party that have unfortunately given this rather green image to the SDLP in recent years. But, as far as Dublin is concerned, I think we should be talking to Dublin at the correct time. I am keen on talks with Dublin and keen on cooperation between Northern Ireland and the Republic. But those talks will be about cooperation between the two parts of Ireland and not about the internal administration of Northern Ireland. Once you get these talks going between unionists and Dublin – and I believe that one can see at the end of the tunnel they will emerge – that will help the SDLP to reach an accommodation with the unionists on the internal administration of Northern Ireland.

MILLAR: John Hume outlined to *The Irish Times* one of their proposals, which was that not only should you have dialogue with Dublin but any new agreement could be put to the people of Northern Ireland and the people of the Irish Republic separately by way of referendum. He says that that would, in fact, constitute self-determination by the Irish people and would make untouchable and unchallengeable any new political arrangements so endorsed.

TAYLOR: I have two objections to that. First, in no way would I agree to the South of Ireland having a say in what is going to be the system of government within Northern Ireland. Secondly, I find referenda a very dangerous way of governing a country and if they can't, with government support, even get a referendum on divorce approved in the Republic, I would be very much afraid of what might happen to such a referendum on the future of the government in Northern Ireland. Because, of course, it begins to raise the extreme republican green flag-waving operation again in the Republic and that would be a very dangerous thing to motivate in the South of Ireland. So I would avoid a referendum on the administration of Northern Ireland in the Republic[...]

4
Looking to the Other Side of the Hill – Peter Brooke 1991

This charming, modest and rather old-fashioned-looking gentleman of (unionist) Anglo-Irish descent did not, at first glance, look like someone set to electrify the political process in Northern Ireland. Yet by the end of his 100th day in office, in November 1989, Margaret Thatcher's appointed Secretary of State had managed to excite the interest of the republican movement while sending a shiver of apprehension through the unionist community.

In an interview to mark the moment, Brooke was asked if the British and republicans had in fact been reduced to 'a Mexican Stand-off'.

Significantly, he allowed there had to be 'a possibility that at some stage debate might start within the terrorist community'. If that were to occur – and 'if in fact the terrorists were to decide that the moment had come when they wished to withdraw from their activities' – then, Brooke continued: 'I think government would need to be imaginative in those circumstances as to how that process should be managed.'

When I interviewed Mr (Lord) Brooke two years later I suggested that the search for a political settlement in conventional terms was doomed to failure – that if the republicans weren't 'part of the solution' they would remain 'part of the problem'. The Secretary of State was emphatic that he could not contemplate 'any posture other than that which the [British and Irish] governments have consistently taken about the IRA'. He was also crystal clear that in fundamental terms the objectives of the British and the declared objectives of the republicans were mutually exclusive: 'The fundamental objective is patently mutually exclusive because one says that the ballot box and the ways of democrats will prevail and the other says that they will not.'

That said, he did not appear resigned to the inevitable continuation of the IRA's 'long war' without end: 'One of the problems, as I see it, in terms of the other side of the hill, is that just as it is difficult for me to read them, so I suspect it is extremely difficult for them to read me or to read the government because of the particular circumstances in which they find themselves. Therefore, if one can identify by anything that they choose to say, to journalists or whoever, which represents a really massive misconception, which is taking them down a cul-de-sac which has no future at all, then one does have some responsibility for finding ways – not in terms of direct communication, but in terms of public communication – that that is a total illusion, because, as I say, it is their coming to the conclusion that they cannot secure their objective which is the way in which we come back to peace.'

It would later fall to Brooke's successor, Sir Patrick (Lord) Mayhew, to explain that the British government had been operating a secret channel of communication with those still 'on the other side of the hill'. Yet even this confirmation of what they had long feared and suspected did not quite convulse the unionist community. Nor in the end, crucially, did it prompt the unionist leadership to renounce the famous three-stranded agenda that was to prove the essential Brooke/Mayhew bequest to New Labour.

FROM *THE IRISH TIMES*, 23 SEPTEMBER 1991

MILLAR: Obviously, speculation about the timing of an election may retard your attempts to resume all-party talks. Assuming you do get them back on the road, can I ask in broad terms about your objectives specifically, can I ask whether you are seeking an alternative to the Anglo-Irish Agreement of, as some suspect, devolution of a kind which might co-exist with the provisions of Hillsborough?

BROOKE: I cannot help going over former ground in responding to that, but the structure, announced on March 26th having been agreed by everybody, which then became the structure used between April 30th and July 3rd, was multidimensional. It did involve looking at the internal arrangements in Northern Ireland. It did involve looking at future arrangements between the Republic and whatever institutions emerged in Northern Ireland. And it did involve the potential consideration of an alternative to the Anglo-Irish Agreement. But it is worth reiterating three things present in that multidimensional structure – in no particular order. The first was that as we set out the arrangements and as we moved forward, it was necessary for the convoy to remain intact. In other words everybody was going to have the right to walk away from the table if they decided that there was some aspect of the procedure which they could not approve. Secondly, it was agreed that all aspects of the problem could be raised by anybody and that implicitly, leaving aside the question of walking away from the table, others would be prepared to respond to any matter that was raised. Finally, it was agreed that nobody would be asked to conclude anything until they were looking at the total package and a comprehensive picture, presumably with trade-offs in various directions. And I think, if you're actually going to get a settlement or a conclusion which would stand the test of time, all those conditions continue to be relevant even if you might modify the way in which you got to them. So you would emerge with all those elements that I have referred to – and they are interrelated. Because the nationalists in the North would find it difficult to come to a conclusion about internal arrangements in the North unless they knew what relations with the South were going to be; it would be difficult for the unionists to agree what arrangements they were going to have with the South unless they had a clear idea, for instance, of what the Irish Constitution was going to say; and it would seem quite possible that the Irish Government, before it embarked on something as substantial as modifying its Constitution, would want to know in what cause it was doing it. So I think the things are inevitably interrelated. One other remark about devolution: although I have said in the original speech in Bangor in January, 1990, that I thought devolution (I am using shorthand) with some form of power-sharing arrangements was the most likely internal solution to secure the sort of overall, universal, uniform support that we were seeking, I did not go into the exercise with a blueprint. The critical thing from my point of view was going to be something around which people could unite.

MILLAR: It is hard to see, though, how you could have a genuine alternative agreement if there was not created in Belfast a substantial devolved structure.

BROOKE: I think on *a priori* grounds that might be right.

MILLAR: I ask these questions because there is a belief that there are very real limits to the powers which the British government would be prepared to devolve. Is that the case?

BROOKE: It would certainly be the case, at least in the early stages, and particularly if you have an emergency continuing to prevail. There would be constraints both on security and presumably on finance. When I say finance it would simply be that the source of the finance would continue to be the British Treasury and if there was a continuing role for the Secretary of State, which it is likely there would be on security grounds, then under those circumstances it would be the Secretary of State who would be negotiating with the Treasury to secure the extra finance.

MILLAR: But if those security powers remained with you in London – and London felt a continuing need to liaise with Dublin on those matters, as it does currently through the Anglo-Irish Conference – would you really be talking in those circumstances about an alternative agreement? Given that the administration in Belfast would be so circumscribed, would not you be left with a devolved structure more in the way of an appendage to the existing Anglo-Irish structure?

BROOKE: We get into something of a marsh in this area, and I describe the marsh rather than seek to enter it. The unionists' views about those clauses of the present Anglo-Irish Agreement which might lead to a devolved administration are ones which they would effectively not recognise. Yet the Anglo-Irish Agreement itself does envisage the possibility of there being in parallel a devolved administration in Northern Ireland or activities that would be devolved within Northern Ireland. Where you enter the hypothetical in this area, of course, is whether – if you were to secure a settlement which was agreed by everybody else – the terrorists in those circumstances would wish to continue or not. I have consistently said, and indeed those participating have consistently said, that we were not engaged in a peace conference – we were engaged in an examination of political development, initially in Northern Ireland. But it is equally clear that if you actually were to have arrangements which had been agreed by everybody in the island, it would remove a substantial locus of such a case as the terrorists at the moment would advance.

MILLAR: But would your expectation not be that, if you did secure the kind of political agreement you seek, the response would more likely be a massive escalation of terrorist activity?

BROOKE: As I say, that necessarily has to be a hypothetical question.

MILLAR: It is hypothetical. And it is a marsh. But there is a seeming conflict between the unionists' declared objective to seek an alternative agreement and the very serious constraints that exist on the powers that might be devolved even if they were willing and the basis for devolution were to be agreed. Apart from the rather general aspiration that perhaps the whole thing would come together and the terrorists would stop and reconsider, constructing the bridge, to take you from where you are to where you need to get, seems difficult.

BROOKE: Yes, though if we were to secure the kind of comprehensive settlement which I have just mentioned and which was certainly envisaged in the plan we set out on March 26th, then by definition you could not reach that point without a greater degree of trust, not only between the parties and the British government in Northern Ireland, but also between the parties and the government of the Republic and conceivably the two governments themselves. Therefore, while I did indicate that there would clearly be constraints about the amount of security responsibility which would be devolved ... the fact remains that what you actually achieve in terms of devolved arrangements would require a formalisation of the communications about security matters which at the moment might occur informally between opposition parties and the government. But you cannot ask those who are democratically elected and are carrying substantial responsibility in the province, assuming a settlement, and who are doing so within the present climate within the province, and not treat them very seriously indeed in the discussion of security policy.

MILLAR: So there might, as part of some end structure, be devices built in which would involve elected representatives – though not in government, and not directly responsible for security policy – in consultation and liaison?

BROOKE: As I say, because we were necessarily exploring matters in the talks on which we embarked in April, there are aspects which would need to be explored in detail and from the point of view of those who were entering arrangements – in other words those who were endorsing whatever settlement we reached – would need to be satisfactory.

MILLAR: In order to get the sort of comprehensive settlement that we are discussing, how important is it, do you think, that the Republic should amend or withdraw Articles 2 and 3 of the Constitution?

BROOKE: I am on record as saying that I do not personally find Articles 2 and 3 of the Republic's Constitution helpful, and I say that in particular because the *de jure* claim which they constitute is overtly at variance with the *de facto* acceptance in Article 1 of the Agreement as to what the situation in Northern Ireland is – and that seems to me to be a slightly general inconsistency and incoherence in the Republic's position. Therefore, I think in the process of building the trust of which we spoke a modification of Articles 2 and 3 would seem to me to be an extremely powerful instrument and the Republic could demonstrate – given their attitude and the attitude which is expressed in Article 1 of the Agreement ... If I may be more explicit: if in your written Constitution you are expressing a claim about the six counties of the island that are not at present part of the Republic, but you are saying that you recognise that the people of those six counties should be allowed to decide their future, then if those two decisions are mutually consistent I would have thought that seeking to persuade those who lived in the six counties that your larger claim would be a sensible conclusion, a sensible way of ending up, would be a fairly central objective of what you were about. But I referred a moment ago to a marsh – the one thing which I patently should not do is to presume to assert the interests of the Republic.

MILLAR: I think that that will be of some interest to people in Northern Ireland and in the Republic. You were not involved in it, you are not held by anybody, it seems, responsible for it: with hindsight, do you think the British government in 1985 was mistaken to sign the Anglo-Irish Agreement without securing a commitment to reconcile Article 1 with Articles 2 and 3?

BROOKE: We are in a situation not dissimilar to the scenario I was describing for this set of talks. In the end, each of those who decides to sign up for something has to decide whether the deal, the package which they have got, is adequately responsive to their own interests and, insofar as it includes aspects which are helpful to your partners, is not counterproductive to yourself. And the government in 1985 clearly took the decision that the Agreement which they had negotiated did represent, on balance, an agreement worth signing.

MILLAR: If and when you get to the talks and this is an issue that is on the table, I take it from what you have said that the British government, certainly if you were leading the delegation to those talks, would not be neutral on this, that when the issue comes up you would be urging the case for an amendment to the territorial claim?

BROOKE: The role of the British government in the whole of this process, right from the beginning, right from January 1990, has been to seek to facilitate agreement among others. In terms of this particular aspect, I can see how modification by the Republic of their Constitution would make an agreement among everybody more likely rather than less. And therefore, in that sense, yes, I would seek to represent to those who would have to make the concession, who would be making the concession – and I am conscious that it is their decision and therefore I should not presume to take their decision for them – but I would seek to indicate to them first why I thought that it was unhelpful, and secondly, why making the concession might actually make a contribution to a wider settlement.

MILLAR: There are some people who think the very fact of the Anglo-Irish Agreement may ultimately make it impossible for the unionists, in particular, to engage with the kind of agenda that would be necessary, in practical terms, to see the thing through. I know you do not want to anticipate failure. But if that should prove to be the case, is that the end of the road so far as you are concerned?

BROOKE: I have been in office for 26 months and I obviously do not know how much longer I would serve in office and of course there will be a successor Secretary of State who will have to decide what he wishes to do. But I am absolutely certain that what we have been about since January 1990, has been worth doing in itself regardless of how many milestones we have advanced along the way. Any Secretary of State who comes to Northern Ireland should not imagine that great achievements, great breakthroughs, are going to occur during his time. That is because of the ancestry of the quarrel and the nature of the issues and their relative intractability. But what he should be doing is leaving circumstances in better shape than they were when he arrived for his successor subsequently to build on. And I think that the climate in Northern Ireland, leaving aside the current level of violence, in terms of cooperation and dialogue and the atmosphere for progress in lots of directions, is better than it was before we embarked on this exercise and that therefore there are other goods that flow out of that.

MILLAR: Granted all of that, I would put it to you that you are in a sense a victim of your own success so far, however limited, in that there are a lot of people who are developing ambitions for you in your current office that go a good deal further. If the talks broke down, you have already made it clear that you would not impose a solution, as some people have advocated. But is it conceivable to you, having already talked to the parties at great length, that there might emerge from this process a role for you as Secretary of State other than as a facilitator?

BROOKE: I have consistently taken the view in terms of the talks we have had so far that if we reached a point where the parties are around the table, and I think I would obviously in particular be saying during the internal arrangements, I think it would be somewhat presumptuous to make that suggestion if the Irish government were also at the table. But when the parties in Northern Ireland were around the table, if we reached a point where they had difficulty in coming to a conclusion but believed that a conclusion could be reached if someone were to put it to them, then of course it would be wholly irresponsible if so invited not to come forward with proposals because sometimes it is easier to accept something which is proposed by somebody else. What I am absolutely clear about, which is why I disagree with the view that you should impose a settlement, is that to do that uninvited is to invite rejection.

MILLAR: The British government, of course, ran that risk in 1985: there was not the same reticence on the part of your predecessors to impose a solution or a framework regardless of majority opinion in Northern Ireland. Why are you so dead set against proceeding with the unfinished business of Hillsborough by the same route?

BROOKE: I am not going to rehearse the history since 1985, but whatever the pluses or the minuses of the Anglo-Irish Agreement as expressed by historians in the future, the one thing which was reasonably clear was that there was a substantial part of the population of Northern Ireland which did reject the principle of the Agreement, let alone parts of the detail. Now in terms of what we are talking about for a settlement – and one has to acknowledge that the Anglo-Irish Agreement was to a significant degree security driven – but in terms of what we have been talking about since January, 1990, where we are looking for a greater degree of political accommodation, I think that what has happened since 1985 is itself a demonstration that unless you can get everybody to sign up, you will not actually have something that will survive.

MILLAR: If you got everybody to invite you to come up with proposals, that would obviously be the ideal. Say they prove a bit more reluctant and the invitation is not as crystal clear as it might be, is it conceivable that you would bring forward proposals and submit them to the test of a referendum, as was done with devolution proposals for Scotland and Wales?

BROOKE: It was done in Scotland and Wales as a result of a very prolonged debate in the House of Commons in which the will of the House of Commons emerged with that particular decision and with backbench supporters of the government in the House of Commons who came from Welsh and Scottish constituencies themselves being among those who built in the referendum conditions. But I think I would have to acknowledge that it would be difficult to implement the scenario I was describing unless it was actually within the framework of talks. But my experience of the talks so far has been – this may seem paradoxical – of a willingness of the leaders when they did collectively want to make progress or wanted to come to a particular conclusion but did not quite know how, to be very ready to allow somebody else make the suggestions as to how we move forward.

MILLAR: So you are not going to impose, but you may well respond to invitations. I ask all of those questions because there is a fear that it may all come to nothing, that the declared flexibility may recede and that you would be tempted to revert to direct rule and the Anglo-Irish Agreement and say: 'Well, that is that! I've done my bit and there is not much more that can be attempted!' But that isn't what you are after and presumably you don't consider that a desirable state in which to leave Northern Ireland.

BROOKE: No. I think where we paused on July 3rd – and I use 'paused' only in the sense of a continuing journey, quite clearly that was a stage of the journey which we completed – we did conclude matters in such a way that if people wanted to come back, they would be able to do so. I hope that in the exploration of ways forward we would in fact be able to conduct it in such a way that either I or indeed any successor of mine would have the early freedom to be able to explore matters forward. Inevitably, what we had achieved between April and July was a curate's egg. There were aspects of it which were disappointing to everybody and perhaps frustrating for everybody taking part. But there were also aspects of that process which were, I think, genuinely revealing to people as to the possibilities capable of being grasped. And it seems to me that providing a framework – providing a stage – on which that exploration can take place is a very valuable role to perform and isn't just the language of sound bites. I have a continuing faith that free men round a table, when confronted with a past as disagreeable as the last 20 years in Northern Ireland, will actually find ways of coming to agreement.

MILLAR: There are some nationalists in the North, and some people in Dublin, who take the view that this initiative is not going to work; they are prepared to support you in testing it to destruction, to borrow one of your phrases, but they are already saying very clearly that if it fails, there is an alternative: that you should greatly expand the work and the area of influence of the Anglo-Irish Conference. I take it that isn't something that commends itself readily to you.

BROOKE: The Anglo-Irish Agreement and the Anglo-Irish Conference is itself an institution which is evolving. The security cooperation under the Agreement, which is obviously directed at bringing terrorism to an end, is itself something that has been evolving over the course of the past six years and there is history which gets in our mutual way in security policy just as there is history that gets in our way in terms of political development. The Anglo-Irish Agreement will overturn itself if it tries to carry more weight than it is at any time capable of carrying: and while absolutely not seeking to use the words 'test to destruction' in the case of the Agreement you do need to test it as you go forward to see whether it will in fact bear more weight than it currently bears.

MILLAR: That is very clear, but lest I was being too delicate in the presentation of this to you, let me put it in even blunter terms. What is being advocated by some people rests on a view that the unionists are not into this, that they are not for real. This is how the argument runs, you must have heard it: they (the unionists) are not going to negotiate in a meaningful way, therefore they need to be left out in the cold a while longer and the Anglo-Irish Agreement enhanced and developed in ways that plainly the unionists wouldn't wish to see, not least for the purpose of turning the screws, as it were, on the unionists. On the basis of what you have said thus far, I take it that if nationalist leaders were to put that to you and to your government, you would be resisting it?

BROOKE: Yes, I would. Because it suggests a different attitude to life than is contained in Article 1 of the Agreement and is contained in the 1973 Act. The whole principle of Article 1 and indeed of the 1973 Act is that free men should be allowed to determine their own future and I certainly would not want in any way to suggest to anybody in Northern Ireland that reality is any different from what it is. The Anglo-Irish Agreement is in being and it has worked but that is a different thing from saying that the democratic will is being expressed in a way that one doesn't like and therefore one is going to take some constitutional means of expressing one's disapproval.

MILLAR: Some of the advocates of this course, I fancy, have a view of British policy – they wouldn't just be nationalists; the mirror image could be found within unionism and amongst many commentators and observers – which is that, in the long run, London's purpose is to oblige Northern Ireland and its people to see their future in terms of ever-increasing cooperation and eventual integration with the rest of the island of Ireland. Is that a mistaken view of British policy and its purpose?

BROOKE: Perhaps it is easier for me to speak for myself personally: it is not my purpose. I expressed elsewhere the distress, if you like, that one of the consequences of partition and of the border has been of the two parts of Ireland growing apart rather than actually living next to each other in the way that you would expect in any other neighbour countries in Europe. The modest proportion of the gross national product of the two countries which is made up by trade with each other seems to me to be an indictment of our mutual relations. And it has a further consequence: if you actually quite deliberately decide not to trade with those who are your immediate neighbours, with whom it would be in every other circumstance totally natural to trade, one of the further consequences of that is going to be that you remain in ignorance of each other. While I am not seeking myself to move the pieces around on the table in order to change reality, I do think that perhaps if there was rather more contact, then some of the realities – some of the perceptions – might change in the process.

MILLAR: But you don't in any sense see the apparatus of the existing agreement as either a torture instrument or a driving force to compel people into degrees of cooperation that they are not ready for and not voluntarily prepared to … ?

BROOKE: No, because that is an offence against my own view of democracy.

MILLAR: On your own view of the union – might the advocates of this course have formed a wrong impression of a speech which you made last autumn when you declared that Britain had no selfish reason and no selfish interest for remaining in Northern Ireland? That was regarded in Dublin and elsewhere as a statement of Britain's neutrality on the question of the union. Might people have made too much of that speech?

BROOKE: What I was seeking to do on that occasion was to say that in terms of history, there were clearly long periods of British history when the control of the island of Ireland was a matter of strategic importance to us, just as there had been earlier eras when what was happening in Scotland and indeed even earlier, what was happening in Wales, was of concern to us. I made the speech in 1990; I was effectively saying that in 1990, such considerations no longer prevail but that a different consideration does prevail – and prevails very strongly – and that is – and ironically everything that has happened in the rest of the world since 1990 has reinforced and underlined it – that decisions about the future of countries should in fact be taken by those people who live in those countries, by ordinary peaceful democratic means and the ancient relationship of the United Kingdom in particular means that you ensure that that condition prevails in all parts of the kingdom.

MILLAR: I am interested that you should mention Scotland. Just to come on from the neutrality speech, the Unionist Member of Parliament for Upper Bann, Mr Trimble, last week criticised you for, as he put it, merely 'accepting' rather than supporting the union. He was specifically comparing and contrasting your position and the government's position *vis-à-vis* Northern Ireland with the Conservative government's antipathy to devolution and Home Rule for Scotland. Are the unionists likewise mistaken in their reading of the British government's attitude on the union?

BROOKE: I hesitate to cross swords with a distinguished academic like Mr Trimble, but my recollection of 1886 and the crisis in the Liberal Party when Mr Gladstone brought forward the proposals relating to Home Rule included observations by a very distinguished constitutional lawyer who was strongly opposed to the principle of Home Rule and indeed took a High Tory position on it, but who did acknowledge as a constitutional lawyer that there was nothing about the Constitution of the United Kingdom which required the manner in which the different parts of the kingdom are governed to be universal.

MILLAR: Indeed, Mr Trimble – or if not Mr Trimble, his party leader Mr Molyneaux – would say that is all very well but they, as partners in the union, don't wish to be subject to separate distinctive arrangements. Their heart's desire is to be governed in every essential respect on a basis of equality with every other part of the United Kingdom.

BROOKE: I would have to say that while I accept that as a point of view, it would not be wholly sustained by the opinion polls that were conducted in July.

MILLAR: So you understand, Secretary of State, that the unionists have great difficulty with your position? I have been coming at you from the point of view of nationalists who have a view of what British policy is. That is augmented by the fact that the unionists think it exactly the same. And the unionists have great difficulty in finding reassurance in all the words that you and other members of your government would seek to offer them because in a very practical sense, their neurosis or uncertainty or fearfulness about your intention is rooted in the continuous rejection of what, for shorthand, I would call 'Mr Molyneaux's agenda'. They see the rejection of the demand that there should be proper legislation at Westminster, a select committee of the House of Commons, a Strathclyde-type regional government, as rooted in a desire, if not to force them into union with Dublin, at the very least to keep them semi-detached within the union. How do you counter that unionist complaint?

BROOKE: I go back to an earlier question which you asked: if you were to reach the point in the hypothesis which you postulated when it was clear you couldn't make way and you couldn't secure widespread support – I mean in the way that I was implying – endorsement across the democratic spectrum for proposals that would involve the delegation of authority and responsibility to within the province – then I would suppose that a government would have to contemplate all the things that Mr Molyneaux suggests. But it isn't quite as easy as that. There is an enormous corpus of Northern Ireland law that goes back to the 50 years when Stormont was in being. If you were really going to carry that proposal to its logical conclusion, you would have an enormous amount of legislation which you would actually have to revise and at least at this moment, it would be difficult to see that the return you were going to get from using up the large amount of parliamentary time for that purpose would in fact be wholly justified.

MILLAR: But if I may say so, similar arguments have been made by other Secretaries of State over 20 years. Direct rule – the temporary measure by which you govern Northern Ireland – is 20 years old next March. Don't the explanations and the arguments begin to wear a bit thin? Or to put it a different way, at what point might the British government have to contemplate …

BROOKE: That goes back to the question which you asked me earlier.

MILLAR: So a British government might some day have to contemplate those things?

BROOKE: Yes, but I would have to say, because it is the other side of a question which you asked me much earlier, that just as we have been seeking to get widespread agreement for the kind of proposals we have been examining now in order to secure stability therefrom, to impose Mr Moylneaux's agenda, which you would effectively be doing, would not of itself necessarily secure the widespread support which would represent stability.

MILLAR: Has it ever occurred to you, Secretary of State, that Mr Molyneaux's agenda would not necessarily find itself in conflict with the essential structure that was put in place in 1985?

BROOKE: In terms of Mr Molyneaux's agenda and if I have appeared unambitious in the speed at which I move on some of the things which Mr Molyneaux suggests and which he would himself say are very modest proposals, there are clearly things in Mr Molyneaux's agenda that you could in fact advance.

MILLAR: To summarise that: you are going to continue as far as you can. You believe that there have been positive gains already; even if the talks don't resume, there have been achievements to date; you would hope that you or a future Secretary of State could carry the thing still further forward and you will not be tempted to use the existing Anglo-Irish structure in an expanded form as some means of leverage on the unionist community to have them address an agenda which they would otherwise be resistant to? Is that a fair ...

BROOKE: All I would say is we have used the Anglo-Irish Agreement in the course of the 26 months that I have been Secretary of State to advance cooperation in a whole series of areas that perhaps we were not doing previously. I would hope that that exploration would go on. But nobody has yet suggested to me scales of expansion that would endanger the structure.

MILLAR: Presumably, there are costs as well to any expanding North–South, East–West activity. Have you encountered any difficulty or had any cause to worry about the Irish government's capacity to match the rhetoric and the scale of ambition at a practical level?

BROOKE: I wouldn't want to get into the entrails of an Anglo-Irish Conference but there have been occasions when we have had to press them to carry forward some of the things that would appear to us to have a particular relevance in terms of the two sides of the border where it might at first blush not be their first priority.

MILLAR: So, if Mr Major hasn't gone to the country, you wouldn't expect Mr Major and Mr Haughey, when they have their promised summit in the autumn, to announce a new dimension to Anglo-Irish relations which would overshadow or preclude the Brooke initiative?

BROOKE: When they met in June, they indicated that they would meet again and they would conduct a review of the state of relations and it may well be that the Irish government would want to put proposals to us; that would be something to which we would have to listen.

MILLAR: Thinking of the grand strategy, Mr Hume has long argued that, almost before you discuss the detail of any package, it would be equally important to decide the means of effecting any agreement that might be made. And you know he has a long-standing proposal that a package would be put by way of dual referendum North and South. I take it from all that has gone before that we are talking, as far as you are concerned, and as far as all parties are concerned, about a political structure and settlement predicated on the assumption that Northern Ireland will, for as far ahead as one can see, remain within the United Kingdom?

BROOKE: Yes.

MILLAR: For all the potential conflict between Article 1 of the Agreement and Articles 2 and 3 of the Constitution, do you think that in Dublin, and within the nationalist community in the North, that is generally accepted?

BROOKE: I have got no grounds for thinking otherwise.

MILLAR: Finally, Secretary of State, on the subject of the IRA, there are people who say it is all very well talking about politics, and you do your best and you will try your initiative, but nothing is going to come of it because at the end of the day you have got the IRA. They have been able to sustain themselves for 20 years; they have got armaments; and they don't, moreover, have anywhere else to go and if somebody doesn't engage in a radical gesture or change of direction to make them 'part of the solution' they will remain, of necessity, part of the problem. Have you ever been tempted to think that perhaps they are right? Not the IRA but those who say 'count them into the political process', that you have got to grasp that nettle?

BROOKE: I cannot contemplate any posture other than that which the two governments have consistently taken about the IRA. That said, a constitutional politician who had responsibilities to the people of Northern Ireland or indeed the people of the Republic would be failing in his duty if he did not spend some of his time seeking to work out, in the Duke of Wellington's phrase, what was happening on the other side of the hill.

MILLAR: What do you think?

BROOKE: I don't know, but that does not mean that I shouldn't actually spend some time thinking about it.

MILLAR: If you were persuaded that some republican leaders genuinely were seeking a way out of the violence, can you envisage circumstances in which you would authorise representatives of your office to engage in discussion with them?

BROOKE: What we have said is what we mean; in other words, that we will not be engaged in dialogue with them but the process of working out what is happening on the other side of the hill does mean that you conduct yourselves, as indeed we have been seeking to conduct ourselves in past years, in a manner which makes it more likely that terrorism will come to an end. We have been pursuing economic development, the removal of unemployment. We have been pursuing political development in the way I described. We have been seeking to remove perceived injustice and to have a social policy which reduces fertile ground in which some of the seeds of terrorism fall and the decision which we took last year that our third priority beyond law and order and beyond economic development should be the targeting of social needs, so that you were looking, across the face of government, at ways in which you could reduce differentials, increase the sense of involvement and ownership in society by everybody, was quite clearly directed to that.

MILLAR: But you clearly have been intrigued by recurring suggestions of an internal republican debate. Do you have any sense of where that debate is currently at?

BROOKE: I think that it would be odd in human affairs and it would be odd in what I know of terrorism in other parts of the world if there was not such a debate going on – not necessarily at this moment but had not gone on and would not be going on in the future – since there will be a spectrum within terrorism in the same way that there is a spectrum within, let us say, my own political party about aspects of public policy. Therefore, I would not in the least be surprised to hear that a debate were going on. But the aspect which would particularly bring terrorism to an end on top of the sense that ground was being lost in the areas I have described is the conviction that you cannot succeed in the objective that you set yourself by the means that you are using; in other words, that the democratic society just will not give way. In that regard, I think that the talks have been a valuable start in showing democrats working among themselves to provide a democratic framework within Northern Ireland that underpins the resolve of the whole of society that the terrorists should not win.

MILLAR: But can you see any circumstances in which Britain could offer the republican movement an agenda and a particular political process which would enable republican leaders, if they were so minded, to successfully lobby to call off the campaign of violence? Or are the short- and long-term objectives of Britain and the republican movement inevitably mutually exclusive?

BROOKE: The fundamental objective is patently mutually exclusive because one says that the ballot box and the ways of democrats will prevail and the other says that they will not, so by definition those are exclusive in that sense. No.

MILLAR: Is there any possible convergence? Given that the fundamentals are mutually exclusive, doesn't that mean that the cold war and the actual war just continue?

BROOKE: You were asking about what government can do. One of the problems, as I see it, in terms of the other side of the hill, is that just as it is difficult for me to read them, so I suspect it is extremely difficult for them to read me or to read the government because of the particular circumstances in which they find themselves. Therefore, if one can identify by anything that they choose to say, to journalists or whoever, which represents a really massive misconception, which is taking them down a cul-de-sac which has no future at all, then one does have some responsibility for finding ways – not in terms of direct communication but in terms of public communication – that that is a total illusion, because, as I say, it is their coming to the conclusion that they cannot secure their objective which is the way in which we come back to peace.

MILLAR: But in doing that, that should not be construed by others as representing an overwhelming desire on your part to count them into the political process?

BROOKE: No, not at all. But they have to make their own determination as to where their best interests lie and the best interests of the community whom they say they represent, and in that regard the clearer they are about the score the more likely they are to make a good decision.

5

In From the Cold – Gerry Adams
1994

In September 1991 Peter Brooke had been trying to discern what might or might not be going on 'on the other side of the hill'. By the time this interview appeared in November 1994 the IRA had called its first 'cessation of military operations' (31 August) and Gerry Adams was pressing for London's promised imaginative response.

Sinn Féin would have a long wait before clearing the many obstacles to its participation in multi-party talks. John Major's government pressed for reassurance that the ceasefire was intended to be 'permanent'. In the absence of that, Sir Patrick Mayhew demanded that the issue of IRA weapons decommissioning be addressed as part of 'the practical consequences of the ending of violence'. Republicans, with SDLP and Irish government backing, objected to this precondition – many seeing it as evidence of the Major government's increasing dependence on Ulster Unionist votes at Westminster as its declining parliamentary majority came more and more under threat. The British were able to counter that the requirement for a handing-up of arms as a signal of republican good faith had also been raised in the first instance by Irish Tánaiste Dick Spring. Unionists, moreover, saw it as the logical outcome of the position acknowledged by John Hume in the original interview published here: 'You can't expect anybody to sit around a table with somebody who reserves the right to pull a gun if he doesn't get his own way.'

The SDLP, it must be said, was not always clear-cut or consistent on the question of decommissioning that would attend David Trimble's negotiation of the Belfast Agreement, dog his attempts to sustain it and, ultimately, condemn him and his party to crushing electoral defeat in the British general election of 2005.

In November 1994, however, I decided that my limited time available with the Sinn Féin leader would not be profitably spent pressing him on what might be expected from the IRA on the issue, or when. I was also more interested to know how Adams saw the republican movement fitting in to a political process already focused on a much more limited agenda than that canvassed by the republican leadership.

Given Hume's new thinking on self-determination for the peoples of

Ireland – and that unionists were never going to consent to Irish unity, or even joint London/Dublin authority – the big questions exercising the other parties appeared to centre on things like the scale and role of cross-border bodies and whether a new Stormont Assembly should have legislative or only administrative powers. Did Mr Adams have a preference?

The Sinn Féin president was naturally insistent: 'We're not talking about changing constitutions. We're talking about constitutional change.' However, the exercise was instructive, as I realised on the morning of publication when I received a call from a senior Irish diplomat congratulating me. 'For what,' I asked, pleasantly surprised. 'For treating him like any other politician and asking him the same questions everybody else is having to grapple with,' came the reply.

FROM *THE IRISH TIMES*, 21 NOVEMBER 1994

Gerry Adams left London on Saturday morning still awaiting confirmation that the British government intended to open exploratory talks with Sinn Féin in mid-December. But, as he concluded his two-day visit to Britain, Mr Adams told *The Irish Times* that Mr Martin McGuinness would head the Sinn Féin delegation in that dialogue.

During the interview, at the Roger Casement Irish Centre in north London, Mr Adams said the priority in the exploratory discussions would be to 'rationalise Sinn Féin's position', and then proceed 'as urgently as possible' to multilateral talks.

Mr Adams said it was 'useful to work on the broad notion' that nothing was agreed until everything was agreed, but he could not say definitively that Sinn Féin would automatically accept the 'three-stranded' talks process. The talks structure, he maintained, was for discussion, although Sinn Féin would not necessarily want to 'upend it, if there is agreement'.

But whatever about the structure, what most people found hard to conceive was what Sinn Féin could talk to the other parties about. To try and get a sense of that, I therefore asked Mr Adams about some of the issues believed central to the ongoing negotiations between London and Dublin.

Mr James Molyneaux thought a new Stormont assembly should, initially at least, have purely administrative powers. Others, including the British, favoured legislative powers as well. Did Mr Adams have a preference? 'My position is quite simple,' he replied. 'An internal settlement is not a solution. A settlement has to include fundamental political and constitutional change.' How far they could move was a matter for discussion. 'We would have a preference, obviously, of ending the

British jurisdiction and bringing about an agreed, new, Irish jurisdiction. And within that context all these matters take on a new significance and become almost transitional matters.'

Save in that transitional context, Mr Adams resisted the idea that devolution is an essential ingredient of a new deal: 'In the way that Mr Molyneaux speaks of it, and in the way in which it appears the British government are speaking about it – it would be a mere repeat of all that has failed in the past.'

But, realistically, didn't the Sunningdale agreement represent the likely outer limits of anything the unionists might agree to? Mr Adams didn't seem enamoured of the invitation 'to go back 20 years' because 'the unionists have started to come to a realisation ...'

Reminded that the unionists might not even go as far as Sunningdale, Mr Adams seemed to place his hope in the 'cut and thrust' of 'quite unprecedented talks'.

I reminded him that there has been quite a lot of cut and thrust already in the liaison group of British and Irish civil servants. Dublin, it appeared, might abandon Articles 2 and 3 in return for amendment of Section 75 of the Government of Ireland Act. Would Sinn Féin welcome that?

Mr Adams resisted, first suggesting that his information on what Dublin was prepared to do 'would not marry exactly' with the proposition outlined. But before dismissing the whole discussion about the Irish Constitution as 'a distraction' and 'in many ways an orange herring', Mr Adams repeated the unchanging republican position: 'I'm not interested in semantics. There is no point in amending the wording of the Government of Ireland Act if the Acts of Union underwrite the position ... What we need is a completely inclusive, negotiated settlement, which will bring about – to what extent remains to be seen – fundamental political and constitutional change. And, of course, as Sinn Féin has advocated, we need a new Irish national constitution.'

So, just to be clear – when Sinn Féin talks constitutional change, it's talking about a hell of a lot more than amending the Government of Ireland Act? Mr Adams is straightforward: 'Oh, of course. We're not talking about changing constitutions. We're talking about constitutional change.'

So what about all this talk of cross-border bodies, Mr Molyneaux's Foyle Fisheries model versus Mr Hume's European-style Council of Ministers? 'Our objective in negotiations will be to end the British jurisdiction and replace it with an Irish jurisdiction. But it is in that context that we would judge any sort of transitional cross-border arrangements,' comes the reply.

Mr Adams says he can understand the reluctance of unionists to negotiate, their perception that 'in talks they're going to have to give'. Everybody has to give, he asserts. But he does not reject the contention that, as far as his own supporters are concerned, the unionists will have to give more, referring instead to Mr Molyneaux's 'very, very dishonest' reference to 'a perception of discrimination' under unionist governments in the past, and the demand that people like himself be given 'some sense of citizenship'.

I put it to Mr Adams that whatever new dispensations unionists might agree to, they would never consent to Irish unity. He conceded only that 'at this time, the unionist position is as you have outlined it'. However, he believed 'ordinary punters' didn't want the present opportunity squandered, observing that 'the two governments have a role to play'.

Mr John Hume had suggested that any new agreement should be put to the test of referendum, north and south of the border, on the same day. If not the intended purpose, was not the likely effect of that to copper-fasten partition? And would such a dual referendum, in his book, constitute self-determination by the Irish people?

Mr Adams was clear: 'It would not constitute self-determination by the Irish people. But it could constitute a very worthwhile way of measuring agreement, on whatever had been agreed.' 'Self-determination,' he said, 'can never be reduced to a mere plebiscite or referendum, so let's not mix the two.'

The Sinn Féin president resists my suggestion that he knows he simply won't get his way. But did he accept that, whatever emerged from a talks process, he would have to live with it? Mr Adams repeated the mantra that Sinn Féin would accept whatever was decided by the Irish people, free from external interference.

It was not for Britain to dictate. Yes, Britain would be involved. And yes, if unionists withheld their consent, the outcome would not be 'an agreed Ireland'. But if there is not to be an agreed Ireland, could Mr Adams support a return to 'armed struggle'? The former West Belfast MP chooses to accentuate the positive: 'What we have at the moment is the IRA having accepted that there is an opportunity for a negotiated settlement, remaining committed to its republican objectives, and ceasing its operations to facilitate that. Let's make that alternative work.'

Pressed further, Mr Adams says: 'As far as I'm concerned, we've left all of this behind us.' But he had previously supported an Armalite and ballot box strategy. Could he ever go back to that? Mr Adams speaks first of Sinn Féin's success in developing its own 'unarmed strategy', before turning to the possible implications of his investment in it: 'Whatever happens, Sinn Féin is committed to developing and promoting the peace. And Sinn Féin is concerned only with that. If there is a resort to conflict in the time ahead, that means we have failed. And at this point I do not envisage failure.'

But if he does fail? Can Gerry Adams' leadership of Sinn Féin survive a resort to violence? As he answers, the implication seems to be that it cannot. 'I consider myself to be a servant of the republican struggle. If I have failed in this leadership role, then it is up to those involved in Sinn Féin to decide what other role I would have.'

Mr Adams says he is not aware of any three- or six-month time limit set by the IRA's Army Council, at which to review progress made during the cessation, although there is a sense of needing to keep it moving.

But if it fails to move in the direction he has described? If, at the end of the day, the British jurisdiction continues, and the supreme authority remains with the crown in the parliament at Westminster? Will republicans one day come to think that he has betrayed them?

Mr Adams says that will be for them to judge in the time ahead: 'But you will note that I said, in my speech welcoming the IRA announcement, that the struggle is not over. And it isn't over. And it won't be over from a republican perspective until the union is replaced by an inclusive, democratic, agreed Ireland.'

But is the 'armed struggle' over? 'One can only read the IRA's statement and accept the British government's working assumption that is the case.'

6

New Labour, New Irish Policy –
Tony Blair
1995

Even as Gerry Adams tussled with the Tories, some in the republican command were clearly preparing to deal with the Labour government, by then more or less guaranteed whenever John Major finally called a general election. Whether marking time through frustration or seeking to strengthen the republican negotiating position, the first IRA ceasefire would collapse in a massive explosion killing two British civilians at Canary Wharf in London on 9 February 1996.

Some unionists immediately claimed vindication for their suspicion all along that the cessation was predicated upon republican assumptions of a guaranteed – united Ireland – outcome to the process. However, surprising numbers of the majority community in Northern Ireland also bought-in to the shared British/Irish analysis that a return to war was neither intended nor a sustainable long-term option, for the republican leadership.

Unionist fears persisted, fuelled by Mo Mowlam's energetic and effective behind-the-scenes efforts to assure nationalist Ireland that an incoming Blair government would be ready to do serious business. Some, like David Trimble, on the other hand, were also investing heavily in Tony Blair's promise that, on the key constitutional issue at least, he would be dealing on precisely the same basis as his Conservative predecessor.

At the start of a two-day visit to Dublin in September 1995 the then Leader of the opposition confirmed the effective end of Labour's traditional policy of Irish unity by consent. When I asked if he thought this transcended the Joint Declaration with its emphasis on the consent principle, Mr Blair replied: 'It didn't obliterate it in any way, but I think it changed the context of it. I said at the time, and would say again now, that I believe the most sensible role for us is to be facilitators, not persuaders in this, not trying to pressure or push people towards a particular objective.' Asserting that Labour's 'historical commitment' remained as it had always been, he continued: 'We just wouldn't have been honest if we hadn't recognised the change that the Joint Declaration and the Framework Documents made.'

'DEMOCRATIC PATH ONLY WAY, SAYS BLAIR'

'Any attempt to force North into United Ireland would be counter-productive, says Labour leader. Mr Blair believes that his party should be "facilitators, not persuaders" on the Northern question.'

FROM *THE IRISH TIMES,* 14 SEPTEMBER 1995

At the start of a two day visit to Dublin, the British Labour leader, Tony Blair, says he regards a resolution of the Northern Ireland question 'as important as any issue in British politics'. The message of this week's visit is that the search for a settlement will continue regardless of any change of government in London.

Q: Mr Gerry Adams says the peace process is in crisis, and that Mr John Major and Sir Patrick Mayhew are squandering a historic opportunity. Do you accept that?

A: No, I don't accept that … Anybody who believed that, with this weight of history behind us, this process was going to be easy would have been extremely foolish. There are bound to be difficulties, and there are difficulties and obstacles in the way of a peace that lasts. But I think we have come an immense way, and I don't believe that anybody would ever forgive themselves if they played a part in squandering that peace now. So I think that whatever difficulties there may be, the overwhelming momentum is still there to push that process on, to deepen it, and to achieve a lasting political settlement.

Q: Sinn Féin says the government's decommissioning requirement sets republicans an impossible test. Mr Martin McGuinness on Thursday said the IRA would not surrender a single weapon ahead of a negotiated settlement. Would you accept that might be the reality?

A: Well, I certainly hope that it isn't because I think if it was it would be an unreasonable position … Let us set this in context. There was the Joint Declaration, then there were the ceasefires. There has then been the publication of the framework documents. All have been designed to establish the principle that the future of Northern Ireland should be determined by consent, and that the wishes of the people of Northern Ireland should be paramount in determining its future. The understanding has been that, once peace is established and the context of democratic negotiation is clear for the future of that process, there then should be talks between all the parties, and those talks should focus around the framework documents. And out of that there should be an agreement. That agreement is then put to the people of Northern Ireland, the United Kingdom parliament and so forth. It is essential if the peace process is to work properly that it is accepted by all sides that the democratic path is the one they have taken. And it is difficult to see how it can be acceptable for any party – not just Sinn Féin but any party – that wants to participate in those talks to participate with any explicit or implied threat that if the talks do not go the way they want then they will revert to violence. It is not surprising to me that the British government has taken the view that it is essential that there is action on decommissioning before … that proper context is established in which the talks will take place. Now I can't believe that those within Sinn Féin, who have come this way and have seen the importance and the support within the community for the peace process, believe that they could engage in the peace process and say at the same time, in effect, that if there is a problem here then outside the door remains the Armalite, the weaponry, and we will revert to that if our position is not satisfied.

Q: So, on the specifics of Sir Patrick's so called 'Washington criteria' Labour would support the government's view that there must be the surrender of some weapons to signal the start of a decommissioning process.

A: Yes, there has to be some visible, tangible sign that it is a proper acceptance of the democratic process. That's the real key to this. The reason why the decommissioning of arms is important is not merely in itself – that people want to stop people having access to weapons of killing and injury – it is that in order for these talks to succeed, in order for there to be a lasting political settlement, there has to be an acceptance that the process is to be democratically achieved.

Q: So, if there's a logjam in the process, the problem lies with Sinn Féin and not Mr Major?

A: I don't disagree with the government's position … I agree entirely with what the Northern Ireland Secretary said a short time ago. This is not a question of victory or defeat for anybody. It is a question of making this process work. But it is clear that these all-party talks will not take place unless there is a genuine acceptance that the path of democracy is the path that people are agreed to take. Now the decommissioning of weapons is to be seen in that context … And I don't believe it is beyond the wit of people of goodwill to find a way to ensure that that is made clear.

Q: Would you accept that decommissioning can only be addressed, perhaps through this international commission, if it is in tandem with a credible commitment by both governments to take the process forward to all-party talks?

A: Well, I think the commitment is there to take us toward all-party talks. The problem is that the context in which those talks take place has got to be clear. It's got to be an acceptance of the democratic road. I've obviously read the reports about some independent commission on decommissioning. That sounds to me entirely sensible. I think that will go some way to meet the worries of people who fear that this is just being driven by the UK government. We've got to see how that develops and works. And I think it is important that it's got a pretty short, tight timetable to work to.

Q: The Dublin view is that Sinn Féin and the IRA are unlikely to accept the commission concept unless there is greater evidence than the British government has shown so far, that it intends in a serious way to persuade the unionists to come to the table and to engage in a meaningful negotiation.

A: Well, to be fair, I think that commitment has been given. I believe they are committed to ensuring, insofar as they are able to do so, that all parties take part in those talks provided everyone is accepting the same rules. Let me make it absolutely clear. Whatever conditions we discuss in relation to Sinn Féin we discuss in relation to any of the other paramilitary groups. This is not an issue that relates to them simply. In many ways these things come back to issues of good faith or otherwise. I'm sure there is a feeling in parts of the nationalist community that Britain sort of says: 'If we can stop the violence, then let's just park the Northern Ireland issue somewhere.' I really believe that feeling is misplaced, that everybody understands and accepts that unless a lasting political settlement comes out of proper all-party talks, then there is unlikely to be a peaceful future for Northern Ireland. I think everyone understands there are fundamental political questions that have to be resolved. I certainly do … And it is a matter of huge personal and political importance to me.

Q: Can I ask when you will consider it appropriate to meet Mr Adams?

A: I think we've just got to keep that question under consideration. Obviously Patrick Mayhew has met Mr Adams now ... I think when I consider it helpful to do so.

Q: A lot of people reading this interview may feel it would have been helpful had you done so earlier.

A: A lot of people feel we should have been on the back of the British government all the way through this, sort of pushing them forward, prodding them and all the rest of it. I think that would have been deeply unhelpful to the peace process. And sometimes it's harder to see these things from the outside. But I can tell you that within the context of the House of Commons and Westminster, had we simply played this as an opposition to them it would have been in my view a great obstruction to the peace process. All the way through I've been concerned about: one, is this a genuine sincere process towards a lasting settlement, and not, as I was saying earlier, just an attempt to shelve the issue for a time? And my view has been; yes it is. And secondly: has it, within the context of British politics, been handled with as much vigour as is possible, given the constraints on all sides? And my answer to that again has been basically yes. Now if people say to me: when would you ever depart from the government? When I believe that they are going fundamentally wrong on either of those two points. But at the moment I don't.

Q: Irish government statements have been implicitly critical of London's handling of issues in the process. The sense is that where Mr Major's government has made concessions, for example on prisoners – instead of doing them early and building confidence in the process, it has appeared grudging and a government acting under pressure. Do you feel in any areas at all that Mr Major and Sir Patrick could have done more, more quickly, to engender republican confidence in their bona fides?

A: These are judgments of great fineness you end up making. My instinct and belief is that they have proceeded at the right pace. You have to remember that they have got their own group of people within their own party ... You have to remember, too, that there has been a huge historic shift in the Conservative Party, in a sense, in its attitude to Northern Ireland. In effect it has said: 'Look, we are yielding up some notion of strategic interest over and above the wishes of the people. We are content to abide by their wishes.' That is in many ways a significant change in their position over a period of time. And they've had to take it part by part.

Q: Let me invite you to one specific issue. Is there any justification, once the new legislation takes effect, why London should resist the immediate repatriation of all republican prisoners currently held in London?

A: Well, it is moving in that direction, let's be clear. The change that has been made, in both the remission times and obviously in the transfer of prisoners from Britain to the North of Ireland where they've got connections with the North, is entirely consistent with ordinary prison policy here. Again we can always make this case … but I think they have proceeded at a rate that is sensible. And of course once the change actually happens, I think in November when the reciprocal arrangements are there between North and South, then it becomes easier to do that.

Q: Many nationalists fear that they detect, under your leadership, a significant movement away from Labour's traditional commitment to Irish unity. Is it your view that the Joint Declaration with its emphasis on the 'consent' principle transcended the traditional Labour view?

A: It didn't obliterate it in any way, but I think it changed the context of it. I said at the time, and would say again now, that I believe the most sensible role for us is to be facilitators, not persuaders in this, not trying to pressure or push people towards a particular objective. I may say if we did try and push them toward that objective I think it would be almost certainly counterproductive … If you've made the political breakthrough of saying it is the consent of the people that is important, then the sensible position for a British government, whether Conservative or Labour, is to give effect to the wishes of the people, not to try and start shoving them in one direction or another. Now, that historical commitment of the Labour Party remains as it always has been. But I think we would have been … well, we just wouldn't have been honest, if we hadn't recognised the change that the Joint Declaration and the Framework Documents made.

Q: Many nationalists also suspect that in the event of a hung parliament you might be tempted to seek an alliance with the Ulster Unionists. Are you in a position to totally rule that out?

A: I can absolutely assure you that – I don't believe we will be in the situation of a hung parliament – but I will do no deals with any political party that involves jettisoning part of the peace process, or dealing on the basis that there is to be something given in return for support. My view of this all the way along has been that this is far too important to play that type of politics with it. And in any event I may say that if we attempted to do so we'd almost certainly fail.

Q: Personally, do you hope to see a united Ireland in your lifetime?

A: What I personally want to see is the wishes of the people there adhered to … I, as you probably know, have got relations at least in the South, going back over many, many years. And I have a very long personal historical association with Ireland. But I am happy for the people there to determine their own future.

Q: So you're easy either way.

A: Yes, I am.

Q: As to whether they stay in the United Kingdom or join a united Ireland?

A: Look, if it is their consent that matters, and their wishes that are uppermost, then that is what I want to see implemented. I do not want them forced either way. And I think the vast majority of people in Britain feel the same. They don't feel some compelling desire to control the destiny of people. What they want is to say: 'Look, we should both establish the peace and then the political framework within which you can make up your own minds.'

Q: Let me suggest why your reluctance to be a persuader worries a lot of people. It goes to the core of a nationalist fear that the unionists will never agree to anything, that there is a real danger that peace could be followed by a protracted political stalemate. Would you accept, as Kevin McNamara would have argued, that in such circumstances the two sovereign governments would have a responsibility to frame a settlement and carry it forward?

A: You don't sit and plan for failure, and let us hope that that never happens. But your responsibilities are to continue to search for peace. The one thing that we have surely learned from the history of Ireland is that you are not going to be able to impose a lasting settlement through coercion or from outside. It is going to have to be in the end the decision of the people there, North and South, that they are going to come to an arrangement that works. We live in a different world today. And I think provided you can establish the peace securely, if you get the North–South cooperation there's going to be, you've got the Northern Ireland assembly coming which is …

Q: It might not.

A: Well, you may not. But I believe it is well possible that you will. We must work for that. And the purpose of working for that is to allow a process to develop organically whereby you have the institutions capable of establishing a better understanding in relationship over a period of time. If I was to sit here and say 'well, I want to give effect to the wishes of the people in Northern Ireland but I'm going to be in there trying to tell them they've got to unite with the South', the only result of that would be to incapacitate my government from playing a proper role. If the Major government were to adopt that position now, either way, they would incapacitate themselves completely … I think in a sense the political class in Britain has taken a collective decision that it is the consent of the people that is uppermost. And we have forsworn on all sides that we are going to try and push them into a settlement they don't want. But what we will try and do is to make sense of the situation – that you're going to have to have, will have, indeed have had historically, a relationship between North and South and so forth.

Q: But the outworking of the consent principle may mean that in the short to medium term there is no guarantee of success.

A: Well, there's never any guarantee of success. One thing is for absolutely sure, and that is if the political will does not exist in Ireland to deliver a settlement, then you're not going to be able to impose one from the outside that is inconsistent with the wishes of the people there.

Q: Whatever about Labour's hopes or intentions for Northern Ireland, is it morally defensible for Labour to continue the exclusion of Northern Ireland citizens from membership of the party?

A: Well, it's a very thorny question this, and it comes up every year at

party conference. We've always taken the view that the SDLP is effectively a sister party of ours, and I can't imagine anything much more
combustible than the present state of the peace process if we were to
announce that here and now. And I think in a sense all that whole
debate is pushed somewhat into the background by the Northern
Ireland Assembly and the prospect of that coming.

Q: But can you understand that many people in Northern Ireland feel
deeply aggrieved that they cannot, as citizens of the United Kingdom,
join and vote for a political party capable of forming the government
of the state in which they live?

A: I totally understand the concerns of people who are Protestants in
Northern Ireland and who feel that the SDLP doesn't offer them a
political future and want to join the Labour Party. I totally understand
those concerns. But in the end we've got to decide – both on our relationship with other parties that are members of the same Socialist
International as we are, and also of what we judge to be the best interests of the North. And the position that we have held we have held to
over a very long period of time and I don't see it changing.

Q: Is the door absolutely closed?

A: Well, every time this decision has come up we have decided it in
exactly the same way. And I'm certainly not agitating for it to be
changed.

7

Trench Warfare:
The Good Friday Disagreement –
Seamus Mallon, Chris Patten
and David Trimble
1998–1999

It really was joy to be in Belfast on that famous Friday, 10 April 1998. And it really would have been smart to get some sleep the night before. Throughout the Thursday evening my various line editors had been gently reminding me of the writing commitments already agreed for the planned Saturday supplement. 'Go to bed,' they urged, knowing I would pay no heed.

The adrenalin surge was too strong, the sense of history-in-the-making too immediate. So I spent the night instead with a small band of fellow junkies, at one stage walking in the snow-covered grounds of the Stormont estate with the legendary Nell McCafferty. Author and broadcaster Éamonn Mallie was up-for-it as ever, always amusing and entertaining, fascinated and informed. At one point, in one of the grim cabins passing as press facility, we found Nell, our mutual friend the late Mary Holland and former IRA prisoner and Sinn Féin spokesman-turned-writer Danny Morrison gloomily assessing the news that the SDLP and Ulster Unionists had just signed-off on the Strand One 'internal' Northern Ireland arrangements. What did it mean? Had Bertie (Ahern) done a deal and cut the Shinners adrift?

I cheerfully suggested there really was nothing for them to worry about – unless, of course, they thought Sinn Féin would refuse to play in the new devolved arrangements. For shortly before the final negotiation I had had a pretty broad steer that, not only would Trimble bow to the SDLP demand for a full-blown Executive but he would do so intending that it should provide places for 'the republicans' as well.

I did finally head back to my hotel at around 5.30 a.m. in search of sleep, only to be awakened about an hour and a half later by my colleague Geraldine Kennedy, then political editor of the paper, who had sensibly gone to bed. 'What's the latest?' she asked, fresh as a daisy. While waiting for breakfast I placed a call to the SDLP office inside the Castle Buildings and, using a pre-arranged code, asked to speak to Seamus Mallon.

We hadn't spoken since about 2 a.m. on the Tuesday of that week. A 'crisis' had erupted on the Monday night after talks chairman Senator George Mitchell had presented the first draft of a putative agreement, and the call went out for Tony Blair to travel to Belfast in a desperate bid to save the entire process from collapse. Monitoring developments from London at that point, I took a midnight call from the invariably reliable and well-informed Ulster Unionist MP Jeffrey Donaldson, the key lieutenant who would in turn become David Trimble's chief tormentor before finally defecting to the DUP. 'There's no deal, it's over,' he told me: 'You can write that.'

I had no doubt Donaldson was reflecting the Ulster Unionist mood of the moment. But something held me back from making a call to my editor Conor Brady in Dublin. As it happened I had tried contacting Seamus Mallon earlier on the Monday afternoon. Upon returning to the Stormont hotel in the early hours of Tuesday he picked up the message and rang me back. I told him what I'd heard from a senior unionist source. The key SDLP negotiator told me to disregard it: there would be a deal by close of play on Thursday.

I had backed Mallon's judgment throughout the rollercoaster ride of that week. And it was a deeply emotional moment when he came on the telephone on the Good Friday morning to confirm that the Belfast Agreement would be announced later in the day. It was a couple of hours later when Alliance leader John (Lord) Alderdice greeted me in the Stormont grounds with a massive bear-hug. A relieved and exhausted John Hume was doing the rounds too, shaking hands and receiving hearty congratulations. A respected BBC Belfast colleague wondered aloud if we as journalists should be shaking hands with the politicians at all, and I took the point. But we were citizens, too – and how many of us had ever thought to witness such a day?

'They really did make history here,' I wrote in the cover piece for the next day's supplement: 'In joy and wonderment, and something approaching disbelief, friends and allies – and even some old adversaries – allowed themselves the luxurious embrace of fresh hope and the sense of new beginnings.' As one local broadcaster had put it: 'Think of all the bad days we've known here. Bloody Sunday, Bloody Friday, Bloody Monday. Bloody, bloody days. This really will be Good Friday.'

While letting the emotion rip, of course, there was need too of cool assessment: 'For in a moment of great personal triumph, Mr John Hume reminded everyone of the barriers and obstacles ahead. This was not the end, or even the beginning of the end, more the end of the beginning.'

A separate inside piece noted the 'last-gasp scare over decommissioning paramilitary weapons' as a reminder of the potential hazards ahead, and warned of the risk run by the Ulster Unionist leader: 'By any standards, Mr Trimble has made a bold gambit. As the howls of protest gather around him, he could be forgiven for pondering the price he might yet pay.'

The Rev. Ian Paisley led the external howls of protest, while Jeffrey Donaldson articulated the pain and angst of those inside the UUP bitterly opposed to what Trimble had done. Even with Tony Blair's powerful presence on the campaign trail, if a majority of unionists voted 'Yes' in the referendum the following month it was only by the narrowest of margins. On his own in the June Assembly elections that followed, Trimble struggled to contain rising unionist anger at the planned release of paramilitary prisoners and the proposed reform of the RUC. Alongside open dispute between the pro-Agreement parties about its provisions for weapons decommissioning, this was a toxic mix for any unionist leader.

Trimble won, but with sufficient internal dissidents on board his Assembly team to deny him the kind of secure majority necessary to carry the project confidently forward. When I met Gerry Adams on the first day of the count at Belfast City Hall he already grasped that the divided state of unionism meant 'trench warfare' ahead. Not even he could have imagined how long it would last, or with what end result.

Within weeks of the election Seamus Mallon, Hume's nominee for Deputy First Minister, was already running out of patience with the UUP leader – warning that he would have to 'reinvent himself' and start 'selling' the Agreement. Mallon would still be waiting over a year later for the appointment of an Executive in even 'shadow' form, while Trimble found himself almost undone by the report of the Patten Commission on policing. Yet the storm over the loss of the RUC's 'Royal' title would be nothing to the damage incurred in November 1999 when Trimble finally lost the argument over decommissioning as 'a precondition' for Sinn Féin's entry into government – and found himself obliged to 'jump first'.

In his book *Great Hatred, Little Room*, Jonathan Powell – who was Downing Street chief-of-staff throughout Tony Blair's premiership – would eventually declare the Belfast Agreement 'in essence ... an agreement to disagree'. The following interviews with Mallon, Patten and Trimble illustrate the point.

'MALLON CHALLENGES "PETULANT" TRIMBLE ON AGREEMENT'

The deputy leader of the SDLP has said a 'petulant' David Trimble must 'reinvent himself again' and start selling the Belfast Agreement in a positive and dynamic fashion. In a direct challenge to the Ulster Unionist leader, Mr Seamus Mallon insists the transitional arrangements defined in the Agreement – including the creation of a shadow Northern Ireland Executive – must follow immediately upon the Assembly elections.

During an interview with the *The Irish Times*, Mr Mallon refuses to be drawn on whether he might emerge as Deputy First Minister in the new Assembly. He issues a blunt warning to Sinn Féin that it will face 'a growing imperative within the body politic' to ensure 'verifiable evidence' of progress on decommissioning during the two-year period prescribed by the Agreement.

FROM *THE IRISH TIMES*, 18 JUNE 1998

The Newry and Armagh MP is in good heart after an SDLP canvass in Belfast's Markets area. He senses a distinct change in the atmosphere as a result of the Agreement which he, as his party's chief negotiator, played a key part in bringing about.

Would he like to be Deputy First Minister in the new Assembly? The answer is predictable – that's not a decision for him; his effort is to win three seats in Newry–Armagh. But if John Hume were to decide that European and Westminster commitments would prevent him doing the job, would Mr Mallon be happy to assume leadership in the Assembly? Again no give. 'I will wait and see what decisions are made. It would be presumptuous of me to pre-empt any decision by anyone else.'

OK. I wonder how he thinks Mr Trimble would perform as First Minister? Mr Mallon has ready praise for Mr Trimble's courage in making the Agreement, but is clearly perplexed by his pre-election manoeuvrings, particularly his opposition to the Bill providing for prisoner releases.

'I think he has to, as it were, reinvent himself again. We had the pre-agreement Trimble, which wasn't very acceptable to the vast majority of nationalists. Then people started to see him in a new light when he showed considerable courage during the talks, and in the final week especially when he did sign the Agreement.'

'Unfortunately,' he adds, 'since then, in the Westminster vote on the sentencing legislation, he seemed to contradict what he had signed rather ham-fistedly, rather petulantly. I think there again we saw the petulant Trimble acting on what seemed to be the spur of the moment, making an important decision for not very good reasons.

'He is now in an election campaign and, rather than leading pro-agreement unionists in a positive and dynamic way, he seems to be sliding back into the realms that have been occupied by Paisley and [Robert] McCartney.'

He continues: 'If he doesn't stand by this agreement – and I mean positively selling it to the unionist community – then again he's justifying the arguments made by Paisley and McCartney, and he could find himself in a bog between the very courageous position he adopted on the Agreement and the quagmire they have created for themselves.'

Mr Trimble has cast a question mark over the transitional arrangements to come into play before the actual transfer of powers to the Assembly. Specifically he has said the shadow Executive need not come into being until close to Christmas, 'if then'.

Does that accord with Mr Mallon's understanding of the Agreement? He replies directly: 'It's completely at variance with those arrangements. It's absolutely essential that the First Minister, Deputy First Minister and the shadow Executive is set up immediately.' He says this is vital first to ensure stability in the process itself. To leave any void would be damaging.

Second, it is important that officials and civil servants who have been running the show for nearly 30 years get the message that there is a new dispensation.

Most crucially, he says, the Agreement stipulates October 31st for completion of plans for the implementation bodies of the North–South Council. It would be impossible 'to decide upon these unless the Northern Ireland departments had been agreed and there were ministers in place to make decisions and work-up the type of arrangements necessary'.

By 'immediately', Mr Mallon expects these key appointments – the presiding officer and his deputy, the First and Deputy First Ministers, and the shadow ministers – to be appointed by the middle of July. If Mr Trimble refuses to accept this, it will be 'incumbent upon the Prime Minister, Tony Blair, to make clear that the British government, the Irish government and the other parties have signed this agreement and that he cannot have a veto on it'.

Nationalists 'bit their lip' when, on three occasions at least, Mr Blair 'came here to bail out' the Ulster Unionists during the referendum campaign. Mr Blair 'went as close as he could to changing the terms of the Agreement without doing so'. If he does not use the same influence to ensure the Agreement progresses, he says serious questions will be asked of Mr Blair, not least by the Irish government.

Are there challenges also for Sinn Féin? Again Mr Mallon doesn't hesitate: 'No question or doubt about that. We have the unease with-in the unionist community about their position. We have the unfin-ished business of the question of the holding of arms. The agreement is specific about that.' But is it?

Dr Paisley, Mr McCartney and others say the Agreement does not guarantee any decommissioning. Mr Mallon agrees 'that is probably an accurate assessment in terms of the Agreement as it is written'. However, he adds: 'I think the overall requirement – in terms of the global assessment to be made by the Secretary of State, the way in which parties are going to have to work together – means there will be a growing imperative within the body politic to ensure that within the two-year period specified, there is verifiable evidence that decom-missioning is progressing.'

He goes on: 'I think Sinn Féin must realise this agreement can only work by consent, that consent is required from both sides and if they – as the unionists seem to be at the moment – play games with this issue, they are going to make a working agreement difficult if not impossible. I would suggest to Sinn Féin that their act of faith in the Agreement and the future working of the Agreement would be a very positive response in terms of the removal of arms and the weapons of war.'

'COMMISSION CHAIRMAN SURPRISED AT DAVID TRIMBLE'S INTERPRETATION OF BELFAST AGREEMENT'

Patten responds to Trimble's criticism.

FROM *THE IRISH TIMES*, 11 SEPTEMBER 1999

Hardly surprising: Chris Patten looks tired, the eyes a bit puffier than usual. The morning after publication, he says, 'feels a bit like a hangover'.

But he shakes off the fatigue the minute I remind him of David Trimble's critique of his 'shoddy piece of work'. According to the Ulster Unionist leader, Mr Patten simply hadn't grasped the point of the Belfast Agreement, namely that, with Northern Ireland's constitutional position settled, emblems and titles shouldn't have been thought contentious.

Chris Patten says he listens carefully to what Mr Trimble says about the Agreement because obviously 'he was one of the creators of it'. But he declares himself 'surprised by his interpretation of it' and fancies a lot of nationalists will be as well.

'It seemed to me what was settled in the Agreement was that the constitutional position should be determined democratically,' he says. 'But in return for making that manifest, I'd understood nationalists and republicans were offered two things. First, parity of esteem and recognition that there are two traditions in Northern Ireland, and that one shouldn't be seen (whether it is a justified observation or not) to be lording it over the other.'

'And secondly, specific institutions of government were created to reflect that, while nationalists and republicans under the Agreement are obliged to demonstrate their commitment to the democratic process, they're not obliged to owe their primary loyalty to the institutions of the state.'

Looking quite incredulous, he declares: 'I don't understand what the Agreement is about if it isn't about that.' And if that's the case, then he doesn't understand either 'the determination to keep the police service in a position where it's identified with the institutions of the state'.

If, on the other hand, it didn't mean all that, then, Mr Patten ventures, 'some of our terms of reference make no sense at all'. And he goes on to explicitly rebuke Mr Trimble. 'I don't say this provocatively but it really does seem to me that we were given a very clear agenda and I'm surprised that those who gave us that agenda didn't understand what the consequences would be.'

The UUP had warned Mr Patten against scrapping the RUC's title. But had they given him to understand that disregarding their view could see his report rejected wholesale?

The man who saw the Union flag brought down over Hong Kong describes the political submissions he received as hardly surprising. Sinn Féin's was posited on the assumption that only disbandment was acceptable. The SDLP argument was for 'breaking up' the police service. The views of the DUP and 'the various gradations of McCartneyism were based on the assumption – which had a certain logic to it – that we were only doing the devil's work'. And the UUP, he confirms, said 'no change in symbols', before adding: 'So make of that what you will.'

Presumably he means a greater focus on symbols than anything else? Mr Patten confides: 'I have had a leading unionist say to me: 'You may have got a lot of the substance right but if you've got the symbols wrong, you've blown it.' And without any change in tone, he continues: 'And I think that is an argument which a lot of people would think tested rationality close to destruction.'

Does he think David Trimble quite grasps the linkage between Patten and devolution? 'I hope so,' comes the reply. 'This is one thing I feel very strongly about in general, and in relation to Northern Ireland in particular. My experience in government, not only as a minister here but as a minister in a centralising government in Westminster, led me to feel that if you take away people's responsibilities, you can't be surprised if they behave irresponsibly.'

Reflecting that personal belief, the Patten report recommends significant police powers should be devolved as soon as possible once the Executive and Assembly are functioning.

And so its author hopes that the First Minister-designate understands the importance of what has been proposed: 'It does after all reflect a long-time unionist request ... I hope not one that unionism today shrinks from.'

Many people in Northern Ireland and beyond fear that there is a moral vacuum at the heart of the peace process. Does Chris Patten understand that?

'Yes, I do, because as in other cases where you're trying to bring together a divided society you fetch up being obliged to make all sorts of compromises, which cut across values that people hold dear. And I suppose it is the beginning of wisdom in Northern Ireland to recognise that while there are absolute values, there are also relativist views on them.'

He goes on: 'It was borne in on me more strongly than anything else when we did those public meetings that there are two stories in Northern Ireland, two sets of experiences. And, all right, they're to a degree propagandised, mythologised, but a lot of what's said and felt and suffered is genuine and credible.'

This, says Mr Patten, has a direct bearing on what he has to say about policing: 'I heard one unionist politician talking about delivering housing estates and the streets to paramilitaries, to baseball-bat justice. What the hell do they think the situation is today in too much of Northern Ireland? Because we've in effect tied one hand of the police behind their backs by tying them to the hardcore political argument ...'

But hang on. There is another hardcore argument, that the IRA will never permit a police force, deriving its authority from the British state, to gain acceptance in their areas. That, he counters, is the challenge, 'that's where nationalists and republicans have to be put on the spot.'

Mr Patten is equally withering about his critics in the *Daily Telegraph*. Referring to what he describes as 'a sort of barmy smack-of-crop-against-leather-boot' editorial in the paper yesterday, he demands: 'What do they know about what's happening in those estates?' Community policing, he asserts, 'is about winning the real war that people experience when they're having to put their hand in their pocket to pay off a paramilitary'. Far from failing 'to understand the nature of the war' in Northern Ireland, he asserts, 'community policing, a partnership between the people and attested police officers, is the real name of the game.'

Grand vision. But is it believable that Sinn Féin could be sitting on a new police board in the short term at least, given the scale of recent and ongoing IRA activity? To this, Chris Patten's answer is concise, and almost certainly the only one which all sides will readily believe: 'I pray for Senator Mitchell.'

He proves equally nimble when asked if he came to the view that the RUC was institutionally sectarian. The Patten Commission was not in the position of the MacPherson inquiry into the Stephen Lawrence case, he explains, in that it wasn't asked to pronounce on a case and its implications. And he moves swiftly on: 'We read with enthusiasm the forward-looking language of the Agreement and decided to try to operate in the same way.'

Finally, on the question of pain: there was much talk on Thursday of the pain involved for members of the RUC, their families, friends and supporters. Where in all this is the pain for Sinn Féin and the IRA?

The former Tory chairman thinks that, if only some unionists read a little more history, 'then they'd know what the pain is. I hope this will happen, but I don't think anybody should underestimate the difficulty for republican leaders in urging young men and women with republican backgrounds to join the police service in Northern Ireland. If you don't understand that's a challenge to republicans then you don't understand much about the history of this island.'

'TRIMBLE NOT CONTEMPLATING FAILURE BUT TAKING NOTHING FOR GRANTED'

New millennium would be 'excellent time for republicans to decommission'.

FROM *THE IRISH TIMES*, 26 NOVEMBER 1999

For a man whose leadership is on the line David Trimble seems remarkably composed. The voice is calm and quiet; the demeanour purposeful, realistic and deadly serious; the peace of his Commons office disturbed only by the sonorous sounds of Big Ben.

The Ulster Unionist leader might well wonder if the bells toll for him. Certainly this is a deadly serious business, with sudden political death a possibility he cannot rule out.

Mr Trimble denies having shifted ground on 'the fundamentals', and insists a change in tactics cannot be described as 'a colossal U-turn'. But he did recently tell his party: 'Read my lips. No guns, no government.' Does he regret that now?

'We are still in the same position ... We are not waiving the requirement to decommission. We have gone to a lot of effort to get republicans to acknowledge their obligation to decommission, to have mechanisms in terms of the way in which General de Chastelain will operate in place, and, of course, to have the sanction of the action by the governments if it fails to happen.'

Obviously he would have loved to have devolution and decommissioning happening simultaneously. But he goes on: 'If people are saying "we will do this just starting immediately after devolution", would we be justified in refusing to proceed simply because there is going to be a short delay? We have the process starting, the process of appointing the contact person [the IRA interlocutor to deal with the International Commission] will start on the day of devolution. So while the two processes are not exactly side by side, they overlap and one follows immediately after the other.'

Yet Mr Trimble has consistently said he would not sit in government with the representatives of a fully-armed terrorist organisation. Isn't that principle about to be breached?

He insists not. 'No, because I said we would not sit in such an administration with people who are fully armed where there was no decommissioning. Nor are we. Because before we go into it they have given commitments on the issue, committed themselves to action on the issue, and we are determined that that action will be followed through. 'Therefore the principle that we asserted has been sustained. The timing has moved a little. But again, can anyone erect a change of principle out of a shift of a few days?'

That sounds quite specific. Does he really expect actual decommissioning to have commenced within days of the appointment of the Executive?

Not quite, is the answer. Within days of devolution Mr Trimble expects a report from General de Chastelain on the 'modalities' – which he says will embrace 'the questions of amounts, types of weapons, methods of decommissioning'. That will leave the issue of timing: 'But we expect the general will then outline the arrangements for the next phase of the process and so on.'

So is the operative date January 31st? The Ulster Unionist leader insists he does not have 'a precise date' in mind. Indeed, he says: 'I would discourage people from thinking in terms of a precise date.' But for any republican reading this interview, he ventures: 'If they commence the legal process on December 2nd, then it would be an entirely wise thing for them to contemplate the beginning of the new year, the new era, the new millennium, as being an excellent time in which they should do that.'

Eight heady days after the Belfast accord was agreed, Mr Trimble famously won the backing of the Ulster Unionist Council with 72 per cent of the vote. Is he anticipating a similar margin this time? And what margin does he actually need to win over doubtful Assembly members?

There is a certain inevitability to the answer. The UUP leader is taking nothing for granted and resists an invitation to say 60/40 would be enough. 'I know that this issue – because of its sensitivity, because of the emotional impact of dealing with Sinn Féin – is something the members of the council will think very hard about. I see, too, that those who were opposed to the Agreement are redoubling their efforts … So I take nothing for granted.'

But will he resign if defeated tomorrow?

Mr Trimble replies: 'I'm not contemplating that, I'm not contemplating failure. I very much expect and hope that we will have an endorsement by the party.' He then adds: 'Whatever happens, I'm not going to turn my back on the party or this process.'

Said with such emphasis, this is clearly important. However, the meaning is not instantly clear. What if his party turns its back on the process? Will he accept a majority verdict against him?

Again the inevitable from a leader in such a position: 'I expect and hope that the result will be an endorsement. If it's not that, then we shall have to consider very seriously what we do.'

This is important: not least, of course, because some critics think he would not accept defeat as the end of the road. One leading opponent suggests Mr Trimble might do what he calls 'a super-Faulkner' – that he might walk away from his party if he thought he had enough strength in the Assembly to save the Agreement.

Mr Trimble doesn't much care for this. 'You're quite right to say I am persistent. I am. But I'm not another Brian Faulkner, have not been at any point in this process. I have not at any point regarded him as a role model.'

So, no possibility of life for David Trimble outside the Ulster Unionist Party then? 'As I say, I don't intend to turn my back on the party or on what I'm trying to achieve.'

An apology seems appropriate for pressing the point. But it does seem odd that – facing into such a crucial meeting – the leader seems unable to say he will accept the majority will of his party. Odd or not, we have reached the end of the line on this subject, Mr Trimble concluding: 'I've a feeling you're trying to draw me into a discussion of what happens if we lose. I'm not contemplating failure.'

Laughter follows when I ask whether a narrow win might serve to keep the pressure on Sinn Féin. Mr Trimble has been accused of trying to manage his party on that basis for the past two years. It's 'completely false', he says, while confirming he would rather like the comfort of a big majority.

He also takes comfort from the default mechanism outlined by Peter Mandelson, which would see the Executive and other institutions suspended should decommissioning not materialise. And Martin McGuinness, he asserts, is 'whistling in the wind' in saying there is no such provision in the Agreement.

Even so, Mr McGuinness, Mr Martin Ferris and Mr Pat Doherty of Sinn Féin seem to have a common view of what should happen if there is no decommissioning: nothing, save that the institutions proceed. Might Mr Trimble remove the uncertainty by tabling that postdated letter of resignation mooted in *The Irish Times* and elsewhere over recent weeks?

The UUP leader specifically dismisses yesterday's renewed press speculation, describing the claim that he would quit if there is no decommissioning by January 31st as 'inaccurate'. He would, he says, 'regard publicly setting a date as wholly counterproductive'.

His party's final decision may well rest on what he says to them in the privacy of the Waterfront Hall tomorrow morning. Even if delegates are anxious to trust his new-found faith that republicans will deliver, Mr Trimble still has to answer the question: what happens if that trust proves to have been misplaced?

'I know the concern that exists in the party, indeed in the wider community, about an open-ended process, where you get sucked along and then hung out to dry,' he replies. 'I know there's an issue there to address. I think actually when people see the outworking of the de Chastelain commission they will see that it is going to be addressed through that. But I'm aware of the concern, and we'll see what we can do about it.'

Whatever the precise formulation he has in mind, Mr Trimble's intention seems clear. 'It's not open-ended. It's very definitely not. I would say to the party – "Don't worry about having to trust Sinn Féin, or the Irish government or the British government. Trust yourselves. This cannot work without the participation of the Ulster Unionist Party." So, at the end of the day, whatever anyone else might do or say or think, it is our decision ... we have within ourselves the capacity to put a term to things.'

A term to things ... No leader ever likes to tie his hands. But it sounds as if Mr Trimble is getting ready to do just that. And to tie the hands of those who, come Monday night, expect to partner him in Northern Ireland's new government.

8

Suspension – Seamus Mallon, Jeffrey Donaldson, Gerry Adams and David Trimble
2000

From the outset David Trimble maintained that the Belfast Agreement contained the clear commitment that decommissioning should be completed by May 2000. He would also claim Tony Blair's private concurrence that the process should be under way by the time the new Northern Ireland Assembly was elected in June 1998. Unfortunately for Trimble, nobody, save his Conservative allies at Westminster, agreed with his interpretation that the two combined to make decommissioning – or at least a start to it – a precondition for Sinn Féin's entry into government.

Blair's first Secretary of State, Mo Mowlam, would eventually finesse the British position, describing decommissioning as 'an obligation' under the Agreement. In a potentially significant intervention at one point Seamus Mallon also declared if the IRA had not decommissioned by the May 2000 target date he would vote for Sinn Féin's expulsion from ministerial office.

Mallon, however, was freelancing. This was not the official position of either the SDLP or the Irish government. When push came to shove London backed the SDLP and the Irish against Trimble. Hence the 1999 'Mitchell Review' of the Agreement, hosted by Senator Mitchell at the US ambassador's residence in London, ended with Trimble agreeing to 'jump first'.

As on the Good Friday itself – and at so many points in the process – what became known as 'the blame game' intruded. Trimble's over-riding purpose at every point since entering the process had been to end what he saw as the dangerous isolation of unionism, and to secure an agreement that would settle and secure Northern Ireland's place within the United Kingdom. He would later admit he went along with the Belfast Agreement knowing that a battle over arms had still to be fought – calculating to survive and fight another day, rather than collapse the process and have unionism blamed across the world for failure. So again, in November 1999, he was faced with the same dilemma. No longer able to count on Downing Street support on the issue, the UUP leader finally relented – knowing that a refusal to form an administration was a guaranteed way to ensure no decommissioning would ever occur, while catching the blame.

It was the biggest gamble of Trimble's entire career, a certain rallying point for all those inside and outside the UUP determined to bring his leadership to an end. Crucially, however, Trimble attached his own precondition, in the form of a post-dated letter of resignation giving the IRA just six weeks in which to start a decommissioning process. With the institutions of government finally up and running, the republicans calculated that Trimble was bluffing. In any event they clearly reasoned that, having waited so long, the two governments would not allow him now to bring the institutions crashing down. They were wrong – at least in respect of the British. In February 2000 – despite dark and bitter protest and objection by Sinn Féin, the SDLP, the Irish government and President Bill Clinton in Washington – then Secretary of State Peter Mandelson kept faith with Trimble and suspended the Executive and Assembly.

'Kept faith' seems unquestionably the appropriate characterisation of Mandelson's action. For even as he condemned Mandelson – 'he should have been prepared NOT to lose the institutions' – Seamus Mallon in the interview below offered corroboration of Trimble's version of events as they played out during the Mitchell Review: 'What we were told by George Mitchell very clearly was that his understanding was that devolution would be set up on 29 November and that decommissioning would begin end of January.'

When I travelled again to Belfast in April – two years after that Good Friday – Mallon was still trying to break the deadlock, while warning Sinn Féin: 'For any party to even contemplate a political future based on the absolute wounding of unionism … is not just faulty thinking but cynicism in the extreme.' With Trimble already badly wounded, Jeffrey Donaldson was still disavowing a desire to supplant the UUP leader – while looking more and more his likely successor. Gerry Adams was rejecting the Mallon/Trimble take on Mitchell, insisting that 'jumping together' had always meant Trimble leading unionists into the Executive and the IRA engaging directly on its own behalf with General John de Chastelain's international decommissioning commission. The Sinn Féin president acknowledged that Trimble had made clear his position would be untenable unless decommissioning was under way within a time-specific period, while insisting 'he [Adams] had no reason to think this realisable, nor did Mr Trimble'. The UUP leader, meanwhile, was battling suggestions that Mandelson might be signalling a shift in British policy by trying to 'decouple decommissioning from the rest of the Agreement' with his warnings of 'a Mexican stand-off' that might merely guarantee the achievement of neither devolution nor decommissioning.

'MALLON STILL IN SEARCH OF KEY TO THE DECOMMISSIONING DEADLOCK'

Today Mr Mallon, the deputy leader of the SDLP, explains his opposition to the suspension of the Executive by the Northern Ireland Secretary, Mr Peter Mandelson. He confirms his belief that Mr Mandelson should have allowed David Trimble to execute his threatened resignation as First Minister in February, arguing that would have placed the 'imperative' on 'political unionism within the UUP' to back its leader on the floor of the Assembly.

Mr Mallon also reveals for the first time that Senator George Mitchell, who conducted last year's review of the Agreement, told the SDLP 'very clearly that his understanding was that devolution would be set up on 29 November and that decommissioning would then begin end of January'.

Mr Mallon rejects suggestions that the SDLP should proceed in government without Sinn Féin, saying the 'inclusive' principle lies at the heart of the Agreement. But he also says for any party to seek a future 'based on the absolute wounding of unionism' would be 'cynicism in the extreme'.

FROM *THE IRISH TIMES*, 13 APRIL 2000

Nationalist Ireland reacted bitterly to Peter Mandelson's suspension of the Northern Ireland Executive on February 11th – none more so than the then Deputy First Minister, Seamus Mallon.

But looking back on the traumatic events of the past few months, does he think he has played fair by David Trimble? The question clearly wasn't anticipated. After a pause, he says he thinks 'very fairly' indeed, adding that he 'probably went further than anyone might have expected' in terms of decommissioning and the way in which it was raised.

The point is that Mr Trimble, encouraged by people like Mr Mallon, agreed to jump first in the expectation that IRA decommissioning would follow devolution. At the conclusion of the Mitchell review, the SDLP appeared to share that expectation. Yet when decommissioning failed to materialise, Mr Mallon and his colleagues opposed the suspension.

Mr Mallon insists this is wrong. While the other parties were technically involved, the Mitchell Review was essentially 'a bartering exercise' between Mitchell, Sinn Féin and the Ulster Unionists: 'Our party wasn't present at any of the meetings when the understandings that are supposed to have been reached were reached. We cannot point to anything we were part of, or experienced, that would indicate any understanding except what we were told by George Mitchell.'

And what was that? Here, for the first time, and without hesitation, Mr Mallon offers corroboration of Mr Trimble's version of events: 'What we were told by George Mitchell very clearly was that his understanding was that devolution would be set up on 29 November and that decommissioning would begin end of January.'

Yet despite this, when Peter Mandelson moves to avert Mr Trimble's resignation and save the Agreement from collapse, Mr Mallon's criticism is directed at the Secretary of State rather than the IRA. Doesn't this reinforce the unionist suspicion that the SDLP will never break with Sinn Féin?

Mr Mallon retorts: 'It wasn't a matter of breaking with Sinn Féin: that is a completely wrong understanding ... First, I still don't accept the premise that, had suspension not taken place, unionism would not have been saved from itself. I think subsequent events show that was a misjudgement. The way in which unionism and its present leadership could have been strengthened was for them to stand on their own feet, put in their resignations if that was their view, then go back and start to really scrap for the return of the institutions, and to return on the basis of cross-community support within the assembly.'

But Mr Mandelson had explained in the Commons that, if Mr Trimble resigned, he would take Mr Mallon with him and that there was no possibility of an alternative First and Deputy First Minister team being found with the requisite cross-community consent.

'How does Mr Mandelson know that? That was a supposition on his part,' comes the reply. Surely because, even as things now stand, Mr Trimble does not command the required outright majority of the unionist bloc? Mr Trimble having written his post-dated resignation letter, Mr Mallon says the perception then 'was that you had a British Secretary of State toppling the institutions which took 30 years to set up, to save that unionist leadership from itself'.

So Mr Mandelson should have been prepared to lose Mr Trimble? 'He should have been prepared not to lose the institutions because they are the focal point of this whole agreement,' counters Mr Mallon. And who does he think would have emerged in this scenario as an alternative unionist First Minister?

Mr Mallon is insistent: 'I believe unionism then would have had the type of imperative within them to try to ensure that they be able to present a nomination for First Minister that would be carried in the Assembly.'

No, this was not a question of Mr Mandelson calling Mr Trimble's bluff. Mr Mallon accepts the resignation threat was not a bluff, and would have been carried through. But yes, he does mean the Secretary of State should have let the resignation go ahead and faced unionism with the imperative of producing an answer.

And if it doesn't? 'I go back to this: unionism is in as difficult a situation because of suspension as it would have been had the resignations been put into effect.'

One possible way out might be to hold fresh Assembly elections. However, Mr Mallon promptly points out that the electoral validity of the Agreement extends beyond Assembly elections to the referendums held North and South in May 1998. He feels deeply that 'the will of the people ... was actually disregarded'.

Yet if the strength of Martin Smyth's leadership challenge reflects the temper of the wider unionist community, isn't the cross-community principle underpinning the referendum verdict itself in serious question?

'In terms of political unionism, yes,' he agrees: 'But does political unionism equate with broader unionism in terms of their express wishes?'

Mr Mallon thinks not. But if that benign view is to be justified, he accepts a new formulation is required giving unionists confidence that the arms issue will be dealt with.

There is no doubt Mr Mallon's language on decommissioning has often riled republicans. Yet the suspicion persists that, for the SDLP generally, decommissioning wouldn't be such a problem if the unionists hadn't made it so. Is it, for him, a profoundly moral issue?

'It is moral ... not in the accepted sense of a moral issue, but in the sense that it is anti-political. We are in the business of politics. And the holding of illegal arms within any jurisdiction as an alternative to the sovereignty of that jurisdiction surely poses serious political questions with substantial moral overtones.'

Does that mean Sinn Féin's participation in government should be conditional on IRA decommissioning? 'Conditional is again stepping into the bog ... What we've tried to do all along is work out a way in which we could be satisfied, especially unionists, that violence and the use of violence is ended.'

Given resistance to that word 'conditional', did Mr Mallon agree with the Taoiseach that 'it is not compatible beyond a short transitional period [in government] to have that democratic mandate with armed backing'?

Mr Mallon is clearly determined to define his position in his own terms: 'I've always said there is a difference between obtaining decommissioning and dealing with decommissioning. Decommissioning can be dealt with in political terms in a way that might not achieve it. It's making sure that it is dealt with and done that is the important thing.'

Would he agree that any fresh sequence leading to the restoration of devolution would require an explicit timetable for decommissioning? Mr Mallon says it must involve two things: 'One: a belief in the unionist community that it was going to be addressed seriously, that violence had ended, that the use of violence for political reasons would not be resumed. And the logical conclusion of that is that illegal arms will be dealt with. It is that comfort zone more than anything else that unionism needs.'

But why should the SDLP not give unionists the added comfort of indicating that it would proceed in government without Sinn Féin if decommissioning does not occur? Because, says Mr Mallon, that would be to tear up the Agreement. The agreement was premised on the inclusive vision, on parallel consent: 'That's the nature of this agreement. It must be inclusive.'

Mr Mallon resists any thought of alternatives, should the Agreement fail. He maintains it will not, and that neither government will move from it.

He dismisses the idea that some republicans might actually be happy to see it fall, thinking to reassemble a pan-nationalist front behind a demand for something approaching joint authority.

Those 'still dabbling in this notion of pan-nationalism are making a huge mistake,' he says: 'There is – let me put this in inverted commas – a "pan-nationalist position". It includes the Irish government, the SDLP, Fine Gael, Labour – all the political parties except one, Sinn Féin.'

And if he won't support its exclusion, Mr Mallon equally disdains any notion of bypassing unionism. 'For any party to even contemplate a political future based on the absolute wounding of unionism ... is not just faulty thinking but cynicism in the extreme.'

'NOT SEEKING UUP LEADERSHIP – JUST YET'

Jeffrey Donaldson is hoping against hope that the question of David Trimble's leadership does not arise. 'I'm in no hurry to be leader,' he tells Frank Millar.

FROM *THE IRISH TIMES*, 14 APRIL 2000

Jeffrey Donaldson knows well the old political maxim that he who wields the dagger should not hope to wear the crown. During the past two years he has nurtured his future prospects by carefully casting himself as 'the constructive opposition' within the confines of the Ulster Unionist Party. Unlike some of his senior colleagues, he declined to join the Democratic Unionist Party on public platforms opposing the Good Friday accord. Likewise, until the very last minute, he opposed a challenge to David Trimble's leadership at the annual meeting of the Ulster Unionist Council.

But the minute Martin Smyth declared, Mr Donaldson threw his weight behind the challenge. Finally over the dam, does he now think he would be better suited to lead Ulster Unionism?

He is clearly unsurprised by the question. Sure, he regrets that the question of leadership 'is often relegated to questions of personalities'. He backed the Smyth challenge 'to send a strong signal to government and to the leadership of our party ... that we really are not prepared to see the Ulster Unionists jump again [into government with Sinn Féin] without decommissioning'.

He is not seeking the leadership, and sees no reason why Mr Trimble should not survive even the collapse of the Belfast Agreement.

'But if David were to come back to the UUC with a new sequence which fell short of our requirements, didn't deliver actual decommissioning, didn't deliver a timetable indicating that decommissioning was going to follow very quickly and be completed within a short timeframe, I think the Ulster Unionist Council would be minded to reject that.'

Mr Donaldson continues: 'In those circumstances we may well have a crisis within the party because clearly if the leadership are making such a significant recommendation and it is rejected, then that becomes a matter of confidence.'

Does a confidence issue translate into another leadership challenge? Mr Donaldson replies: 'I think it would be very difficult to avoid that in those specific circumstances. Now that is not, let me hasten to add, that is not Jeffrey Donaldson putting down his card for a leadership challenge. I am hoping against hope that such a scenario does not arise. I've made it clear that I'm in no hurry to become the leader.'

Such disclaimers apart, it's pretty obvious he thinks Mr Trimble's continued leadership highly conditional. Isn't it? 'Any leader's hold on the leadership is conditional on that leader retaining the confidence of his party. It's clear from the vote on the leadership and, more importantly, from the vote on the RUC, that the confidence of the party has been seriously undermined.

'What I'm saying is, if we are going to have to go through another divisive vote on the implementation of the Agreement, and jumping back into government with Sinn Féin without actual decommissioning, I think that may well be the straw that breaks the camel's back.'

Mr Donaldson echoes John Taylor's view that May 22nd is the 'sell-by date' for the Agreement, after which the task will be to seek an alternative way forward. And if Mr Trimble has taken a principled stand on decommissioning, he says, he could lead the search for that alternative. However, he fears the UUP leader will come under enormous pressure from London and Dublin to 'jump again'. And does he think he might? 'Before Washington [and Mr Trimble's remarks about a fresh sequence] I felt that, having jumped once, he was going to stand firm on decommissioning. Post-Washington the seeds of doubt were sown ...'

The Irish Times interviewed Mr Donaldson during the critical run-up to the 1998 referendum, at a point when he was under massive pressure from Tony Blair to back the campaign for a Yes vote. Watching him then, listening to him now, the suspicion is that he really is in no personal hurry for leadership, and in truth views the prospect with decided dread.

For who would want to lead unionism in the circumstances he envisages? Whether it's Mr Trimble or himself leading the search, does he really believe there is a ghost of a chance of the SDLP agreeing to stay in an Executive without Sinn Féin?

'I think there has to be a chance. If the Agreement collapses and there is a political vacuum, the losers in it will most definitely be the SDLP.'

Surely outsiders would contend that the one certain death for the SDLP would be to gang up with the unionists against Sinn Féin? He disagrees: 'In circumstances where the IRA are clearly in default ...' But the SDLP and the Irish government don't as of now believe republicans to be in default, do they?

'Clearly we have a problem … What I'm saying is that beyond May 22nd we can go in two directions. We either see direct rule copperfastened, or we can try to find a Plan B. If politics is to work in Northern Ireland, we have to build the centre ground. I say to the SDLP, your failure to build that centre ground with unionism and your fixation with pan-nationalism is going to be the death knell of progressive politics in Northern Ireland for the next 10 or 20 years.'

One possible Plan B which Mr Donaldson favours is an agreement with the SDLP to restore the institutions, leaving space for Sinn Féin to resume its place on the Executive once decommissioning has occurred. Another option is to retain the inclusive principle while stripping the Assembly of its law-making powers and thus removing the need for an Executive altogether.

But isn't this just whistling in the wind? Isn't he merely reviving proposals his own party gave up on in the negotiations preceding the Good Friday accord?

Interestingly Mr Donaldson reveals that Mr Trimble, John Taylor and Mr (now Sir) Reg Empey only abandoned their position on non-executive, administrative devolution in the early hours of that famous morning. And he stresses he was prepared to buy the final 'inclusivity' package, provided the IRA agreed to disarm.

But he quit the talks team in those final memorable hours, precisely because he felt the commitments on decommissioning had been fudged. Could he understand the republican view that it is the triumph of his agenda that has actually led to Mr Trimble being in default?

Whatever about the 'different interpretations', he says, 'republicans always knew they would have to do something … The price had to be disarmament.'

Mr Donaldson rejects the more pragmatic view that Martin McGuinness's participation in a partitionist government is a better guarantor of republican good intent than any amount of decommissioning.

'That hasn't proved to be the case,' he insists, listing a series of breaches in the IRA ceasefire. Nor does he seem troubled by the thought that the British might simply by-pass the unionists and move toward some form of joint authority with Dublin. 'That won't bring peace to Northern Ireland.'

Yet many people suspect that, should he eventually inherit the leadership, Mr Donaldson would end up settling for even less than Mr Trimble secured two years ago. Isn't it the case that unionists always offer too little, too late, while nationalist confidence and expectations grow ever more expansive?

Mr Donaldson attributes this in part to unionism having presented itself 'splintered, divided and split in face of a pan-nationalist front'.

'If pan-nationalism indulges in the luxury of a partisan approach to the process, then I think unionism has to match that, in terms of strengthening its position to strike a better deal next time,' he declares. 'And if this agreement is the only show in town, then we're all in trouble.'

We're all in trouble, of course, if the peace collapses. Isn't it a mistake to risk that peace because guns that are silent, as some would put it, are not yet destroyed? Mr Donaldson, however, sees decommissioning as the only tangible test to prove that the threat of violence has been withdrawn.

Yet, in real terms, aren't republicans in the process of doing so? Isn't the true indication of republican intent that they hope to see Sinn Féin sharing in government, not just in Belfast but in Dublin?

He finds no reassurance here. 'If Sinn Féin can get away with it here why wouldn't they believe they could get away with it in the Republic, if Fianna Fáil were desperate enough in the aftermath of an election?' he asks. 'We've seen enough of politics in Dublin to know that when it comes to cutting deals high principle falls well down the agenda.'

'WITH TIME RUNNING OUT, IS IT POSSIBLE TO REVIVE THE AGREEMENT?'

Gerry Adams believes that his 'huge misjudgment' was trying to deal with decommissioning 'on unionist terms'. As efforts to revive the peace process enter a critical phase, the Sinn Féin leader talks to Frank Millar.

FROM *THE IRISH TIMES*, 15 APRIL 2000

Gerry Adams appears to have a problem. At the end of his review of the Belfast Agreement, Seamus Mallon says Senator George Mitchell told the SDLP his expectation was that devolution would occur on November 29th and that decommissioning would begin at the end of January. Doesn't this call Mr Adams' version of events into serious question?

'No.' Did he share that expectation? 'No.' Does he at least accept this was Senator Mitchell's expectation? The Sinn Féin leader laughingly says he sounds like a unionist. 'No,' again.

Mr Adams hopes 'this isn't going to be one of those decommissioning interviews we could have had at any time in the last four years'. He then insists that the 'jump together' agreed last November was to see David Trimble into the Executive 'and the IRA into the de Chastelain commission'.

And, he says: 'I sought and was given a firm commitment by Senator Mitchell that if it came to it he would make it absolutely clear that there were no assurances, no guarantees from Sinn Féin.'

Mr Adams accepts the Ulster Unionist leader made clear his position would become untenable unless decommissioning was under way within a time-specific period. But he insists he had no reason to think this realisable, nor did Mr Trimble. Might it not have been more honourable then to have told him to hold back, because the thing wasn't going to work?

'Well, first of all, he's a consenting adult. We didn't say it wasn't going to work because there's always a need in terms of negotiation to do your best to make progress.'

Mr Adams says he believes Mr Trimble could have carried the Ulster Unionist Council without the deadline, but chose instead to 'move forward tactically', armed with Peter Mandelson's 'side letter' about suspension in the case of default on decommissioning: 'They went forward with that parachute. So we jumped, and caused huge problems ever since in terms of the republican constituency. David Trimble did a bungee jump.'

Rehearsing the hurt, anger and frustration of republicans, Mr Adams asserts that the Belfast Agreement contains 'no default clause' and that there was 'no basis whatsoever for suspending'.

But isn't there, in real terms? And mightn't this be part of his difficulty as a republican? For wasn't the act and fact of suspension rooted in the legislation establishing a devolved Assembly at all times subject to the authority of the British crown?

Mr Adams doesn't flinch: 'Oh yes, and, in terms of the realpolitik, we have accepted entirely, it's obvious, partition is still here, that the British jurisdiction is still here. That isn't the issue. The issue is that the British signed an agreement in which they devolved power into this part of the island, and also into an all-Ireland interlocking structure.'

The Sinn Féin leader denies having misjudged the British position, or being surprised by the suspension: 'My misjudgment was trying to deal with this issue of weapons on unionist terms. That was my huge misjudgment.' While it was right to try, he gives an important indication of his approach to the renewed negotiation both governments hope is imminent.

Dismissing 'the feeding frenzy' which had Mr Mallon and others criticise Sinn Féin 'when they thought the party's back is to the wall', he makes plain there will be no further reliance on 'this misused word, understanding'.

In words which might actually be welcomed by many unionists, he explains: 'Let's have it out there in black and white, with certainty and great clarity, if there's going to be a deal. And let David Trimble shake hands on a deal.'

Mr Adams is not saying he won't deal from here on in with the arms issue: 'We see this as a process of change which has to be irreversible and we see all these as issues which have to be resolved.'

Picking up on that 'i' word: is Mr Adams' personal commitment to totally peaceful and democratic means irreversible? 'Yes.' And does he personally believe that the IRA's 'war' is over?

'I don't think we can any of us say – which is why I don't say it – with any certainty. And if we were moved, or tricked into saying it, or made the mistake in saying that the war was over, what would happen is someone would go out to try to prove that it wasn't. So I think we're into a whole sidetrack issue.'

Moreover, 'it isn't the IRA's war ...' The West Belfast MP takes me on a tour of the prevailing landscape: ministerial concerns about hostilities between loyalists, and the possible knock-on effect in terms of more attacks on Catholics, the ongoing efforts of dissident republicans, the RUC warning in recent weeks that 17 Belfast-based Sinn Féin councillors are being 'actively' targeted. 'Isn't that the reason why we shouldn't go into a summer unanchored?'

Going back to his earlier answer: do unionists have the assurance that Sinn Féin will not at any point in the future uphold the right of any group to take up arms to advance the goal of unity?

Mr Adams replies: 'Sinn Féin's position is we want to see an end to British involvement in our affairs, we want to see a new Ireland, and we are totally wedded to peaceful and democratic means. The hard reality is that if the war recommences ... you will see the beginning of the end of the present Sinn Féin leadership's reign.'

Whoever came after would have to deal with these issues, says Mr Adams: 'We have tried over a very long time to create conditions in which there is no more war, forever ...'

So success for Gerry Adams' leadership is to end the war?

'It is my view that we will get a united Ireland. We won't get it just naturally, we'll get it if struggle continues ... The only way in which those who are against change can win is if we give up.'

Those words – 'if struggle continues' – seem in many ways to take us to the core. Within the unionist community, including those who have supported the Agreement, there is great uncertainty about the nature of this process.

Is this a peace process, about reconciliation with the unionists, accepting the existing constitutional parameters until such time as there is consent to change them? Or is Sinn Féin's real game – struggle continuing by other means – to destabilise Northern Ireland and show it to be irreformable?

'No, that isn't the case, the second scenario isn't the case.' It would take too long to explore it in the course of this interview, he says. 'But in one discussion, Ken Maginnis made this appalling statement – and I say that advisedly, because Ken is sometimes presented as a counter-insurgency expert. He said the Sinn Féin plan was to take all we could, to get the ministers, and then, up the road a bit, the IRA goes back to war.'

The basis of the IRA being at war, says Mr Adams, was that there was some popular support for what it was doing, because of the degree of alienation of ordinary nationalists and republicans from the state.

'Now people who have an ownership in the future, and given the modifications of the state – because the state in terms of its relationship with the other part of the island was now interdependent and interlocked into structures ... Too weak for a republican, but still we went along with that. Again, I think the decision by Sinn Féin to go into the Assembly was undervalued – we had no notion of going into the Assembly.'

What Ken Maginnis's scenario left out, says Mr Adams, is 'that most republicans don't like war, and that most of those who were actively involved ... did so as a last resort' because they felt there was no moral or political alternative.

'Picture that eight or nine weeks when we had unionists, nationalists and republicans working in tandem, and where there was broad acceptance that they all did a good job. How on earth could the IRA – even if it wanted to, and in my view it wouldn't want to – how on earth could it go back to war in a situation when the people had an ownership in the institutions of the state, and were able to have a man from the Bog and someone from Andytown, with all the others, in places of government?'

Looking beyond the North, to what is widely believed the intended end result of Sinn Féin's electoral strategy, a place in government in the South. Does Mr Adams accept the Taoiseach's view that democratic mandate can be the only basis for participation and that 'it is not compatible beyond a short transitional period to have that democratic mandate with armed backing'?

The Sinn Féin president says that its electoral strategy is misrepresented and misinterpreted by the press and his party relies on its electoral mandate alone. 'If he's referring to us,' Mr Adams declares, 'we don't have armed backing.'

'LET'S SHAKE ON IT, MR ADAMS, AFTER THE CLARITY AND CERTAINTY'

David Trimble reiterated the case for saving the Belfast Agreement in a speech at the weekend. In an interview with Frank Millar, he talks about his disappointment in the nationalist response to the Ulster Unionists' big leap.

FROM *THE IRISH TIMES*, 17 APRIL 2000

In an important speech on Friday night Mr David Trimble again rehearsed his case for the Belfast Agreement. It had secured Northern Ireland's constitutional position, ended 'the cold war' with the Republic, and reduced differences on policing and justice issues largely to questions of symbolism.

Doesn't his global view suggest unionists would be mad to lose the Agreement, and encourage the belief that he will have to take another calculated risk to try and save it?

'What I was saying was that there were good reasons for making the Agreement, but we knew it was not a complete answer,' he replies. The Ulster Unionist leader says he knew on the morning of April 10th, 1998, that massive problems lay ahead, but he believed the Agreement provided a better basis for dealing with them. 'And so it has proved to be. The real problems we have now narrowed down to one ... but that one goes to the heart of it.'

His speech may have struck some as a second instalment of the initiative begun in Washington. In any event, won't he have encouraged nationalist expectations that he will see the Executive reinstated, because he appears to have conceded that decommissioning was not clearly defined as a precondition for Sinn Féin's place within it?

'No, that's reading far too much ... It certainly was not said by me, nor do I think any reasonable implication ...' But the headline grabber was his acknowledgment that, if he had attempted to negotiate decommissioning in advance, there would never have been an agreement. 'The principle was set down. The principle of decommissioning is there,' he insists. But not as a hard and fast precondition?

Mr Trimble clearly thinks the point has been entirely missed: 'I'm sorry. What was not dealt with in absolute clarity was the detail of exactly how and when. But the implication is clear ...'

Tony Blair's side-letter had confirmed decommissioning should start in June 1998, the Agreement said it should be completed by May 2000. 'If you tried to hammer down every jot and tittle you might not have got an agreement. But to take that statement and then say I'm conceding this, this and this ... sorry, there's only one word for that, if you don't mind my using it, balderdash.'

Some critics, including Jeffrey Donaldson, say he should have defined every jot and tittle before signing up for an agreement which would bring Sinn Féin into government. Mr Trimble is having none of it: 'That doesn't square with the facts ... It was better to have an agreement than not, and that is not challenged by the Jeffreys of this world either.'

Nor is Mr Trimble having any suggestion that Peter Mandelson has signalled a shift in British policy, with his warning that people should think twice before linking decommissioning directly to continuance of the institutions of government.

'Sorry, they were so linked.' So is the British position shifting? 'No, I don't regard what Peter Mandelson says as being a statement of government policy.' Does he imply the Secretary of State is out of line with the Prime Minister? 'No ... I don't want to get involved in criticism of the Secretary of State. But you must not presume ... I mean, if the British government were saying now that they've decided to decouple decommissioning from the rest of the Agreement, that would be a massive shift in policy.'

So why does he think Mr Mandelson has been speaking of a 'Mexican standoff' which might merely guarantee the achievement of neither devolution nor decommissioning? 'With respect, I think you should put those questions to the Secretary of State rather than me.'

It seems entirely appropriate to put these questions to the leader of unionism, since Mr Mandelson's comments over a period appear to call the British position into question. However, Mr Trimble is insistent: 'No communication to me has indicated any change.'

Moreover, he repeats this is not just his policy, and that his real purpose in that speech was to focus paramilitary-related parties on the end product of the process. 'The inescapable requirements of this process are that at the end of the day there will be no UDA, no UVF, no IRA. So it's not just the business of how and when you start decommissioning ... I'm saying to those parties, 'this is where it's going to be ... tell us how you're going to get there.'

Since it isn't just his policy, might it be an idea for Mr Trimble to stop behaving as if it is? Might there be a case for leaving the two governments to make their judgment as to republican intent, reinstate the institutions, and leave London and Dublin to see weapons 'put beyond use' in concert with the International Commission?

The suspended First Minister says the experience of recent years suggests that would not provide the necessary confidence in society as a whole: 'Nor would I personally have that confidence.'

Mr Trimble considers the present position worse as a result of having jumped last November. His party's expectations had not been fulfilled: 'That has led to some rather bleak conclusions about the intentions or abilities of those with whom I was dealing.'

He says the question of trust in Gerry Adams or Martin McGuinness is beside the point: 'Either they had no intention of delivering, or they tried and failed. It doesn't matter which is the case because the end product is the same.' He draws no reassurance from Mr Adams' assertion in *The Irish Times* on Saturday that the IRA could not go back to war, even if it wanted, if Sinn Féin were still seated in a functioning Executive.

But he does rise to Mr Adams' demand that any new deal should be spelt out with clarity and certainty, and that he should shake hands on it: 'Yes ... now will Mr Adams please provide the requisite clarity and certainty?'

Even if there is a deal on decommissioning, the Ulster Unionist Council has stipulated retention of the RUC's 'Royal' title as an additional condition. Does Mr Trimble feel bound by that? 'In speaking to his motion Mr [David] Burnside said – 'Of course this is what we want but we all know there's going to be a negotiation and we all know the result of that negotiation, if there is one, will be put back to the council for it to decide.'

However, Mr Trimble is adamant he too wants to save the Royal title, and reacts angrily when it is suggested he knows this battle is already lost. Isn't it the truth that it was lost when he signed up for the terms of reference for the International Commission?

'No ... no, no ... I don't ... quite the contrary.' If the Agreement's terms of reference had been honourably followed by Patten, he asserts, he would have produced a different result: 'The entirely false argument he bought is the argument that, somehow, Northern Ireland is to be a neutral state, with neutrality between Britishness and Irishness ...'

But this view seems widely held, by Dublin and the SDLP as well as Sinn Féin. They think the Agreement is about 'dual consent' and parity of esteem, don't they?

'There are people in Irish nationalism who think this way. They are wrong and are not following the Agreement. Bear in mind I have always said about this issue, that it is the litmus test of consent ... Has Irish nationalism actually signed up for consent?'

So, consent for the constitutional position of Northern Ireland means identification with the symbols of the British state?

Mr Trimble invites me to read the Agreement again. The principle of consent was not new: 'What is important ... is that Irish nationalists said they accepted the legitimacy of that consent and the legitimacy of British sovereignty in Northern Ireland.

'Therefore, it is not a neutral state. It is one sovereignty, and the symbols of British sovereignty flow from that. That is why the Agreement subsequently talks about sensitivity in the use of symbols in public purposes because the symbols used in public purposes will be British symbols.'

And this is why, Mr Trimble declares, the Patten question is capable of destroying the Agreement. 'Has nationalism actually accepted the Belfast Agreement? Because it looks as though they haven't thought through the significance of what they agreed. If it turns out that nationalists only pay lip service to consent, and then immediately pursue their old-fashioned, outdated agenda – then is the Agreement worth anything?'

Unlike his deputy, Mr John Taylor, Mr Trimble is ruling nothing in or out ahead of May 22nd. But I suggest he sounds angrier with the broad sweep of nationalism than for a long time past.

'I have been deeply disappointed with the position some nationalists have adopted,' he confirms. 'Especially after the failure of republicans to carry things through. I'm not going to personalise it, but I've been deeply disappointed that – having been as adventurous as they urged us to be, and having found it didn't work – we have not had the support that was promised.'

9

No More Itsy Bitsy – Tony Blair
2002

Northern Ireland's devolution experience would prove very much a stop–go affair, with in real terms more of the former than the latter. When, in May 2000, the IRA promised to put its weapons 'completely and verifiably beyond use' in a manner designed to maximise public confidence, Trimble returned to government. When the process of decommissioning had not begun a year later he forced a second suspension. Trimble resumed office in November 2001 after the IRA confirmed it had begun the decommissioning process – only to quit a year later in the furore over an alleged republican 'spy ring' operating at the very heart of the Stormont administration.

On 17 October 2002 Tony Blair travelled to Belfast to make a major speech warning the IRA that its latent threat of violence had become wholly counterproductive, a positive vindication no less for those republicans called 'rejectionist' unionists. There was 'no parallel track left', the Prime Minister avowed, only 'a fork in the road', a time of choice, and a need for 'acts of completion'.

When I saw him in Downing Street on 6 November the Prime Minister stopped short of calling for IRA 'disbandment', though it seemed clear that was what he was about. 'When I talk about acts of completion what I mean is we need to try and do this in a big step forward, where the British government fulfils its mandate, the paramilitaries realise they can no longer use force in order to pursue their political ends, and we reach a situation where Northern Ireland's politics become normal, in the sense that there is no mixing paramilitary activity and politics.'

I put it to Mr Blair that, for all his impressive rhetoric, aficionados of the process believed he understood well enough that IRA disbandment would be slow in coming and that, if and when it did, it would be at a price. That seemed to point to still more of the 'choreography' on which the process had relied at critical points – and another round of negotiation, compromise and barter. The Prime Minister insisted it wasn't going to happen that way. Either, he suggested, the republicans would move to end the impasse or it would endure. Nor need republicans think to prosper from the continuing stalemate by way of an alternative, 'Plan B' for joint British/Irish authority: 'If there is an impasse here as a result of confusion over paramilitary and political ends, there is no way I can cook up some solution with the Irish government and slam it down. It is not going to work.'

'WE NEED A BIG STEP FORWARD – THERE IS NO POINT IN LITTLE ITSY BITSY NEGOTIATIONS'

FROM *THE IRISH TIMES*, NOVEMBER 2002

Q: Prime Minister, you've said the IRA cannot continue half-in, half-out of the peace process, that there must now be acts of completion. Does that mean, as General de Chastelain has suggested, that the IRA must now commit to a verifiable and transparent process of decommissioning and disbandment?

A: What I have learnt about in this process is the use of words. Sometimes you can use words and they can end up being an obstacle to progress. But I think everybody knows what we are saying. What we are saying is this, that the process of transition is over. We cannot any longer have a situation where people are half-in, half-out. When I talk about acts of completion, what I mean is that we need to try and do this in a big step forward, where the British government fulfils its mandate, the paramilitaries realise that they can no longer use force in order to pursue political ends, and we reach a situation where Northern Ireland's politics do truly become normal, at least normal in the sense that there is no mixing of paramilitary activity and politics.
I think over the past few months everyone has reached the stage where they say, look there is no point in inching forward any more, there is no point in having another series of little itsy bitsy negotiations, let's work out whether people are really deciding they want this thing to happen or not. Now I want it to happen, I believe the unionists want it to happen, I know the SDLP do. I actually believe that the leadership of Sinn Féin do as well, but we have all got to realise that it is time to put the full cards on the table and get them cleared.

Q: When unionists hear you reluctant to spell out your terms, they will worry that – though you say you can't have another inch by inch negotiation – you will inevitably be dragged into another exercise in peace process choreography.

A: Well we won't, that was the purpose of the speech. As I say, my reluctance to use certain words is that sometimes the words aren't helpful, but I can't be any clearer in saying that the process of transition is over. There has got to be no mixing of the paramilitary and the political.

And you know when people in Northern Ireland say but you let Sinn Féin away with it – I say look, the very reason why there has been now for the second time a suspension of the process is precisely because we haven't let them away with it.

Q: Some would counter the only reason there has been a second suspension is because David Trimble couldn't sustain his position and that – even faced with alleged IRA espionage, the compilation of prison officers' names and addresses and so on – you would still have been prepared to show the yellow rather than the red card?

A: I believe that is unfair. Of course it is true that David Trimble made his own position clear, but I don't think there was much room for doubt in the speech I gave a short time afterwards. The fact is all sorts of options could have been open to the British government, we have chosen the route that we have taken.

People also sometimes say to me, well look there is a contrast between you getting really heavy on al-Qaeda or Saddam Hussein while you are negotiating with Sinn Féin. My answer to that is every situation is different. What you have got to work out is whether there are aims that people can pursue that are politically reasonable, not in the sense that I may agree with them but they are within the normal ambit of politics, and is it possible to get them to pursue those political aims in an exclusively peaceful manner. The answer with al-Qaeda or Saddam Hussein and weapons of mass destruction is no, there is no meeting point at all. The answer with Sinn Féin is yes, it is perfectly possible for them to pursue the aims of equality and justice, recognition of the nationalist identity in Northern Ireland, provided they recognise what they cannot any longer do is pursue those aims by violence.

I think it is interesting this time that with the institutions suspended there is a political crisis but not a security crisis. I don't think six years ago that would have happened.

Q: You've said the IRA, everybody indeed, must take big steps forward. Let me put two reasons why the IRA might not comply. First, within their own communities the demand may be that they resist you because Catholics are subject to ongoing loyalist violence, and because there does not appear to be a corresponding British demand that the loyalist paramilitaries also disband?

A: It is understandable that that feeling is around, but it is comprehensively wrong. First let me make it clear that the activities of the loyalist paramilitaries are not just totally and completely contrary to law, but contrary to any decent sense of humanity. The only difference is that the loyalist paramilitaries are not connected to political parties and government, that is why there is a different situation there. But in terms of the paramilitary activity, of course it has got to cease and cease entirely. The other thing that I would say to you – and you can see this from that appalling attack over the weekend [the 'crucifixion'] which made me physically sick – these people have to realise we are going to come down on them with every single bit of force and authority we possibly can. The new chief constable is absolutely determined to do that. We have already I think arrested 60 or more of these people and they are going to be treated for what they are, which is common criminals. We are not going to play around with it at all or negotiate with it or give any quarter to it at all.

Q: Are we witnessing the beginning of a qualitatively different crackdown on loyalist paramilitaries?

A: I believe that we are, yes. There are two things that we have got to do. We have got to resolve this political crisis. And actually part of resolving it is to come to the point where we treat paramilitaries as criminals. Of course their activity has been criminal, is criminal. But I think now there is actually an acceptance across the spectrum in Northern Ireland that that is precisely how it should be treated.

Q: But the second reason republicans may not be compliant is because of their belief – notwithstanding what you said in Belfast – that it is the threat of violence which gives them leverage. Indeed many others besides believe this is the essence of any peace process between the IRA and a British government. Isn't the fact of the matter that for that reason you can never really treat Sinn Féin as you would any other normal political party?

A: That is a very good point and I agree it is the nub of the issue. And what has changed is that everybody in Northern Ireland who has always been part of democratic politics recognises that as you get the peace process under way, you don't have the Belfast Agreement one day, and total peace the next. They realise there will be a process under which you leave violence behind. What has really happened is that, in part frankly because of the advances Sinn Féin have made democratically, people are now at the point where they say well hang on, I am sorry, everyone has got to play by the same rules. Now if everyone is not going to play by the same rules, there is nothing we can do about that, but you can't have a peace process except on the basis that everyone does play by the same rules. So whatever the position in the past was about leverage, whatever their feelings that this is necessary for the leverage, it is now the obstruction.

Because what is preventing me doing the acts of completion for the British government? The continuing existence of this paramilitary activity. What is the thing that has actually made David Trimble get out of the Executive? The existence of the paramilitary activity. What is the thing that prevents unionist opinion coming behind an agreement that in the end is perfectly good for the people of Northern Ireland? Paramilitary activity. So whatever the past has been and whatever people's feelings – well, this keeps the British government up to the mark, makes them realise they have got to watch us and all the rest of it – you know we can speculate on that, I can give you my views and other people can give you theirs. Today, there is no doubt in my mind, it is the opposite of leverage, it is actually an obstacle, it is an obstruction to the process.

Q: Let's test that in two ways. If they don't comply, what is your sanction against them?

A: Well it is not so much a sanction against them, it is that the political process can't move forward. That is not to say people are not entitled to equality before the law, fairness and all the rest of it in any event. But it is far more difficult for us to make political progress in for example a power-sharing Executive, in having decisions taken by people in Northern Ireland, in having ministers from all the different communities, if that commitment to exclusively peaceful means isn't there.

So it is not so much a sanction. When I walked out of the building after my speech the other week there were some republicans there with a placard saying 'Say no to the unionist veto', and I felt like saying look, the trouble with this process is that everyone has got a veto. It can't move unless people want it to move.

Q: That brings me to the second test. You say not so much a sanction but that the process can't move forward. Some people will be reluctant to believe that because there is a widespread suspicion that republicans think themselves in a win-win situation.

That's to say, if the present Agreement fails, nationalist Ireland as a whole will regroup and press for an alternative solution in the form of joint British–Irish authority. In your Balmoral speech in 1998 you said there would be no question of any imposed solution. Can you confirm that that remains your position?

A: I can, yes. You know people can fall for this delusion again that somehow you can have a lasting peace in Northern Ireland without the main elements of the political parties involved in it.
You can't. That is the reality. And my view is, and again I think this is different, that that reality is understood by all the main political parties. You see the advantage I have is that I meet these people the whole time, I talk to them, have got to know them very well. I have got to know them better than many people who are supposed to be my own political colleagues. I have worked with them a long period of time, and what often happens is that they end up deeply suspecting the other side's motives in almost identical terms. So republicans will tell you, well David Trimble is not really interested, he wants the whole thing brought down because he really wants unionist supremacy back and all the rest of it. I know that is not true, I just know it is not true. Look, for whatever reason and whatever the history of it, he has come to the view that the only viable future for Northern Ireland is a future in which people are treated equally. That is his view. And he will often come to me and say oh, look, this is all a sly game by Adams and McGuinness, what they really want is to trick everyone into a situation where you end up with a solution being imposed by the British government. You can't impose a solution in this situation.

Q: So in terms of any hope there may be within the republican or wider nationalist community – that failure to restore the Belfast Agreement leads incrementally over a period of time to joint British–Irish authority – you rule that out?

A: There is no way that we can go back to that as a solution to a set of circumstances in which the political parties come to an agreement. That is why I said to you everyone has got a veto on this situation and all we can do as the British government, or the Irish government for that matter, is to facilitate. In the end, and this is one of the things I want to say to people in Northern Ireland, there is a tendency sometimes for everyone to turn round and say, well, what is the British government going to do about it, what is the Irish government going to do about it? Look, we can do certain things but I can't make this work without willing partners, and those willing partners have got in the end to come together themselves. So if there is an impasse here as a result of confusion over paramilitary and political ends, there is no way I can cook up some solution with the Irish government and slam it down. It is not going to work.

Q: You've also said you will not countenance a renegotiation of the Agreement. But consent freely given can surely be withdrawn. If you go ahead with an Assembly election and a majority of unionists back parties committed to renegotiate, isn't the reality that you would have to go back to the drawing board?

A: You've always got to take account of the reality of the political circumstances, that is true. But I come back to the point I made to you a moment or two ago, I can only facilitate agreement, I can't force people to agree. And just so that people understand this – when people sometimes say, ah well, what we want is not this Belfast Agreement but a different agreement, and I say to them well, fine, you go ahead and negotiate that then – you are going to be ending up negotiating with exactly the same people, and that is what we were doing. So there is not some magic trick that can be taken here where suddenly everyone wheels into a different position. The fact is you will come back to the same issues to be dealt with in the same way. And at the heart of the Belfast Agreement, whatever adjustments we made along the way, is essentially this deal, that in return for equality and justice and recognition of the nationalist identity, then Northern Ireland shall remain part of the union as long as the majority of people there wish it.

Q: But you don't dispute that its continuation rests upon the enduring consent of a majority of both communities in Northern Ireland? In the end that is the reality, isn't it?

A: Look, we will implement whatever measures we in the British government can implement that are right in their own terms, for example equality and justice and human rights and so on. It is important that we do that in any event, that is something that is the right of anyone who lives inside the UK. But I can't restore a power-sharing Executive, that part of the political process, that can't be done unless the parties themselves want it.

Q: You've said you believe the IRA is further away from war than ever. But post-September 11th – given the climate that now exists and that you, with President Bush, have helped create – do you believe that returning to the war actually remains an option for Irish republicans?

A: In the end that is a decision for them, isn't it?

Q: But could they get away with it?

A: I don't think there is any mileage in it any more. You are right, the world has changed. People just have a different attitude towards terrorism today, they recognise it as a global threat, and the attitude in America is completely different. There was genuine outrage at any association of the IRA and FARC, because people know what FARC is, which is an absolutely appalling sort of narco-terrorist organisation. My view is that Adams and McGuinness know all that perfectly well. And I have said this before and I believe it, I think they are committed to the peace process, they know it is the only future for republicanism, there is no future in terrorism. And that is the other thing that has changed. It is not just that as the process has gone on people have come to a view that the process of transition has got to be over, it is also that the terms of debate have changed post-September 11th. There is no support for it anywhere, there is no real inclination to excuse it any more. I never did excuse it, but I think there were parts of the political spectrum, themselves respectable, who kind of excused it or said, well, we sort of understand why it is happening. It is just not the case any more. You look at Spain in relation to ETA, you look at the activities of the terrorists around the world linked to al-Qaeda, you look at the attitude of the US.
No-one is going to put up with it any more, and so there is no mileage in it. The only question in the end is can reactionary elements, who can't see the world has changed, can they drag the whole thing backwards or do we, as I say, get to the acts of completion that lets everyone see that we all mean it. Because we do mean it. I genuinely want this whole thing to work and I am prepared to do whatever it takes on the part of the British government to fulfil our obligations completely. But I need to know I have got a willing partner, and that is what the whole thing is about.

Q: You've had the first instalment of Mr Adams' response. Do you think he has got the message that it is a case of big steps now?

A: I believe so, yes, because I think that they want that too. They know that it is not now about symbolic acts or gestures, it is about are we a normal political situation or not. You can't have a situation – you can understand why historically these things happen, but you have reached the point at which it is no longer acceptable that they do – whether it is people being beaten up on the basis that they are alleged to be drug dealers or whatever, or playing around with paramilitary activity the world over, there is no support for it, there is no future in it. And in the end people on the island of Ireland know that too. That is why there was such huge support in the Republic of Ireland for this peace process; that is why Bertie Ahern has been a tremendous partner in this process, he recognises that too. And you know I think that that is the common ground now and the rest is about political leadership and vision.

10

Heir Apparent – Peter Robinson
2002

Politicians will sometimes feel moved to complain about the headline put on a story – invariably to the journalist, knowing he or she is not actually responsible. Obviously complaint is justified if the headline writer has failed to get the whole point of an article and produced something that is misleading. Sometimes, of course, an objection might be raised because the opposite is the case – and the headline proves just a bit too sharp, too close for comfort.

I had no doubt about Peter Robinson's frustrations with the politics of unionist opposition and his desire to play a role at the heart of a government in Northern Ireland. But as I read my *Irish Times* on the morning of 4 December 2002 I also had little doubt that this particular headline – spot on as it was – might raise a few eyebrows in the House of Paisley. It read, prophetically as it would turn out: 'DUP deputy leader could be First Minister'.

In the interview itself Robinson dismissed talk of renewed Dublin/London/Washington interest in his potential as a future majority unionist leader: 'It's not how I see the position because it's not something I've looked at … I don't spend one waking moment looking at those issues.'

Maybe, though Robinson knew better than I that many people spent a great deal of time savouring precisely such a prospect. I also knew that any public discussion of it would be regarded by some in the DUP as an affront to the party's founding father, and not least by the leader himself. Might that headline, then, have occasioned some mild discomfort in the House of Robinson? Should I await an angry, or at least mildly irritated, telephone call in protest at our pre-occupation with the leadership issue?

Obviously there was less sensitivity than I might have allowed, and the call never came. If that in itself provided me with some instruction, however, it would also become apparent over time that the big question exercising many British, Irish and American officials about Robinson – could he deliver Paisley? – was not the one likely to yield the answer they sought. When the serious possibility of a DUP/Sinn

Féin deal finally hovered in to view, Robinson and his parliamentary colleagues would be the first to concede it would turn on questions of 'the Big Man's' own changing motivations and ambitions.

That said, Robinson was unquestionably a driving force for change and pragmatic judgments. From a 2008 vantage point, indeed, it would seem reasonable to ask if the entire history of unionist politics in the post-98 period might have been different had greater attention been paid to the earliest signs of the DUP's intended direction of travel.

In 1998 the still-firebrand Ian Paisley had denounced David Trimble with characteristic venom: 'The worst and most loathsome person in society is the traitor – the Judas, the Iscariot. Who dares to excuse and whitewash treachery but he who is a party to the treachery?' Yet the DUP also managed to reconcile promised undying opposition to the Belfast Agreement with the decision to appoint so-called 'ministers in opposition' to take their places in the Trimble/Mallon Executive. It is unlikely that Dr Paisley would have arrived at that position on his own.

'ROBINSON CLAIMS CORE PRINCIPLE OF BELFAST' AGREEMENT ELEVATED TERRORISTS

'The central feature of any government is that there must be trust between the parties. I don't trust Sinn Féin.'

FROM *THE IRISH TIMES*, 4 DECEMBER 2002

The spotlight is turning once again on Mr Peter Robinson, potential majority unionist leader-in-waiting. As the peace process stumbles from crisis to crisis, some – particularly in Dublin – wonder if he might be the better man to deal with.

In the quiet of his Westminster office, I put it to him that, while this may irritate Mr David Trimble, it will hardly please Dr Paisley either. Is he at all embarrassed by this attention?

A: I usually find that when the Democratic Unionist Party is reaching a critical stage and it's vital we maximise our support, our traditional opponents attempt to suggest there's some division there and that Ian and I are following different agendas. It isn't the case. I don't think Ian and I have ever had a cross word over all these years. We sit in meetings on an almost daily basis. We are following the same agenda, we are agreed on the way forward, there is no difficulty at all within the party.

Q: But people see Dr Paisley isn't getting any younger. There is an obvious question mark over Mr Trimble's position, and an increasing focus in Dublin, London and Washington on your personal position as a possible future leader of unionism. Is that how you see the situation shaping up?

A: It's not how I see the position because it's not something I've looked at. My focus is on what's happening here and now, and how we can get out of the mess that Trimble and the Ulster Unionists have got us into. I don't spend one waking moment looking at those issues. They are of no importance in the overall scheme of things.

Q: Your critics, of course, would say that you're actually David Trimble-in-waiting: that demonising Trimble is a function of what you intend to do, which is tinker around the edges of a renegotiation, blame the deficiencies on the Ulster Unionists, and then accommodate yourself to the essence of the Belfast Agreement.

A: The Belfast Agreement was fundamentally flawed. The core principle was that instead of confronting terrorism you actually elevated terrorists, gentrified their leaders, accommodated their wrongdoing and rewarded their evil. That's the antithesis of the policy that I pursue. And having been an opponent of David Trimble on the Belfast Agreement, it would only be my enemies who would attempt to associate me with it.

Q: Let me suggest why some may be disinclined to believe you. In a recent profile in a Dublin newspaper, your colleague, Jim Wells, predicted you would be the next First Minister of Northern Ireland. That hardly suggests he expects you to pull the entire edifice down.

A: The policy is that we use the election in order to secure a unionist majority in order to force negotiations and get a new agreement. Whether the new agreement provides devolution – it would be my hope that it would – whether the devolution provides a First Minister or not I don't know, but presumably it will have someone in that position, and who may be in the leadership the electorate will decide.

Q: So, while your intention is to renegotiate the Agreement and if possible secure devolution, you're not pretending that you necessarily can.

A: My intention is to have a new agreement. Some people interpret renegotiating the Agreement in the sort of terms you spoke of earlier, which is simply to tinker and trifle with the existing agreement. I think it's fundamentally flawed in a number of areas but centrally it's all around the issue of accountability. Accountability within the Assembly, accountability North/South-wise, the democratic controls. Power is exercised by ministers, not by the Assembly. Those are issues we can go into … I want devolution to be the outcome. But devolution to be an outcome must be built on a basis that is sound and practical. If the only form of devolution being offered is a form that is effectively going to have an IRA veto, then that is not in the interest of the unionist community. Therefore the form of devolution must be one that the unionist community can give its support and allegiance to.

Q: Your opponents say your position is either extremely naive or actually fraudulent. You're going to renegotiate the Agreement but you won't negotiate with Sinn Féin. Surely you can't have one without the other?

A: It depends what you mean by this terminology. Did David Trimble negotiate with Sinn Féin?

Q: He sat in the same room as them, took part in the same talks.

A: That's the inaccuracy of it all. Immediately the talks were over, Trimble confirmed publicly that he had never once negotiated with Sinn Féin, that his negotiations were with the honest broker George Mitchell, and at times with the Prime Minister. I have no objection to negotiating with the Prime Minister, the Secretary of State or anyone it is agreed should be the honest broker in such a process.

Q: So you're happy to negotiate with people knowing they are negotiating with Sinn Féin?

A: I cannot regulate the procedure or the behaviour of others; I can only regulate my own behaviour. I'm not negotiating with them through any honest broker. I am negotiating with the honest broker. The people who take the decisions are the government. We will attempt to convince them. Who they speak to as a government is a matter for themselves. It is my job to get the best deal for unionists that I can speaking to the government who have the responsibility.

Q: Sinn Féin are convinced you'll eventually talk to them because, like David Trimble before, you know there is no alternative. Indeed, some of them look forward to this because they believe that if Sinn Féin and the DUP emerge as the majority nationalist and unionist parties they are going to be better placed to make a deal and make it stick.

A: If Sinn Féin believe that then they must be looking to a time when they're going to start behaving themselves, give up violence and stand down the IRA. All of those issues will be coming before any Democratic Unionist would ever engage with anybody from Sinn Féin. Our position is clear and we didn't set the criteria. It was set by the so-called two governments, namely that the only parties that could be involved in the democratic process were those committed to exclusively peaceful and democratic means. Now, if Sinn Féin is saying they are going to become democrats, are going to take part in politics on that basis, then that's a new set of circumstances. I don't see it. There's nothing in their present behaviour that suggests that they are going to reach that stage.

Q: You're suggesting you'd be better equipped than Trimble to put better democratic manners on Sinn Féin?

A: No, we're saying we will have nothing to do with them until they reach that stage.

Q: But you'll sit in a government that affords them places?

A: The central feature of any government is that there must be trust between the parties that are in it. I don't trust Sinn Féin.

Q: Sinn Féin might say you're not required to trust them; that the point about the Belfast Agreement is that it constructed an inclusive system of government that reflected the mandate of the parties.

A: That doesn't work.

Q: Well it did work, and you were a member of it.

A: It doesn't work. It has collapsed four times. You see this is the nonsense of that kind of argument; that something works because it stays up for five minutes. That's tantamount to saying you can have a telegraph pole without cementing it in the ground because it will stand up for two seconds before it falls. It works but it doesn't work for long and it doesn't work for long enough. And for any stable political structure to endure there is a requirement that the parties who are a key part of it trust each other. That doesn't exist under the present system, and the present system requires that level of trust in order to endure. That's why it has been punctuated by crisis after crisis, that's why it's collapsed four times.

Q: Do you see circumstances where there could be that degree of trust between you and Sinn Féin?

A: No, I take the opposite view. I say if the system that you have requires trust that is absent then it's not going to work. Therefore you need to have a system that doesn't require that degree of trust.

Q: How would you reconstruct the Executive to overcome that problem?

A: Well, that's one of the issues that I've made clear to the Secretary of State. If he wants to see those cards he'll have to put his money on the table.

Q: Might you be seeking to insert something that wasn't there in 1998, namely collective responsibility in the Executive?

A: No, I think you're going in the wrong direction. If the existing problem is that there isn't sufficient trust to operate the system, then you need to change it to a system that doesn't require trust, not a system that requires more trust.

Q: Does that new system provide an inclusive government in Northern Ireland, and a role without precondition for Sinn Féin?

A: You see, I'm indicating that we will fight the election on seven principles and I am not going to reveal the hand of the Democratic Unionist Party to other parties when other parties are refusing to reveal theirs.

Q: But there's no possibility of you having any form of devolved government from which Sinn Féin is excluded?

A: That's a statement you have made; that's your view. I accept that Sinn Féin are likely to be the dominant nationalist party and that the system that we have in Northern Ireland must recognise that that is the case.

Q: So whatever your system is it will be inclusive?

A: No, it will recognise the size of the Sinn Féin vote.

Q: But you're not going to have anything that isn't a power-sharing administration?

A: Why do you say that?

Q: What, you believe it's possible to have a form of majoritarian government?

A: Well, why do you say that? You seem to be so boxed in with the past and systems that have existed …

Q: Well, take me to the new system then.

A: I don't want to take you to it. Because why would I reveal my position before an election and before negotiations when others are not doing so?

Q: So, the DUP has come up with a system for the future government of Northern Ireland that nobody has previously thought of?

A: Very clearly the proposals we have are different from anything that has happened before in Northern Ireland. Yes, of course.

Q: And it provides a role for the DUP in government, a role for the Ulster Unionists, for the SDLP …

A: The problem is that we're talking different languages.

Q: I thought we were talking about, preferably, a devolved government in Northern Ireland.

A: Yes.

Q: Can there be a structure of devolved government that does not command the consent of Sinn Féin?

A: You see again you're coming back to principles that are built upon existing types of structures, and I am not confined by the box that you are in. I'm looking at proposals which can gain the support of the electorate and at the same time do not require the level of trust that the existing system requires. And I really am not going to give any detail of those proposals, either in essence or in practical detail.

Q: I understand that. You're not talking, are you, about …

A: Well I'm not talking at all.

Q: … about some system where you dole out packages of power to the different tribal chiefs and make them directly answerable back to the Assembly?

A: You're absolutely right. I am not talking about any proposals at all.

Q: Presumably one criteria for your form of government would be that it be cohesive?

A: I will respond to that question because you specifically asked it. But in responding to that question I will make it clear that I'm not going to respond to any others of that type because I'm not going through a process of elimination and I'm not looking at the kind of proposal you're suggesting.

Q: Do you accept as a matter of principle that there will be no system of devolved government in Northern Ireland that does not command the consent of a majority of both communities?

A: First of all, I don't accept your premise that we've been operating on the basis of consent. Or else David Trimble is an unmitigated liar because change after change has taken place which he has indicated publicly he is opposed to. And if his consent hasn't been given to it then clearly the premise on which your question is asked isn't true.

Q: As a principle for the future?

A: As a principle for the future, I believe you can only govern through consent and any attempt to govern without consent – and I do refer to that as being consent from both sections of our community – and I've argued the case over and over again that past systems have fallen because there was an absence of consent from one section of the community or another. Therefore, it follows that it is necessary to have the support from both sections of our community …

Q: A majority of both communities?

A: Well, I don't think you have the support of a section of the community unless you have the support of a majority of that community.

Q: But you won't sit down in government with republicans until they do what?

A: We won't sit down with anybody unless we judge that they are committed to exclusively peaceful and democratic means. That's the criteria, not set by us but set by the so-called two governments.

Q: In terms of your criteria, republicans may think: 'We'll never be able to satisfy any of these people because they're constantly raising the bar too high.'

A: Maybe they never will satisfy us because they never will meet the criteria.

Q: But you can devise a system of government that includes Sinn Féin, includes the SDLP, even if they don't satisfy your criteria and win your trust?

A: I can't choose who the electorate return. We have to deal with whatever the electorate throw up. Therefore you have to have a system that isn't dependent on the outcome of an election, which isn't dependent on the good behaviour of those who are elected. That's the reality. It must be a system that has sufficient shock absorbers to be able to deal with the kind of bad behaviour that we have seen from the Provisional IRA.

11

Guns and Government -
David Trimble
2004

Against a rising tide of 'rejectionist' unionist sentiment, Tony Blair had one last card to play on David Trimble's behalf. Despite Sinn Féin and SDLP, Irish and American objections, the Prime Minister in 2003 postponed scheduled fresh elections for the then suspended Northern Ireland Assembly, twice – insisting there was no point in an election that would not produce a new Executive. By the time Trimble entered a final, fateful negotiation with Gerry Adams that September, however, Blair had already promised Sinn Féin the election would proceed in the autumn. Trimble would admit in the interview below that it was 'hubris' led him to think he could negotiate a better deal with Sinn Féin than Tony Blair and Bertie Ahern had managed.

The result was a fiasco at Hillsborough Castle the following month, when General de Chastelain reported on another phase of IRA decommissioning but, crucially, with none of the detail necessary for Trimble to restore public confidence in the process. Taoiseach Ahern would later tell the Dáil he had not wanted to travel to Belfast that day, knowing that what was on offer from the republicans was not going to do the trick. But Blair had decided to trust to Trimble's luck holding one more time.

Against such an inauspicious backdrop Trimble's Ulster Unionists did remarkably well in the 26 November poll to trail the triumphant DUP by just three seats. However, the picture was instantly transformed when Jeffrey Donaldson and two colleagues defected to the DUP, turning Dr Paisley's margin of advantage to nine. There would be no way back, and in the British general election of 2005 Trimble lost his Upper Bann seat while his party returned just one MP to the new House of Commons as against nine for the DUP.

Between these two seismic developments in the affairs of unionism, I decided to write a book about Trimble. It would have struck many as an odd time to do so, given the consensus by the summer and autumn of 2004 that he was already 'yesterday's man'. Despite two other books already devoted to the subject, however, Trimble felt – and I agreed – that he had not been properly heard. So *David Trimble: The Price of Peace* was designed by way of a series of extended interviews to let him explain why he had risked everything for the Belfast Agreement.

A number of friends and colleagues reacted enthusiastically to the publication, liked the interview-based approach, and flatteringly suggested it might make the basis for a mini series on key figures in the peace process. I had to tell them it sounded good in theory but that the project had only worked so well because of David Trimble's willingness to subject himself to lengthy and rigorous questioning – and because of his quite remarkable candour. I think this chapter is illustrative of that, and of his stature.

FROM DAVID TRIMBLE: *THE PRICE OF PEACE*
by FRANK MILLAR
(LIFFEY PRESS, 2004 AND 2008)

It was the belief that he could bring unionism back from the margins which carried David Trimble through the tortuous negotiation which led to the Belfast Agreement. He has frequently characterised its achievement for unionists as twofold: the acceptance by all the sides of the principle of consent, and the consequent participation by republicans in a partitionist settlement. But has he not greatly exaggerated this 'achievement', and paid a heavy price for it, because 'consent' was there in the Anglo-Irish Agreement in 1985 and has in fact been the operative and guiding principle of British government policy since it was defined by Edward Heath's government as far back as 1973?

Trimble's memory and knowledge is greater than mine and he takes me further back: 'Oh, you can go further back than that because consent is the operative element of British government policy, as and from 1920. It's not clear until 1920 that consent is British government policy. The reason why unionists organised the way they did in 1912 to 1914 was because they feared their consent was going to be ignored. But a fair bit of the political establishment was veering towards consent by 1914 and by 1918 they were at that point and it is written into the 1921 agreement that created the Free State. So in that sense consent is there, and in that sense too the Irish Free State in 1921 and again in the 1925 Tripartite Agreement clearly bought into consent. But then de Valera repudiates consent. John Hume never actually gets his head round the concept. The Irish state in Sunningdale in 1973 does not accept consent. The Anglo-Irish Agreement gets to a sort of a fudge position where people say "there will be no change in the status of Northern Ireland without consent", but without defining what the status was and without asking people to consent to that Agreement. It's sort of saying, "We're going to impose this upon you but we promise we won't impose anything else." Now there's a certain credibility lack in that and of course our shibboleth in this is Articles 2 and 3 of the Irish Constitution, which laid claim to the territory of Northern Ireland irrespective of the wishes of its inhabitants. So one of the things that is undoubtedly an achievement of '98 is we get change in Articles 2 and 3, and in fact the Agreement writes a double consent provision into the Irish Constitution. There has to be a separate consent in the Irish Republic to the admission of Northern Ireland to a united Ireland, which was their idea, not ours. I find that fascinating. So you get consent then coming into the Irish Constitution and you get consent being accepted now by the SDLP, I believe, in a wholehearted way. And when the SDLP subsequently start to try and develop a language of a post-nationalism I think that's genuine on their part. The fact that they [later] allowed themselves to be scared by the Shinners didn't help.'

So it's consent of a very different quality, augmented or made real by the withdrawal of Ireland's constitutional claim?

'It's the withdrawal of the claim, and the formalisation of consent, approved by the people North and South in the dual referendums. That I think does change the context quite significantly. But it's not just that. I think there were other things that we did. We got a new architecture and completely neutralised the whole issue of cross-border stuff, and we've got cross-border structures and arrangements now that actually work satisfactorily and don't cause any problems for us. They are largely symbolic from a nationalist point of view, that is significant.

'What I thought was the big thing and what I kept going over in all the meetings we had with the SDLP during the talks was that our two parties were the centre of gravity in Northern Ireland and what we had to do was work together. I kept pressing them on that. Subsequently I talked about our two parties providing 'the voluntary coalition' within the compulsory coalition. I thought the thing was only going to work if the SDLP and us worked closely together. Part of the reason why, on the very last night when we were signing off on the internal devolved arrangements, that I go a little further than some people thought I should in terms of conceding the title of minister and a few of the other 'safeguard' provisions to the SDLP was because in my mind the business of entering into a genuine partnership between us and the SDLP was the core of this. If I'm curmud-geonly and grind them down in negotiations, there's the danger that they become easy prey for Sinn Féin, but there's an even bigger danger that they become resentful of me and of our approach to it. This is the start of a partnership between the two of us and we've got to do it in terms of being friendly with each other. So at the point when I abandoned my preference for 'departmental secretaries' and conceded the term 'ministers', Hume actually burst into tears and they all started throwing their arms round us and that seemed to me to be laying the foundation for what was going to happen. But it doesn't work out that way as you well know.'

One of the big mysteries for me through all of this has centred on this question. Why – having, as he saw it, done 'the big thing' for the SDLP, and agreed to the full legislative Assembly and Executive demanded by them, as against the Welsh Assembly/regional administration model favoured by his own party – did Trimble not go for a weighted majority by which the Ulster Unionists, SDLP and the Alliance Party would exercise executive power? Under such an arrangement Sinn Féin would have been handed the prospect of power but would first have to work their passage and overtake the SDLP. Why instead did he not only construct a bridge to bring republicans 'in from the cold' but a bridge which would bring Sinn Féin into the Stormont cabinet office in one fell swoop?

Trimble counters that it was Molyneaux who had 'saddled' him with the d'Hondt formulae which would subsequently be used to allocate the ministerial jobs between the qualifying parties, and that this principle of 'proportionality' had been UUP policy since 1992.

But come on. In all fairness to Jim Molyneaux, he and his colleagues certainly weren't talking about putting Sinn Féin in government back then?

'No, they weren't. But they weren't talking about excluding them.' That, surely, was because the suggestion of including them had never arisen in 1992. Wasn't the real point anyway surely that Trimble consciously decided to include them when he agreed the basis for devolution in 1997?

Trimble recalls hints by Molyneaux, the Rev. Martin Smyth MP and others that they could envisage talking to Sinn Féin after a period of 'quarantine' and is anyway insistent: 'I want to put the record straight here. If you look back at the Unionist Party proposals for the Strand One talks in 1992, about the purely internal Northern Ireland arrangements as part of any settlement, it's d'Hondt.'

Yes, but nobody until the final week of negotiations in April 1998 had the faintest notion that he was talking about a full-blown government that would include Sinn Féin?

Trimble is determined, as he has argued over the years, that a fully inclusive and proportional arrangement was in fact part of his bequest from the Molyneaux/Paisley talks with earlier British governments. 'No, no, no. It's perfectly obvious from '97 onwards that when they [Sinn Féin] come into the process, having won so many seats in the Forum, that if you stick to proportionality ... Now we have hung our hat on proportionality from '92 and for five years we'd been banging on about proportionality. If I suddenly turn round and say, "Whoops, changed my mind, I don't want proportionality, we'll go for weighted majorities instead", and it's obvious that you're doing it to exclude Sinn Féin, it puts you in a slightly queer pitch in the matter. And our effort in the negotiations is to try and link proportionality to things like decommissioning. But let me say this: to have a link to decommissioning so that Sinn Féin doesn't get the advantage of proportionality until they have genuinely done the business.'

So you were thinking they would probably still be excluded because you didn't expect them to do the business and qualify for office?

'That was one of the factors that we had in mind during the negotiations and of course when it came, and we see the final draft at the end of the day, the biggest thing was that the linkage between holding office and decommissioning wasn't as strong as it should be.'

I still don't quite get this. It is possible now to forget the magnitude of the policy shift with which Trimble was proposing to bounce his party. In a final repudiation of the Molyneaux years he had agreed the creation of a power-sharing government at Stormont, in which John Hume or Seamus Mallon would serve with him as co-equal First and Deputy First Ministers. Having conceded to the SDLP, surely all he had to do was take Hume or Mallon aside, explain the facts of life as he saw them, and reason that while he could win party backing to share power with the SDLP he would be wasting his time if Sinn Féin had to be part of the equation? Why did he not seek at that moment to detach the SDLP from Sinn Féin and go for a centre-driven government?

'Well, we thought we were doing that. Okay, this may be one of the things which in retrospect one would have to pin down more clearly. But this was about constructing a good relationship with the SDLP. We also left the SDLP in no doubt about our position on the linkage between IRA decommissioning and the rest of it. Now implicit in that is the position that, if they do decommission, yes ... I went to see unionists in some parts of the west of the province who would say to me in one breath, "Oh I can't have Sinn Féin, can't, terrible", and then take a pause before adding, "The SDLP are no different from Sinn Féin at all". Wait a minute, hold on, where are you on this? And there is also the fact you have got to bear in mind that if the republicans are actually turning their back on terrorism and coming into the political process then what is the difference between them and the SDLP?'

Most unionists of course saw a world of difference between the SDLP and Sinn Féin. Trimble has said himself he saw the republican movement as being in transition but wasn't at all sure they would complete it. In an interview with the *Irish Times* in April 2000 Trimble expressly rejected my assumption that somewhere along the path of his original tactical engagement in the talks chaired by former US Senator George Mitchell he had made the leap of faith and accepted the bona fides of the republican leadership. If he wasn't convinced of their unequivocal commitment to purely peaceful methods, why on earth was he considering bringing them into government at all? Why not pursue the other option and push the SDLP to go it alone with the unionists and Alliance? At the very least why not put the SDLP to the test?

Very deliberately he tells me: 'I don't think that was a viable option at midnight on Thursday 9 April 1998. The structural issues on Strand One [the internal arrangements for the governance of Northern Ireland] had all essentially been pre-determined even before the Mitchell talks began in 1996. Go back to the talks unionist leaders had with Secretaries of State Peter Brooke and then Sir Patrick Mayhew circa 1991–92 and the Agreement on Strand One. Now the Agreement wasn't finalised but the broad shape of it was, and we went into the '96 talks with our '93 position, which was based on d'Hondt and with the principles of proportionality and automaticity at the heart of it.'

But that UUP policy was hardly drafted with power-sharing with Sinn Féin in mind, I persist.

'I know that, I know that,' Trimble replies now sternly. 'But let me explain to you the situation as I saw it. We go into talks largely bound by the power-sharing mechanism that had been developed in '92. There isn't a formal Executive in the '92 model but we knew that there was going to have to be movement in that direction because we knew that the model that we were sticking to in '92 was unworkable, let alone not being acceptable to other parties. And I mean all through '92 and again through '96 and all the rest of it, people knew we couldn't even have run Belfast City Hall by this model. In City Hall we do have a General Purposes Committee which effectively is the Executive. So we're going to have to have something there. Now to turn round at the last minute and say, 'Hey boys, because we've Sinn Féin in the process I'm going to tear up everything and start from scratch' would have destroyed the process in any event. But there's another factor, and this is where you might have a different view of me. It comes back to where you are with regard to what is happening with republicans. Where they were as I saw it in the '90s, particularly when we had the revelation of the secret contacts with the British in 1993, was that the penny for a variety of reasons was dropping with republicans that violence was counterproductive, that quite apart from the moral considerations it just wasn't going to work and was making the situation worse. Worse for them as well as worse for others. And that the republicans were in the process of dropping the armed struggle. If republicans dropped the armed struggle and engaged purely in ordinary politics, even if they still remained totally committed to a united Ireland, that is a hugely beneficial thing, right? And that's why then when we got to '97, our position vis-à-vis republicans was predicated on the basis that they would move to being a normal political party. And if they did that, then it would not be right to exclude them from the benefits of the structures that had been already tentatively agreed. So the emphasis then was really not on excluding republicans but rather on getting republicans to complete the transition and excluding them if they didn't deal with the transition. That is quite a different position, and that basically is the position we were in.'

That seems clear enough. David Trimble didn't quite believe Gerry Adams and co. when the Agreement had to be concluded – but he wanted to believe them and he believed they should enjoy the full benefits of an unequivocal embrace of politics. But wasn't the problem that would come to haunt him – and finally prove his electoral undoing – that he failed to make the linkage to IRA decommissioning, the scrapping of IRA weapons and the completion of the republican transition, a condition within the terms of the Agreement everybody else signed up to?

'That was the huge problem with the Agreement, no doubt about that. Our position through the negotiation of the Agreement was that republican participation in the Executive should be made conditional on decommissioning.'

Yes, but the problem was that he didn't succeed in making it a condition of the Agreement. He may have wanted it but he went ahead with the Agreement anyway and accepted a procedure which, assuming Sinn Féin got enough votes, would entitle them to seats in government. He also accepted an 'exclusion' mechanism which – because it would require 'cross-community', that is to say SDLP, support for any action against Sinn Féin in the event of the IRA defaulting on decommissioning – people knew from the outset simply wasn't going to work. Isn't that the reality?

'But wait a minute. That was the huge problem on 10 April, because our position was that republican participation is conditional on decommissioning, right? And then we get a linkage which is not robust enough, where the high degree of probability is that it wouldn't have worked. I couldn't have said with certainty, but looking at it we sort of say, "This is the weak point." Now that was the position on the afternoon of 10 April 1998, because when we worked through everything else we were left with two issues: prisoner releases and IRA decommissioning. And by decommissioning what we had in mind was the linkage of decommissioning to holding office. That was the whole point of it. And when we had to decide which was the key issue, we decided the key issue was this. Then the question for us is, "Are we going to say, simply because of this, there will not be an agreement?" – bearing in mind I was coming from a position when I accepted the leadership of having a unionism that was marginalised, a unionism that was losing out steadily?

'When Mo Mowlam arrived in '97 she said the status quo was not an option and some people were getting excited, and I said, "Look, the status quo's not an option for us either because the status quo post the Anglo-Irish Agreement was the status quo where unionism was weak and marginalised, where the system was being run for the benefit of nationalism and the long-term effect of that was going to be disastrous from the point of view of the union with Britain." And if we were going to get ourselves back into the centre and have any hope of clawing back ground, we knew we were going to have to make a deal. We knew a deal was going to involve difficulties. But the question we had to look at on that Friday afternoon was whether we would be better off or worse off accepting the Agreement. And the view of most, with difficulty and with reluctance, was that we would be better with the deal. Now, there was the problem about the linkage of decommissioning to holding office. But I didn't regard, and I don't regard, the Agreement of April '98 as being Holy Writ. I knew there were unresolved issues that we were going to have to have a fight over in the period afterwards. And I was looking at the situation, thinking, "We've got a number of things so far on this, we don't want to throw them away, and we've got outstanding problems, we want to position ourselves ...."'

I interrupt at this point just to clarify this. Does this mean that after all the presidential phone calls from the Clinton White House, after Senator Mitchell flew home to his wife and young child, after an exhausted but delighted Bertie Ahern returned to Dublin and a jubilant Tony Blair finally got to join his family for their Easter holiday in Spain – and while news of the historic breakthrough was greeted with acclaim across the world – David Trimble did not regard himself as yet committed to sitting in government with Sinn Féin?

'No,' he tells me. 'Look, on that Friday afternoon there was a fair probability that Sinn Féin would reject the Agreement, and Sinn Féin did not actually accept the Agreement on 10 April 1998.'

I interject again with what may appear a stupid question but which to me seems blindingly obvious. Whether Sinn Féin would finally accept or not, whatever about their procrastinations, their 'need to consult the republican base' and all of that, why couldn't the condition Trimble sought be made explicit in the Agreement? Why couldn't he just say, if it was what he thought, 'God almighty, these people or their pals have been murdering members of my community for thirty years; we're talking about bringing them into a government, and the Agreement must be explicit that the IRA must do X, Y and Z within a designated timeframe if Sinn Féin members are to hold office before I go anywhere near my party with this deal'? Would nobody else go along with that? Did the Ulster Unionist leader even ask them?

'At that time of the day, yeah, at the time we saw the draft with its weak linkage. Now I've mentioned what our position was in terms of there having to be linkage. When Jeffrey Donaldson and I went to Chequers a couple of weeks before to prepare for the last bit of the negotiations, there was agreement that there had to be a provision excluding Sinn Féin if they didn't decommission.'

Are we talking here about what became known as Tony Blair's 'side-bar' letter after the Good Friday accord was concluded?

'No, no, before we got on to that. What I'm saying to you is this. When Jeffrey Donaldson and myself left Blair and John Holmes [Blair's Private Secretary at the time] at Chequers on that Sunday afternoon we understood all four to be agreed that if Sinn Féin did not decommission they would not go into the Executive. So it wasn't a matter of weighted majorities or anything like that. We were expecting a mechanism that would do that. Now I don't have this in writing but that's where we were at Chequers, that's where we were in the run-up to and through the last week of the negotiation. At times we would remind the British government that of course we have to have an exclusion mechanism – "Yes, yes we're agreed on that" – and then when it emerges it emerges in a weak form. Five of us go up to see Blair late in the afternoon – and by the way this is long before any telephone call from Bill Clinton – and we say this is the problem, we need an effective exclusion mechanism, and Blair says, "Look I can't unravel this now, everybody is … you know … this is where we are, we can't change this document now."'

So Blair suckered him?

'I don't know if that is true or not,' Trimble admits.

Yet if this was such a big thing – and he and Donaldson had left Chequers understanding they were all agreed on the exclusion mechanism – how come they were only seeing it inadequately presented in the final text, on the last day, and when it was seemingly impossible to change presumably because the other parties would not agree to do so?

'Because there weren't texts until late in the day. There was the earlier Mitchell text which we said had to be binned or dealt with, and this was one of the things that had to be dealt with. Did Blair sucker us? I don't know, he may very well have been genuine both at Chequers and in the last week. Whether he did or he didn't, I then made the suggestion of the side-bar letter.'

The essence of this letter was a promise by the Prime Minister that if the exclusion mechanism in the Belfast Agreement proved inadequate, he would bring forward legislation to change it. Most people thought at the time, and think still, that the letter was no more than a last-minute attempt to cover Trimble's embarrassment and was otherwise of no value or significance since it was not included in the text of the Agreement itself or endorsed by the other parties as forming part of the Agreement. David Trimble holds to a very different view.

'The letter was my idea, and it was the same idea that I used to solve a problem over the Strand Two talks about the future relationship between Northern Ireland and the Republic. And it wasn't even new then. It goes right back to the original concept of "rolling devolution", and beyond that. I reminded people of what happened in 1921–22, following the Government of Ireland Act 1920. Elections to a Northern Ireland Parliament in May of 1921, some powers devolved in December '21, other powers over the course of the six-month period after that, and security powers not actually devolved until May '22. I was saying, "Have your election, and then use your post-election period to resolve issues."'

So the 'Agreement' concluded on the Good Friday was really just a work-in-progress?

'Yeah, but what that was doing was using the period post the election to solve the problem. Now before I put that idea to the Irish on the Wednesday night, I spoke to British officials, and I asked what they thought was a likely period of time between the Agreement, the referendums, the Assembly election and the earliest point at which power could be devolved. And they said they couldn't see power being actually transferred before February '99. So I was working with that, saying that there was going to be this period from May through to the subsequent February – nine to ten months, something like that – in which these issues could be sorted out. Now that was Wednesday night. Then we come to the Friday afternoon, we're at a situation where we've got a lot of good things in the Agreement, the Agreement is on balance in my view a good thing for unionism, and we've got this problem over decommissioning. If they do decommission, then yes, it's fine for them to be in the Executive, but we've got to get the decommissioning. I said I was looking at the period post the election to solve this issue. And that's why, when Blair said he couldn't get the thing renegotiated, I asked for commitments from him to be in a letter which I thought would strengthen our hand post the Agreement in order to achieve this.'

But what status or authority did Trimble think that letter carried?

'Well, you see, that's why I was so anxious to have the letter circulated, that's why when Clinton phoned me I said, "There is this idea which might solve our problems but I need the nationalists and the Irish to back off", because if they had dumped on it and said, "We don't agree with that, it means nothing", then we wouldn't have had an Agreement. The letter was important, but it was important not just as a means of easing the party into taking a decision, but important for what was to be done in the post-election period.'

Important to him and the Ulster Unionists clearly. But, again, what was its status? According to Trimble: 'Its status was an authoritative interpretation of the Agreement, of the decommissioning section. Someone actually did say to me afterwards that we should have gone to court over the whole decommissioning question at the time when republicans and others were saying, "Oh, there's only an obligation to use their best efforts, they don't actually have to do it." Which if they'd thought about it is a contradiction anyway. Some people did say at the time to go to court to get an authoritative judicial interpretation of the decommissioning section of the Agreement because that did impose an obligation on republicans to decommission.'

What, the Blair letter? 'No, the Agreement itself did. I think the proper interpretation of that clause requiring the parties "to use any influence they may have" to secure the disarmament of all paramilitaries was just a good faith clause. The section as a whole says that they commit themselves to achieve total disarmament and that put an obligation [on them] and the Blair letter confirms that interpretation.'

The British government did indeed subsequently confirm this view in terms. Mo Mowlam said that while IRA decommissioning was not a precondition for Sinn Féin entering the devolved government, decommissioning was 'an obligation' under the Agreement.

If the Ulster Unionists and the British government were broadly of the same view, and republicans disputed it, why didn't he then go to the courts?

'If you're going to any sort of court, whether a British court or an international court, to say what is the impact of the decommissioning section of the Agreement, then the court would have determined there is an obligation to achieve decommissioning, total disarmament, permanent, of all paramilitary organisations, by such and such a date. So that bit of the letter about the interpretation I think was legally significant. It has to be said too that the British government, and I think arguably the Irish government, never resiled from the position that decommissioning was an obligation. That's actually important, particularly for those unionists who, driven by their own ambition, were going around saying, "There is no obligation to decommission." I really was infuriated at the time with the hypocrisy or stupidity of the people who were saying this.'

But it wasn't specified in the Agreement as a prior requirement for Sinn Féin joining the Executive. And I put it to Trimble that he was forced in the end by that simple fact, and by the logic of the argument, to 'jump first' and form the Executive in November 1999 without any decommissioning taking place.

'Oh, I don't think I was forced by any logic, the logic of any argument, to do that. I don't think that was at all in my mind. In my mind Blair delivered on the letter, and he did so twice. The first way he delivered on the letter was in the Northern Ireland Act 2000, by introducing legislation giving the British government the power to suspend the Assembly. The whole issue comes back in the spring and summer of 1999, when we've reached the end of the transitional period so far as making arrangements for creating a new administration and still no decommissioning. We get republicans to accept in the spring of '99 that they have an obligation, we don't actually get them to do anything. And then Blair's saying, "The only way we're going to achieve this is by setting up the institutions." He's come back to the "linkage". We say, "Well, we're quite happy to set up the institutions if the Shinners are not there." At the time when Blair came to meet my Assembly group, they were pressing him on this, and Blair's response always was, "I can't force people to serve on the Executive." Now, decoded, that means, "If I legislate to exclude Sinn Féin, SDLP will refuse to serve." He wasn't saying "I can't exclude", he was saying "I can't force people to serve." That is the origin of the legislation to suspend. He said, "The best I can do is to have a mechanism that rolls everything right back to the status quo ante if they don't decommission." He was saying to us at that time, "We believe there's been a seismic shift; they are about to decommission but they'll only do it immediately after you've formed the Executive." We were saying we weren't going to go in beforehand without there being a certainty of them decommissioning. The certainty that Blair could offer us was, "Well, if they don't decommission, we'll go back to the status quo ante."'

But however he rationalised it, the massive downside for David Trimble was that he would then be damned for abandoning the 'no guns, no government' policy on which his party had fought the Assembly election. No matter in the first instance that it was for just six weeks before he forced the first suspension of the Assembly. Having vowed that he would not, Trimble 'jumped first' and was seen to go back on his word and, crucially, to have lost the argument. Wasn't this the moment that marked the beginning of the erosion of trust which would finally see the rival Democratic Unionist Party triumph in the second Assembly election in November 2003?

Trimble delivers a cold and steely dismissal of this analysis. 'But I never went back on my word. I never abandoned my "no guns, no government" policy. Maybe I should have but I never did, and when there were no guns I made sure there was no government. And when DUP people say to me now, "no guns, no government", my reaction is, "What the hell do you think the position is? We've actually got some guns and there's no government because they didn't give enough guns and they didn't do it in the right way." So as far as that phrase is concerned, I regard myself as having stood absolutely on the principle and maintained that principle at some cost to myself right through the negotiations preceding the election in autumn 2003 until now. Funnily enough, the people in the DUP who accuse me have in their policy papers floated as an option going into a form of government in the Assembly with no guns at all, and without there ever needing to be any guns given up.'

As Trimble sees it, he joined battle on this issue that Good Friday afternoon even before the ink was dry on the Agreement. 'I knew there were battles still to come, that there was going to be a battle over putting the IRA out of business. But for me on 10 April 1998 having an agreement – yes, with that battle still to fight – was much better than having no agreement, and the world blaming me for there not being one.'

I'm pressing hard on this because many people have never been able to comprehend the UUP failure to tie decommissioning to Sinn Féin's entry into government explicitly in the body of the Agreement. Likewise, they could not believe that the highly controversial provision for paramilitary prisoner releases was not similarly tied to disarmament. Why wasn't it?

'Hold on a second,' comes the sharp reply. 'I didn't ... the Agreement did.' Really? How so? 'Oh, the Agreement isn't a legal document, again that's another mistake a lot of people make. They assume that this is a big legal document and they're looking for the certainty that a conveyancing lawyer would have about anything.'

Is it not an international treaty signed by and binding of two sovereign governments? 'And how many treaties are precise, without their opacities and all the rest of it? This is actually very clear. Look, a two-year period for decommissioning, a two-year period for prisoner releases. It's obvious, you really have to be stubborn not to see ...'

But surely the two-year 'deadline' for decommissioning was entirely aspirational? May 2000 might have been mentioned in the Agreement but it came and went without any decommissioning whatsoever and its absence did not halt the prisoner release programme. Moreover, Trimble himself incurred the wrath of some traditional Conservative supporters in the House of Commons when he failed to join them at Third Reading in opposing what became the Sentences Act 1998, precisely because it failed to make the linkage between prisoner releases and decommissioning.

'Look, there were two years for prisoner release, two years for decommissioning, obviously set side by side. The mistake was made by the British government in legislating for prisoner releases that would take place irrespective of the circumstances. Because they were so embarrassed at the thought that they were releasing people because of a political context, they dressed it up as a special new remission-type arrangement, and they legislated in such a way that gave them no leverage at all. That was a huge mistake. Now we blamed Mowlam for it but I'm not sure if the responsibility shouldn't be placed elsewhere.' With Blair himself? 'Yes.'

I want to leave this subject. However, it seems to me that Trimble has made a very telling point which goes to the heart of my still-nagging doubts and confusion both about the decommissioning requirement in the Agreement itself and, in particular, about his actual stand on the issue. He says the Agreement is not a big legal document. But isn't that the nub of the matter? It is in these vital respects much more a politicians' draft. Lawyers would have had no difficulty producing a document which explicitly tied together decommissioning, prisoner releases and Sinn Féin's entry into government had they required to do so. But Trimble was acting and deciding as a politician rather than as a lawyer. Isn't the fact of the matter that he left it vague and imprecise because he knew he wouldn't otherwise reach political agreement? And is it possible that, had he won the 1998 election with a more comfortable majority, he would have given decommissioning less priority than he was otherwise forced to do by the internal unionist arithmetic at Stormont?

That to me would seem to make sense of the ambiguity. But Trimble is insistent I've got this wrong: 'Oh no, no. Obviously I wanted to get an agreement, I wanted to get a situation that brought unionists in from the margins to the centre. But there was an even bigger prize there because if there was a genuine transition taking place amongst republicans from violence towards democratic politics, then you had the prospect of actually settling once and for all the instability that there had been in Northern Ireland. But if you're going to get them down that path, you know … I've complained about the process being "all carrot and no stick", and I've complained about there not being enough "push as well as pull". That's not to say that I don't recognise that there has to be a pull as well.'

In other words, he was distrustful while wanting to believe the republican leadership was for real? 'I wanted a transitional period. Even if Gerry Adams and Martin McGuinness were absolutely genuine and totally wanted to do this, there was no guarantee that they would succeed. So there was absolutely no point saying, "Because I've looked these men in the eye and I know they want to do this, therefore I'm quite content." There was no point doing that because their people might not have wanted to do it. I was not in any event convinced of their good faith in doing it. While I saw there was the prospect of a transition, and that if that transition was achieved it would be a good thing, I was not of the view that republicanism was an entirely willing participant in the transition. They'd partly got into this situation as a result of the security force pressures that were on them. They were travelling down a path that was deeply repugnant to a lot of republicans because it meant slaughtering their sacred cows at every stage along the way. So there was no point in me buying into the pose that "they really do want peace and therefore everything in the garden's rosy". I knew that there would have to be a constant struggle. It's taken longer than I expected, yes, but I expected that there would be something like this and I thought that once it started down this road, unionism had the stickability to see it through, and I'm sorry about the fact that a significant number of unionists lacked the stomach for doing what was necessary.'

Does he think people sufficiently recognised his achievement in actually delivering the Ulster Unionist Party in the first place? 'Well, this goes back to my private secretary's comment about the way in which the Irish government look at things. You know, their view is so skewed that they understand nothing about the nature of unionism, so the achievements you're referring to – they're something they expected to happen. Coming back to October 2003 – and you have written about what the British government did to me there ... I mean they and the Irish government got into the habit of assuming that, no matter how difficult the situation was, somehow I would manage to pull some rabbit out of the hat and everything would be okay. They never really actually had any gut feeling for the political situation I was dealing with.'

One other problem Trimble had, which helped undermine him greatly, I think, was that – while he saw the Belfast Agreement as 'a settlement' and a line in the sand over the IRA's challenge to the Northern Ireland state – Sinn Féin characterised it as 'a process' pushing remorselessly toward a united Ireland. And, of course, a great many unionists were prepared to believe Adams rather than Trimble.

He readily recognises the truth of that. 'Absolutely, absolutely. This is epitomised by that great comment by Adams after the UUC decision to endorse the Agreement: "Well done, David." He said that you know there are those unionists who don't realise, in terms of this and of virtually everything that happens, that republicans find it laughably easy to wind up and manipulate unionists.'

What was the effect of Adams' words, and what did Trimble think when he heard them? 'Oh, I knew exactly what he was doing. I knew it was done deliberately, that this was him winding up unionism ... It also has to be said that Adams would not have been able to get all the concessions that republicans have made past his own people were it not for the howls of outrage from unionists.'

Trimble has complained in particular about the Irish government's lack of awareness of unionist sensibilities. Presumably he had that in even larger measure from a republican leadership which affected at least to believe that unionists were merely clients of a British government which could command their compliance?

'They always have that, they approach things in much that same light and the consequence of that is that they tend not to understand or to try to understand the political dynamic within unionism. I mean, in the past they didn't bother. It has to be said that for quite some time now republicans have been making efforts to try and find out how unionists tick.'

But on that question of the Agreement as 'settlement' or as 'process': some of the loyalist politicians certainly entered the negotiations acutely conscious of the possibility that unionism could be required to concede a great deal to reach an accommodation with nationalism only to discover that republicans regarded any outcome

as the departure point for a further negotiation and still more concessions. And some I think entertained the idea that in return for a generous deal – and in order to overcome the predictable opposition of the
hardliners on their own side – unionists should seek to stipulate that
any subsequent change in Northern Ireland's constitutional position
should require something more than a simple majority. Did that ever
become an issue? Not for Trimble: 'I don't think – I never have
thought – that there was ever any prospect whatsoever of there being
a majority in favour of a united Ireland. I don't think that's ever going
to happen, ever, ever.'

So it wasn't worth bothering about? 'I may be completely wrong
about that but if I am I'll never see it. Why expend energy on something that's just completely irrelevant?' he replies laughing. Yet there
is a serious point here surely. The Belfast Agreement for example represented the triumph of John Hume's argument that majoritarianism
does not work in a divided society. In consequence, Trimble and
Seamus Mallon required a majority of unionists and a majority of
nationalists to elect them First and Deputy First Minister. If dual consent is required for the formation of a regional administration within
the United Kingdom, is it not arguable that a higher threshold than a
simple majority should be required to effect a change of sovereignty?
And even as a matter of practical politics, does Trimble think a simple
majority in a Northern Ireland referendum would provide a workable
basis to take Northern Ireland out of the United Kingdom and into a
unitary Irish state?

He says he thinks 'this is possibly why the Irish put in what they
did, that there would have to be a double referendum before there's a
united Ireland with votes in both the six and twenty-six counties'. But
would a bare majority actually be enough to effect a successful change
of sovereignty? 'Unfortunately you do have the democratic principle
which says in theory you ought to,' he reminds me before lighting on
my reference to the world of 'practical' politics: 'You said "practical".
On the practicalities, obviously not. I presume this is why some SDLP
people have said – and interestingly some in Sinn Féin – that if there
was a change in sovereignty it wouldn't affect the existence of the
institutions of Northern Ireland as a unit and that the local administration established by the Belfast Agreement would continue as
before. All it would mean would be instead of sending MPs to
Westminster you'd send them to the Dáil. Now none of that's in the
Agreement and I don't see that it in any way logically follows from the
Agreement. But they have said that, and I presume they have said it
as their own way of acknowledging the point that you make. As I say

it is my view this will never happen, and I don't think there will be any change in sovereignty.'

In fact, rather than the Republic assuming responsibility for the North, Trimble ventures: 'I think what is happening, has been happening for some time and will continue to happen, is that the Irish Republic will get closer and closer to the United Kingdom. That has been happening for some time but I think it's going to happen further in the future. I don't suppose that the Irish will return to the pre-1921 union. But they'll get very close to the British.' Why so? 'There are so many factors, there's the shared language, the shared culture, the shared history, the shared economy, the shared peoples, the closeness, the movement of people. You've got a situation where – if you just take passenger numbers, flights, London–Dublin, London–Belfast – many more people go London–Dublin than go London–Belfast.'

Given all this closeness, is there not in fact an argument for some voluntary sharing of sovereignty, some sort of confederal arrangement within these islands?

Trimble's answer is true to the letter of his unionist beliefs but surprises me nonetheless: 'Again, the British state will never go down that path in formal constitutional terms. But it's getting close to that path in practical arrangements, in practical working.'

So the boundaries between Britain and Ireland, nationalist Ireland and unionist Ulster, are becoming more and more blurred, less and less meaningful and relevant all the time? 'They're blurring all the time but the people I see who are threatened by this are Irish nationalists.'

Ignoring the threatening and sticking with the spirit of closeness, I wonder how far boundaries have blurred. Could he comfortably now consider himself 'a citizen of these islands'? But I should have known it was a stupid question, at least to put to him. 'Well, I am,' he cheerfully affirms. 'Everybody is actually because the famous provision in Section 2 of the Ireland Act 1949 says that the twenty-six counties are not a foreign country. So in a sense the British government has never fully accepted that the Republic of Ireland is really foreign. After all, are we not all part of the British Isles?'

12

Back to Stormont – Dermot Ahern, Gerry Adams, Peter Hain and Ian Paisley 2006

Was the triumph of the 'extremes' inevitable? Some in London and Dublin certainly appeared to accept Sinn Féin's 2001 eclipse of the SDLP and the DUP's 2003 triumph over the Ulster Unionists as the logical outcome of the peace process. Others, not so philosophical perhaps, could see that once Sinn Féin had gained the upper hand in the nationalist and republican community the tribal imperative pointed to a Paisleyite hegemony within unionism.

Seamus Mallon would eventually charge London and Dublin with losing the 'centre' parties as a matter of deliberate policy. Specifically, in 2007, he would accuse Blair of betraying Trimble by proceeding with the 2003 election after the Hillsborough debacle. Trimble remained inclined to give Blair the benefit of the doubt, while suspecting the Northern Ireland Office of sharing the view that the Sinn Féin/DUP ascendancy was only to be expected. The Prime Minister undoubtedly failed Trimble in the end. However, there is no supporting evidence that he ever thought to. In the aftermath of the DUP victory, moreover, Blair would prove slow to persuade there was any possibility of a breakthrough on the Rev. Ian Paisley's watch.

That said, by 2004 an extraordinary chemistry had developed between Blair and Paisley, and negotiations were resumed at Lancaster House and then Leeds Castle. Failure did not prevent Blair and Ahern travelling to Belfast in early December to claim 'comprehensive agreement'. But it had been undone by the IRA's rejection of the DUP demand for a photographic record of the complete weapons decommissioning programme otherwise now seemingly guaranteed.

Had the Agreement gone ahead at that point, Paisley and the DUP would have found themselves spectacularly undone by the pre-Christmas news of a £26.5 million robbery at the Northern Bank which police on both sides of the border – and Taoiseach Ahern – swiftly concluded was the work of the Provisional IRA. The wheels appeared finally to have come off the peace train by March 2005 when President George W. Bush snubbed Gerry Adams in favour of the sisters of murdered Belfast man Robert McCartney at the annual White House St Patrick's Day festivities in Washington.

Yet less than a year later, on Saturday, 18 February 2006, *The Irish Times* was able to reveal Tony Blair's plan to restore the suspended Stormont Assembly, this time with 'an absolute deadline' of the following November for the appointment of a new power-sharing Executive.

Irish government sources initially denied the story. Then, after talks between Prime Minister Blair and Taoiseach Ahern in London, it appeared reinvented almost as an Irish initiative. As suspicion grew that the whole idea had in fact originated with the DUP, meanwhile, the recurring suggestion was that Sinn Féin might 'pull the plug' and refuse to participate.

But they would be there in the end, as was *The Irish Times* with a mini-series of interviews with key players in the week before the 'Return to Stormont'. Intriguingly some DUP 'modernisers' complained at its conclusion that the series laid 'too much emphasis' on the last great outstanding issue – policing, and Sinn Féin's refusal still to endorse the Police Service of Northern Ireland. This might have offered some encouragement to Secretary of State Peter Hain and, in particular, to Irish Foreign Minister Dermot Ahern. The minister apparently managed to annoy his own Taoiseach, the SDLP and the Americans with an interview suggesting the Patten reform of the PSNI remained incomplete – while insisting policing would not be a precondition for a power-sharing deal. However, there was no encouragement for ministers from Dr Paisley, who left the author in no doubt about the importance he attached to the policing issue, and the priority it must yet command. While the British and Irish governments continued to display almost incomprehensible reticence on the question, meanwhile, from Gerry Adams came the unmistakable signal that he was in fact preparing to resolve it.

'POLICING ISSUE WILL NOT BE A PRECONDITION' FOR DEAL IN NOVEMBER – AHERN'

FROM *THE IRISH TIMES*, 9 MAY 2006

Next Monday sees the recall of the Northern Ireland Assembly, tasked to appoint a power-sharing Executive by November 24th. The British and Irish governments insist the deadline is absolute. However, many suspect London and Dublin have got their timing wrong and that the politics of next year's election in the Republic might prove the undoing of this latest devolution initiative.

And there is one other potential obstacle, little discussed in detail, yet every bit as complex as the negotiation of the Belfast Agreement itself. Even assuming the Rev. Ian Paisley might be tempted to conclude a power-sharing deal with Sinn Féin, does Dermot Ahern accept that the DUP leader would first require Sinn Féin to endorse the Police Service of Northern Ireland?

Mr Ahern makes clear 'the policing issue wouldn't be a precondition' for a November deal, before recalling that both parties appeared content to put the issue 'in the middle distance' when negotiating around the 'Comprehensive Agreement' proposals in autumn 2004.

There is of course a question as to whether the parties were negotiating for real back then. But be that as it may, many would say had that deal gone ahead it would have come quickly unstuck precisely because it did not contain a resolution on policing.

Yet my sense is that the minister shares Mr Hain's expectation that it might only be resolved in the context of the future devolution of policing and justice powers.

'That would be our view,' Mr Ahern confirms. 'But I agree with people that it follows as night follows day that if parties are going to go into an Executive there has to be an understanding that there is a move toward full acceptance of policing.'

The problem with this scenario is that there appears a considerable time lapse between the darkness and daylight.

'What I'm saying is Sinn Féin have work to do, and they accept that,' says Mr Ahern, adding that he always agreed with Séamus Mallon 'who said policing would be the key issue in any resolution'.

Yet Mr Mallon might argue that by successfully delaying a resolution, policing is the issue Sinn Féin is now using to complete the destruction of the SDLP.

Mr Ahern doesn't think so: 'Sinn Féin recognise they need to move on policing. Equally, others need to recognise that Sinn Féin have to be part of that policing hierarchy.'

I put it to the minister that he would not sit in government with anybody who did not, as a matter of first principle, support the Garda Síochána.

He instantly confirms: 'No I wouldn't.'

So why should any unionist politician sit in government with people who refuse to support the PSNI?

Mr Ahern is clear cut: 'You're not dealing with like with like between the South and the North.'

What's the difference?

'You're dealing with 35 years of history, the very strong suggestion that over 35 years people within the security services had been involved in some criminal activities ... You haven't got that in the Republic, you're dealing with a normal democratic society and I think it's unfair to equate the two.'

Mr Ahern volunteers the same applies to the political question – why should Sinn Féin be considered eligible for government in the North while rejected in the South? Again: 'You're dealing with a normal democratic society in the South, whereas you're dealing with a situation as per the Good Friday Agreement where it's accepted by the vast majority that the only way forward is by cross-community partnership. The Patten proposals were all designed ...'

But they've all been implemented, surely? 'No they haven't been fully implemented, but they were designed to bring us to a stage ...'

Which substantial pieces of Patten have not been implemented?

'The parties haven't totally subscribed,' replies the minister. 'For instance, Sinn Féin aren't part of the Policing Board.'

But that's hardly Patten's fault?

'I accept that.'

So which parts have not been implemented?

'The point I was making was that there are still gaps in that parties have not fully implemented Patten.'

Does the minister accept that Patten has been implemented? 'I think you'd have to leave that to the Oversight Commissioner.'

I wonder if the implication is not that the SDLP has been stupid about all this, and actually jumped too soon? The minister is making no such suggestion. Yet a nationalist or republican reading this interview might want to know his judgment as to which of these parties has got it right.

'I can't speak for either party,' insists Mr Ahern: 'Given the fact that I personally have been very supportive and requiring of people to support the PSNI, despite all the history ...'

But is there any reason he can see why somebody should still refuse? 'You'd have to ask those people who are not doing that,' Mr Ahern tells me: 'They continuously articulate, with some clear evidence ...'

Yes, but we knew all that at the outset, that's why we had Patten. And the Irish government endorsed the SDLP's decision to accept the PSNI. Mr Ahern accepts that. So, is there a legitimate policing dispensation available to the Catholic community in the North, or not?

'There is,' is the minister's unequivocal reply, before adding he does not think Sinn Féin could join the policing board before endorsing the PSNI. 'No. I think it has to be with the clear ultimate goal of accepting that these are the people who will enforce law and order.'

Without raising difficulties for the management of the process ahead, the minister also expresses confidence that this is the direction in which Sinn Féin is ultimately headed:

'I think to be fair, if they are to make a decision to join the policing board it will clearly show there's a sequence of movements to happen. They've always been strategic in that way.'

What then of Dr Paisley's possible strategy for the process ahead? We've already identified what unionists consider the double standard, whereby they are encouraged into government with Sinn Féin while the parties in the Republic keep them at arm's length. Why would Paisley do it? The minister reminds me we are 'not dealing with like with like', and I get the point that coalition is prescribed for the North by 'the template' that is the Belfast Agreement. However, we are surely dealing with the same underlying democratic principles in both states – the core issue being whether the republican movement has turned its back on violence and fully embraced exclusively peaceful and democratic means. Why would any unionist embrace Sinn Féin in government while Irish ministers are about to fight an election saying they are not fit or to be trusted in government in Dublin?

Mr Ahern replies sharply: 'We're not saying they're not candidates for government.'

No, isn't it rather that they're not considered fit for government? 'We haven't said they're not fit for government.'

The point being that they're just not candidates for Fianna Fáil? 'Yeah, that's the point we've made time and again.'

Why not? 'One very big reason is that they're an extreme socialist party, they've no like policies with us, they want to increase corporation tax to 17 per cent which would send everything out of this country.'

How could they be bad for the Republic's economy yet good for that of Northern Ireland? 'Again you go back to the premises upon which the future of Northern Ireland is set down, the Good Friday Agreement and the principle of partnership government.'

Mr Ahern may cite economic reasons but I put it to him that other ministers like Mr McDowell and Mr O'Dea cite the continued existence of the IRA and its constitution as inimical to membership of an Irish government.

'I think it's fair to say if you look at what Michael McDowell has said in relation to any of the recent Independent Monitoring Commission reports it is in the context of the ability of Sinn Féin to participate in government.'

Mr McDowell hasn't resiled from other statements he has made about the republican movement in relation to its activities in the Irish state? 'No, but I think it's fair to say a lot of the utterances of Michael McDowell are couched in terms of the political scene in the Republic, let's be straight about it.'

So Gerry Adams is right to say much of this is electoralism? 'Well, what's wrong with electoralism?' demands the minister: 'Parties have to put out their stall, and we do.'

I suggest what might be wrong with it is that Southern politicians are playing politics with the issue, while solemnly telling everybody in the North they have to abide by different rules.

'We have them [Sinn Féin] as part of our democratic system,' argues the minister.

And they are elected to the House of Commons and the North's district councils, and can participate as they wish, I counter. Mr Ahern is adamant: 'We deal with them purely in the political realm.'

But is that true? The Minister for Justice certainly sees them as a threat to the state?

'No, he doesn't say that in relation to Sinn Féin, he says that in relation to the IRA.'

Does Mr Ahern consider the IRA a continuing threat to the state? 'No, I do not. The security advice I receive is that the IRA are in effect gone out of the scenario, that what is clear to our security services is that there is a complete and unequivocal move to politics.'

Like every other democrat, Mr Ahern says he 'would love to see the IRA disband' while not thinking it possible because some people 'will say that's a bridge too far'.

But like Dr Paisley he is hopeful of seeing them become 'an old boys' society' and asserts: 'In effect that's what's happening.'

If Sinn Féin go into an Executive with adherence to the policing service, he concludes, 'it follows that they are recognising that the IRA are off the scene once and for all.'

'ISSUE OF POLICING IS CAPABLE OF BEING RESOLVED, SAYS ADAMS'

FROM *THE IRISH TIMES*, 5 MAY 2006

Despite deep misgivings about the strategy adopted by the Irish and British governments, Sinn Féin will be at what Gerry Adams calls 'the [Peter] Hain Assembly' when it convenes at Stormont next week.

Months of negotiations lie ahead, and we know what republicans hope to see at the end of the process. But before the hard bargaining gets under way, I put it to the Sinn Féin president that his party's influence is in fact diminishing, and that he may have to settle for considerably less than he achieved in the Belfast Agreement back in 1998.

Mr Adams acknowledges 'that would certainly be a concern' if it proved the case. 'Our objective is straightforward. We will make a serious effort to create the conditions where the DUP become part of the power-sharing arrangement in the terms of the Good Friday Agreement.

'There aren't any other acceptable terms ... We go in with a good will and will make a big effort, and I've actually been telling republicans we should suspend our scepticism about the DUP.

'In terms of the process, this is probably the last effort there's going to be in the lifetime of Ian Paisley to get this straightened out, and the Paisley deal is the best deal. So let's see if we can get that.'

Yet there are reasons for thinking Mr Adams might be disappointed. Sinn Féin has lost in David Trimble a willing unionist partner; doesn't it now face in Dr Paisley a leader mandated to reverse what unionists regard as a process of concession-making to Sinn Féin?

'Let's see. I don't underestimate the difficulties for unionism, nor the fact that the DUP had its position on these matters. But the DUP are now the leaders of unionism and they now have a responsibility to figure out the best way forward.

'Of course the DUP will try to figure out a way forward which is best for unionism.

'But there will be no return to majority rule. There can be no situation where the inequalities which were inherent within the six-county state can be accepted.

'There is a whole raft of measures in terms of the Good Friday Agreement which have to be delivered on, and the DUP has a veto only over one, and that is whether they will participate in the power-sharing arrangements or not.

'I would like to see them participating. But if the DUP decides it's not going to be part of this, that's its decision. Sinn Féin will continue to do what we are doing in terms of trying to proceed with reform and modernising ...'

As, I observe, they've been forced to do for a long time now, given the suspension of the institutions for longer than they ever operated. Indeed, isn't this the point? Sinn Féin is now dealing with a DUP which is confident, not least because they believe the republican movement has lost the leverage that came from the IRA campaign. Like the British state, the DUP also calculates that the IRA can't now go back to 'the war' and thus that Sinn Féin's influence is diminished the longer peace takes root.

Mr Adams doesn't flinch, recounting the familiar charges about the UDR, security force collusion in sectarian killings, and what he sees as a state of denial within the unionist leadership 'for the situation which developed into conflict', before issuing his challenge: 'We should be pleased that the war's over. If we're thoughtful about this, and I think there are people in the DUP who are thoughtful about this, the last 30 years wasn't good for anyone, particularly in terms of those who were bereaved or who have injured family members. But without the last 30 years, had unionism been allowed to continue, the situation would just be desperate.'

Even the unionists he appeals to will hear in this a defence of the IRA's work over those years. Mr Adams says 'they shouldn't be surprised at that' while insisting: 'Let's not go into re-fighting the war.'

Except that unionists still see him as the enemy. They distrust where he's coming from and where he wants to take them. Their constitutional purpose is inimical to his. They will naturally seek the best terms. And again, they're more confident now – courtesy of the end of the war and, incidentally, assurances from Peter Hain and Dermot Ahern that the alternative to power-sharing will not be joint London–Dublin authority.

With the territorial claim in Articles 2 and 3 of the Irish Constitution gone, and the principle of consent established, unionists might think relatively benign direct rule plus a bit of North/South cooperation is something they can live with. They've nothing to fear, have they?

'And Sinn Féin continues to grow across the island,' comes the reply. 'Sinn Féin's going to continue to be an influence which will radicalise and popularise these broad republican concepts. Now, we can sort of divide across the island – orange in this little northeast corner, and the rest of the island becoming increasingly green – or we can try to find accommodations and I think the Good Friday agreement is a good accommodation.'

In terms of helping the DUP to an accommodation, does he accept the Belfast Agreement's assertion of Britain's sovereignty in Northern Ireland, subject only to the principle of consent?

'I would put it in slightly different terms. I accepted the Good Friday Agreement, I was part of the group that negotiated it. We're for the Agreement. If the Agreement doesn't work, all the elements in it are still necessary to bring about the type of rights-based society which is required.

'One of the significant dimensions of the Agreement which is very clear is that the British government has said that it will only stay there for as long as the majority of people want ... like a couple deciding they will get divorced, but will wait until the children are grown up.

'It isn't as British as Finchley. It isn't the absolute commitment to the union. It isn't the same arrangement as there is for England, Scotland and Wales.

Does it go as far as republicans would want it to go? No, but it is still a sizeable movement forward. And, you see, we have to stop shaping ourselves in the shadow of Britain.'

But doesn't that expression speak of Mr Adams' profound and continuing failure to understand the nature of unionism? Unionists don't see themselves living 'in the shadow of Britain' but rather in the country, and under the government, of their choice?

But no: 'Unionism is much more paranoid about the Brits than I would ever be, feels much more insecure about the Brits than I would ever be.'

Unionism, he says, can decide to maintain a 'not an inch' approach, look after what are seen as unionist concerns 'and continue with this living in the shadow of Britain' or 'be genuinely confident and try to work out an accommodation'.

Supposing Dr Paisley was confident enough to contemplate an accommodation, isn't it certain he would require Sinn Féin's upfront endorsement of the Police Service of Northern Ireland?

Mr Adams maintains his traditional line, asserting that Sinn Féin will resolve its attitude to the PSNI 'when the British government completes the commitments they have made' on the issue. But will that be good enough this time?

President George Bush's envoy Mitchell Reiss says it is a requirement of any party seeking to enter government that they support the police. Mr Adams advises: 'Do not heed what Mitchell Reiss has said. Mitchell Reiss will not be sorting these matters out.'

DUP chief whip Nigel Dodds also says endorsement of the PSNI is 'a prerequisite' for any party sitting in government anywhere in the UK. 'Well, let's talk about these issues,' he offers.

But Dr Paisley almost certainly won't see much to talk about. Does Mr Adams really think the DUP leader will sit in government with Martin McGuinness, a Sinn Féin Deputy First Minister who doesn't support the police?

He insists, to the contrary, 'the big issue is whether Ian Paisley will go into a power-sharing government'. But say he is prepared to do so, and policing emerges as the DUP's bottom line?

'Well, the issue of policing has to be resolved anyway.' Yes, and I might have been told that in any one of a number of interviews since the Belfast Agreement.

This debate has been going on for years. Can it be resolved at least in principle by November?

Like any politician Mr Adams can 'talk the talk'. However, while the DUP may remain sceptical, longer term students of the republican 'process' will almost certainly find his answer instructive.

'Policing may be a necessary element in the resolution of the outstanding matters to do with the Assembly. But policing needs to be dealt with anyway, if there was no Assembly. If there was none of this issue you have articulated bearing down upon the process, policing still needs to be resolved.'

So will Sinn Féin step up to the plate?

'There is no issue that is not capable of being resolved, including the issue of policing, that's the best answer I can give you. If the DUP cast about for reasons why they will not be involved in power-sharing, that's their choice. But I think we have clearly said the policing issue needs to be resolved.

'Given the British government propositions to resolve it – and they've agreed to proceed on those – that will then bring the onus back on Sinn Féin, so that's going to happen anyway in my view.'

'GOOD FRIDAY AGREEMENT REMAINS THE ONLY SHOW IN TOWN – HAIN'

FROM *THE IRISH TIMES*, 12 MAY 2006

Peter Hain has said that November 24th is an absolute deadline, and that either the Stormont Assembly forms a power-sharing government by that date or it closes down. Does he accept he might thus be inviting the Rev. Ian Paisley to preside over the final death of the Belfast Agreement?

'No, what we're saying is the process can't continue and go on being an end in itself. I don't think the public in Northern Ireland will stand for this, and the Good Friday Agreement remains the only show in town. I think there'll have to be some legislative amendment to it – in terms of Strands One to Three [the Northern Ireland, North/South and British/Irish components], in the sort of territory there was in the comprehensive proposals of 2004 – for the DUP to take their seats in a power-sharing Executive. But there's no other show, and if anybody thought they could bring the curtain down in the interests of burying the Good Friday Agreement they couldn't be more wrong.'

But can that be right? Mr Hain will recognise the proposition is that of Mark Durkan. The SDLP leader said that not the least of the risks in this British/Irish initiative is that if Dr Paisley sits tight, for whatever reason, that's the end of the Assembly and the end of the central piece of the Agreement.

'The alternative is dragging this on year after year with the process becoming an end in itself, going on and on and on, and Assembly members not doing the jobs for which they were elected, drawing salaries and allowances, which the public won't stand for. The problem I think Assembly members have got themselves into is that they're not having an argument with me about this deadline, they're having an argument with their voters.'

He says it can't go on and on. But the DUP doesn't believe him. If Dr Paisley or Peter Robinson declare in November 'great progress made, not there yet, but getting there', they don't believe that Tony Blair would close it all down.

Mr Hain insists: 'They couldn't be more wrong. Whether it's the DUP or the SDLP, they could not be more wrong. At midnight on November 24th the curtain comes down, the Assembly's put on ice, the salaries will stop. In the late summer – if they don't think we're going to get an agreement, or they're not willing, or don't have confidence we can reach an agreement – I'll be advising Assembly members then to tell their staff to find new jobs. They'll also need to do something else in the summer and advise the landlords of their advice centres that they're not going to be able to pay the rent. I don't say that as a threat, because they themselves will bring the curtain down, not me, and the public won't stand for millions and millions of pounds going to waste in this fashion.'

Then comes an interesting caveat: 'If they go to one minute past midnight in the expectation that we're going to blink, well we won't blink first. Now, if they then decide voluntarily to go on the dole, sack their staff, close down their advice centres, and then come back to me after one month, two months, three months, six months, and say, "We think we got it wrong, now we're ready to run it again", well my door's always open. But I'm not going to be chasing after them.'

A strange thought occurs. If Mr Hain is to be taken at face value about the deadline, in an odd way – and certainly in a way he would never have intended – this reflects just how far Northern Ireland actually has come. Because presumably, while he would like devolution, he is also calculating there will be no political or security crisis if the devolution project fails. And therefore we've arrived at a point where, whereas previously devolution was considered an essential part of ending the conflict, we can now have peace without it.

Mr Hain concedes: 'You may be able to have peace without it, and I think you will have peace without it, because, you know, Northern Ireland is as night and day compared with what it was in past years, even in April 1998.'

However, he also argues: 'Actually you'll have a completely artificial situation because you will not have democracy there. You may have, we like to think, a very effective group of direct rule ministers who are making the decisions in the public interest. But we're not accountable, I'm not accountable to anybody in Northern Ireland, I don't have any voters who can kick me out.'

Notwithstanding what Mr Hain says about a democratic deficit, doesn't this reinforce the suspicion that Dr Paisley has got the soft option here, compared to where David Trimble was in 1998? The Irish constitutional claim is gone and the IRA's 'war' is over. As he says, Dr Paisley can have peace, albeit imperfect peace, without devolution. For all that Mr Hain talks tough, direct rule is relatively benign and will continue to be. With nine seats in the Commons, the likelihood of more electoral success to come, Mr Blair running out of time and the possibility of a hung parliament next time, a lot of people in the DUP might think their prospects rosy enough without the pain of having Martin McGuinness as Deputy First Minister.

Mr Hain is determinedly unimpressed by such lack of conventional political ambition. 'It's one thing for Northern Ireland MPs to enjoy being at Westminster, but their power is very limited. And actually a lot of the policies we're implementing, not that they have that ambition, are fiercely opposed by the DUP in particular ... the seven councils, the reform of education, the water charges, a long list of things. I'm not doing these to knock anybody on the nose. I'm doing these because I strongly believe – and have the support, I believe, of civil society, including the business community, the trade unions and the voluntary sector – in building a world class Northern Ireland. This is what this agenda's about. But they [the DUP] say they don't like them. Well it's a profoundly dissatisfying and unsatisfactory position for democratically elected politicians to be in, where they're actually saying, "Be my guest, make these decisions that I don't like."'

It was the accidental loss of meaningful local government alongside the suspension of the Stormont parliament in 1972 which created what has long since been described as Northern Ireland's democratic deficit. And with the proposal for seven 'super councils' Mr Hain might be said to be filling it. The DUP does not like the seven, but with proper levels of parliamentary representation, and their dominance of it, it might be democracy enough for the DUP.

'But you see that didn't work in Scotland and it didn't work in Wales,' counters Mr Hain. 'And you didn't have the bitter history in either of those two nations.'

Yet it might work for Northern Ireland, and for the unionists in particular, precisely because the bitter history creates an aversion to sharing power above a certain level.

Mr Hain is unconvinced: 'I don't think there is, I think there's a problem of trust and a failure of leadership, and too much followership and not enough leadership, by all the parties by the way.'

What single act of leadership could Gerry Adams engage in between now and November 24th?

'I think Sinn Féin do need to put themselves on the road – and I think they have started off warily down this road – to cooperating with the police. I'm not saying, "Join the policing board tomorrow." But there is a commitment they have given, which I'll expect them to honour, that when we've got royal assent for the bill devolving policing and justice, they then need to take positive moves to call a conference. They've promised that and I'm sure that they will.'

That's the assent for the bill, not the actual transfer of powers? 'No, until you've got institutions to devolve to, you can't devolve.' And the timetable for that? 'Well it's due to get royal assent by the summer recess, by the end of July.'

Mr Hain says he can't be certain of the timing of any Sinn Féin árd fheis, and declines to speculate as to whether the party might actually be ready to join the board and endorse the PSNI in time for a November deal. He also stresses: 'There's a radical difference between trying to solve problems and difficult issues like policing, which is what we're doing, and using those difficult issues to erect a hurdle to power-sharing ... I agree with what Dermot Ahern said in *The Irish Times* on Tuesday, that there's a danger here of continually shifting the goalposts.'

Yet he is also confident: 'Provided nobody's playing games, then it's in Sinn Féin's interest – since their declared objective is to get into government with the DUP and the others – to build trust and remove an excuse from unionists and everybody, because we all want them to cooperate with policing. It's in their interests to remove that excuse which could act as a final obstacle.'

Finally, again on the subject of leadership, does he think Ian Paisley wants to end his days as First Minister? 'Well, I think Ian Paisley over his extraordinary political career has been incredibly courageous.'

Courageous? 'Yes, I think he has shown a lot of courage as an individual. You can agree or disagree with what he's done and I'm not going to go into that territory, but I think he's shown a lot of courage, and I think he would like to see his political career concluded with peace set in concrete in Northern Ireland, with democracy flourishing and with the party that he created leading that new democracy. So yes I do, I think that's where he wants to go.'

'THERE IS NO WAY FORWARD WITHOUT RESOLVING POLICING ISSUE – PAISLEY'

I said to Taoiseach: 'We're not sitting here in friendship and ecumenical kisses ...'

FROM *THE IRISH TIMES*, 13 MAY 2008

Can Ian Paisley understand that many Catholics in Northern Ireland would find it difficult, indeed repugnant, to wake up one morning and find him as their First Minister?

There isn't the slightest hesitation before his reply comes laughing back: 'I think I wouldn't be the unionist I am if they didn't ... I mean, I have said that personally to Bertie Ahern, and his whole cabinet when I met them. I said 'you are bound to be against me because I am against you. We're not sitting here in friendship or ecumenical kisses ... We're sitting here because we are opponents on a vital issue.'

The leader of unionism is in rude good health and high humour. But before answering my questions he wants to address some vital issues by way of reply to Minister Dermot Ahern's interview in the *Irish Times* last Tuesday.

Dr Paisley rejects what he considers Ahern's presumption in 'setting the parameters' within which he must work. 'And the first parameter is the important question of the police. How do you support the police? Joining the Police Board is not an act of supporting the police, because you can go on to the board without making any statement whatsoever, you can carry out your own plan of operation to further what you have in mind, and you are not supporting the police. But we are being sold that the best thing is to get Sinn Féin to support the police and the best way to do it is get them to join the board. That is not supporting the police at all.'

Ahern and Secretary of State Peter Hain have said the DUP must not raise policing as a new 'precondition' to power-sharing. Is that what he's doing?

'I resent very much them saying I am putting forth preconditions,' the DUP leader says. 'These are the conditions I set out in all my talks with them. I fought an election on it. I won my majority on this very issue. And the issue is a simple one. Number one, there could be nobody in the government of Northern Ireland except they accept the forces of law and order. And by accepting them, they hand to the state all the information they have on lawlessness.'

So this issue will have to be resolved if there is to be an agreement in November?

'Yes. Except we have the police issue resolved, there is no way forward. The talks have no future until everyone who's going to be in the government of Northern Ireland is a complete and total support-er of the police. That doesn't mean he can't criticise police activity. But he's not going to be planning activity against the police, he's not going to withhold information, he's not going to use his position on the Police Board to tip off fellows to clear the country …'

Since they clearly want the issue resolved every bit as much as him, why does he suppose the British Prime Minister and the Taoiseach are not demanding this of Sinn Féin at this stage?

'I think they've been told strongly by Sinn Féin they're not getting it.'

The SDLP and the British government have been intrigued by comments made by Sinn Féin president Gerry Adams in this series, and seem to anticipate movement. However, time to park this debate and move forward or, rather, back to my first question.

I advance it by way of an invitation to Paisley. As is evident from what has gone before, much of the political discourse centres on his views about what republicans still have to do. The invitation is to con-sider what Tony Blair would call 'the big picture' from the other end of the lens, and how far republicans have already travelled, even against the continuing backdrop of loyalist terrorism. In the ninth year of the second IRA cessation, and following confirmation that their 'war' is over, does Paisley recognise the situation is already trans-formed beyond recognition?

'Yes,' he replies, before adding the qualification. In the Commons recently he challenged Hain: 'I said, "Who is it that brought about those changes? Was it your policy or was it my policy?" Our pressure had a lot to do with it, our pressure was successful. Then you say to me throw it all in now. You don't throw away successful policies, you pursue them.'

Paisley has anticipated me. I remind him that when he addressed the opening session of the (Peter) Brooke talks in 1991, he warned: 'No political agreement short of the impossible, that is surrender to the IRA's demand for a 32-county republic, will cause the IRA to go away.' Thus he said no political agreement would give Northern Ireland peace.

I put it to him, many, including disillusioned republicans, think he has succeeded beyond his wildest imaginings. No constitutional com-promise is demanded of him, much less surrender. He has the peace he never thought to see, and the opportunity now to cement it with political stability. The obvious question – in terms once posed to unionists generally by the Progressive Unionist Party's David Ervine – is whether he is going to grasp defeat from the jaws of victory?

'No, because the ultimate victory is a foundation upon which we can build democratically.'

The DUP leader contends 'a democracy' cannot be built on what he says 'is lacking' in the Belfast Agreement, and refers to his proposals to the British government for change.

'We have said, at the end of the day the IRA gives up all its arms, the IRA genuinely has no more truck with criminality, the IRA supports the police and called for its people to support the police ... You do all that, but that is not sufficient.

'We must be able to build upon something that is a democracy, and we haven't that. Now they promised they would change the Agreement in the way we suggested it could be changed, so that we would have a firm democratic foundation, because you can make a quick deal and then, when you start to build, you'd be on sinking sands.'

Paisley confirms this means provision for 'collective responsibility' in any Executive, 'and especially the fact that you cannot forever be stuck, that you have to get agreement between two diverse agencies. There's bound to be a time when we have to go to a majority weighted vote. I am prepared to have a weighted majority. I'm prepared to go as far as any real democracy goes, but I'm not prepared to tie my country in with people who at the end of the day want to destroy it.'

I'm not sure where that leaves Sinn Féin. Does he mean they want to destroy his country? 'Yes, their aim is a 32-county Ireland and they're not going to give that up.' But it's a legitimate political aspiration? 'Ach ...'

Imagine if I had told him in 1991 we'd be sitting in his office in these circumstances ... with Articles 2 and 3 of the Constitution gone, Sinn Féin having already worked a partitionist Assembly, the principle of consent established.

In the terms in which he addressed those Brooke talks – nobody is asking him to go into a 32-county state. What he's being asked to do is have a power-sharing administration within the United Kingdom.

'Yes, but that government must not be an interim government. They cannot tell me I must take a step, but it's only a step to another step and another step ... I mean Adams made that clear, that we're on a progress [to a united Ireland]. That progress is not going to descend on this Assembly. And I do not see this Assembly ever being a real true democracy unless changes are made.'

But these changes don't preclude Sinn Féin being there as members of an Executive? 'No, provided the other questions of the police and all are dealt with.'

On one specific, he has previously said he would not accept the concept of co-equal First and Deputy First Ministers. Is that an absolute position?

'I can't see how you could have an absolute position with that, that before you can get agreement you have to have the Agreement of a person who has already said 'this is only a step'. I mean they talk about the peace "process".'

But doesn't he think they're bluffing? I mean, he's already claimed success for his policy? 'Yes, but to a degree, we're not out of the woods yet.'

In this respect Paisley records particular concern about the closures of military bases west of the Bann, and the proposed seven-council reform of local government, before declaring his fear that events are actually moving toward 'a repartition of Northern Ireland'.

So he's not yet satisfied as to where the political process is taking Northern Ireland? 'No,' he confirms, 'I am shrewdly suspicious of the British government, I don't put my faith in the British government.' And in a seeming warning against any temptation to go behind his back, he adds: 'I think the British government would like somebody else where I sit, and would make a deal. Well I intend to sit on and sit tight … I'm not interested in office. Do you think I have come to 80 years of age to sell my soul? No, I'm not.

'What I'm interested in is to have a broad base of democracy on which we build, and then, come hell or high water, that edifice is going to stand.'

Does the IRA have to disband? 'I think they have, yes, I don't see any use for them otherwise. But the whole organisation of the IRA as an army … I say that that must change and we can't have them.'

He's going to be accused of raising a whole list of impossible demands. 'I know that. But I haven't said anything I haven't said before and they are on record.'

Yet here he is, the undisputed leader of unionism. He fears no man. Why not sit down and negotiate the terms face-to-face with Gerry Adams?

'Because my principle says to me you don't negotiate with terrorists.' And that's how he still sees him? Despite everything? 'Yes.'

Whatever Paisley says about him, Adams says 'the Paisley deal is the best deal', if it can be had.

'But you know why? He knows I can deliver … Well, to be in my position and know you can deliver makes me more careful. I'm not going to take one step that's going to in any way hinder my power to deliver.'

Yet he's been to the Bush White House, and he agrees terrorism is not an option in the post 9/11 world. Isn't that his greatest assurance? But no: 'My assurance is that there's a God in heaven, a sovereign God, and he works in a mysterious way.'

13

American Intervention – Mitchell Reiss 2006

At events to celebrate the success of the Northern Ireland peace process, British and Irish politicians take due care to acknowledge the important contribution made by the United States under the leaderships of both President Bill Clinton and President George W. Bush. In the inclusive spirit of the post-agreement times such tributes could also comfortably embrace Mitchell Reiss, who was appointed presidential envoy to succeed Richard Haas in 2003.

By late 2006, however, it was difficult to find members of the British and Irish establishments with much good to say about the part being played by Reiss, at least in private.

During the St Andrews negotiations in October of that year I asked one Irish source if the ambassador was making any contribution, and found the source seemingly surprised that I should even ask. A senior British source simply shook his head in casual dismissal of my inquiry. The inquiry, of course, was really by way of seeking confirmation of a growing suspicion, later confirmed, that Reiss had in fact made a significant contribution that the British in particular found discomfiting.

It was Reiss, after all, who had imposed fundraising restrictions on Sinn Féin and had Gerry Adams dropped from the White House guest list in response to the Northern Bank robbery and the murder of Mr McCartney. Downing Street was also well aware that the special envoy thought Jonathan Powell and Tony Blair very poor poker players, overly indulgent of the republicans and dangerously relaxed about the IRA's continuing involvement in criminal activities.

Ambassador Reiss also 'got' very early on something about which the British and Irish remained in seeming denial up to and through the St Andrews negotiations – that the resolution of the policing issue and Sinn Féin's endorsement of the PSNI would be absolute requirements of any deal for Ian Paisley.

Mary Alice Clancy, the author of an excellent thesis on 'The United States and post-Agreement Northern Ireland', reported that the Americans were so troubled by the Dermot Ahern interview reproduced in the last chapter that they asked for a clarification of the Irish government's position. Certainly I had no doubt it was because of the supreme importance he attached to the policing issue that Ambassador Reiss volunteered for this interview, which appeared as an addendum to the 'Return to Stormont' series.

'BUSH'S ENVOY SEES POLICING AS KEY ISSUE FOR SINN FÉIN'

FROM *THE IRISH TIMES*, 10 JUNE 2006

It's routinely stated and generally accepted as a matter of fact, and yet some wonder: does America still have a meaningful role to play in the Northern Ireland peace process?

US special envoy Mitchell Reiss is in no doubt: 'Absolutely. I think you can't just view this moment as a snapshot but rather, looking back over the previous few years at the substantial contribution the US and Irish America has made to the efforts of the two [British and Irish] governments and the political parties to restore a normal society in Northern Ireland ... At this particular moment I think we are part good offices, cheerleader, a source of ideas and encouragement to everybody who's involved, to try to get everybody over the line so we can restore the Assembly and have local government.'

I put the question for a variety of reasons. Sure, at summits and on set-piece occasions the Taoiseach or the British Prime Minister will attest to America's ongoing importance. Yet even President Clinton's role was probably less in his second term than in his first. The world has changed after September 11th. The Irish question, inevitably, has slipped down the agenda. And, of course, the Belfast Agreement itself changed the dynamics by imposing a direct burden on the local parties, thus reducing the role of outside facilitators.

Ambassador Reiss agrees: 'That's absolutely true. The distance we had to travel was clearly much further in the past. Where we are today is a product of that success.' However, he still hears from both governments and across the political spectrum the desire for continuing American involvement, and appreciation in particular for the role of President Bush, 'given all the other things on his agenda, for him staying involved and allowing the US to help'.

I also put the question for a particular reason, namely Sinn Féin's apparent antipathy to Mr Reiss's own involvement. In his recent *Irish Times* interview, Gerry Adams told me to 'pay no heed' to the ambassador, the republican charge being that Mr Reiss has further reduced American influence because of the position he has taken on the vexed question of policing in the North.

The man chosen by former US Secretary of State Colin Powell packs a mean diplomatic punch. First gently suggesting that it's never totally useful 'to have a discussion through the media', Mr Reiss responds: 'I think what Gerry Adams said about my not having any authority in Northern Ireland is absolutely correct, and that the key decisions are going to be made by the political parties and the two governments. But I think it's also correct to say that the United States does have a fair amount of influence, and it's how we decide to use and leverage that influence that defines the role we play in the peace process.'

Sinn Féin's complaint is that he has chosen to use that leverage by way of a ban on Mr Adams raising funds in the US as part of an overt attempt to force the pace of the internal republican debate on the policing issue.

Again, the diplomatic language doesn't quite mask the envoy's fairly uncompromising stance: 'I'm not going to speak for them or how they interpret events. As I've explained on a number of occasions, this really isn't about fundraising at all. It's all about giving the decent, law-abiding people in republican and nationalist communities the type of police service they deserve, so that they're not confined to ghettoes. It's about policing, it's about normality, about having a police service that reflects the personality and the wishes of people of the communities.'

Sinn Féin would say they are the better judge of how to conduct the debate with that end goal in mind than Mitchell Reiss. 'Well, they certainly can say what they like. But I think I've heard it from enough people in these communities, and from others, that I think the people in these communities are a little ahead of where the party [Sinn Féin] is. And Al Hutchinson [the Oversight Commissioner] gave a report the other day in which he said there is no reason for Sinn Féin any more not to join the Policing Board and support the Police Service of Northern Ireland.'

Specifically, and intriguingly, they say Mr Reiss has shaped a position rendered irrelevant by their prior agreement or understanding with London as to how the policing issue can be resolved over time. And indeed we've heard reports in the past week that Northern Secretary Peter Hain is pressing the envoy to lift the fundraising ban.

However, Mr Reiss insists: 'I'm convinced, persuaded ... that there is no difference of opinion at this moment between the British, Irish and American governments on the issue of policing. Everyone recognises how essential this is to getting a normal society in Northern Ireland.'

In terms of the fundraising ban on Mr Adams: 'The British and Irish governments have always stated that this is an internal American decision. We've had consultations on this all along. On my recent trip to London and Dublin, we discussed the matter at some length. So I think the story that appeared recently [in the London *Times*] that there was a disagreement between Secretary of State Hain and myself was wildly overblown.'

Looking ahead to the latest British/Irish 'deadline' for a deal at Stormont, does Mr Reiss think the policing issue can and should be resolved by November 24th?

'I certainly hope so,' he replies, interestingly without the usual British/Irish caveat about it being a requirement but not a precondition: 'I think it's important to recognise the steps Sinn Féin has already taken and some of the work they are doing internally with their own constituency. I think they need to do it for their own reasons, regardless of whatever the governments say, what other parties say. Sinn Féin needs to do it on its own for its own constituents. I think they understand that, and for whatever reasons they do decide to do it, it will be a very good day for the people of Northern Ireland.'

But when London and Dublin say it's not a precondition for a devolution deal come November, does America stand four-square behind them?

'We're always supportive of the governments,' he replies: 'Again, as I've said before, I think Sinn Féin need to do it. They're moving in the right direction. We just want them to follow through.'

The worry for many people is that even if Sinn Féin resolves the policing issue, the DUP will simply find fresh obstacles. Is he saying that Sinn Féin signing up for policing should be seen as the last act, so to speak, of republican decommissioning?

Again, Mitchell Reiss says he doesn't want to presume to know the DUP's position, while his own seems clear: 'I will say that I've been encouraged by the objective criteria they have set out for joining a government with Sinn Féin. The two issues Peter Robinson articulated when he visited the US in April were a commitment to supporting the police and an ending of IRA criminality. I think those are completely reasonable for the DUP to stake out – and again, if they should be met, then I can't see any reason why the DUP wouldn't be willing to stand up in Stormont immediately.'

I note Mr Hain thinks republicans have to all intents and purposes already passed the test, with the historic decision now to be made by the DUP. Mr Reiss in turn notes the potential importance of October's Independent Monitoring Commission report if convergence is to be secured with Dr Paisley: 'I don't think the DUP is quite where Peter is at this point. I hope they will be after the October report.'

Worryingly for the DUP, perhaps, Mr Reiss also appears robust in support of Mr Hain's approach to the Plan B alternative spelt out by Taoiseach Bertie Ahern and Prime Minister Tony Blair in April, when they spoke of their obligation to provide 'joint stewardship' of Northern Ireland in the continued absence of devolution. He maintains 'there are risks for both parties' if the stalemate prevails on November 24th and persists for any length of time thereafter.

Any possible allowance for 'injury time' after November strikes me as interesting in light of renewed speculation that the DUP 'modernisers' now think May next year their best bet for delivering a deal. My immediate difficulty, however, is to see the risk for Sinn Féin in a Plan B which would inevitably be seen as a 'greening' of direct rule if not a prototype for some form of joint London/Dublin authority.

Mr Reiss disputes the contention that Plan B as defined is all 'carrot' for Sinn Féin and 'stick' for the DUP, and argues both sides will lose from a sense of their collective failure: 'It really depends on what form joint stewardship takes. But I think there's a larger sense that decisions will be taken by people other than Sinn Féin or any of the political parties in Northern Ireland, and I can't see how that's anything but uncomfortable for leaderships that have staked their reputations and careers on being the stewards of their own people.'

14

'Dr No' Says Yes – Ian Paisley

2006–2007

When Ian Paisley finally sat down with Gerry Adams on 26 March 2007 in confirmation of the historic DUP/Sinn Féin agreement to share power, I reflected on the moment when it had all finally begun to look inevitable.

'FIRST SIGNS OF FIRST MINISTER'

FROM *THE IRISH TIMES*, 13 OCTOBER 2006,
THE FAIRMONT ST ANDREWS HOTEL, SCOTLAND

When we were finally admitted for Prime Minister Blair and Taoiseach Ahern's press conference at the end of the three-day negotiation that set the scene for Monday's agreement, I noted that the front row of seats had been reserved.

Dermot Ahern and the rest of the Irish ministerial team occupied the first four. They were promptly followed by Peter Hain and his two colleagues, leaving just two seats at the end. These in turn were taken by Dr Paisley and his wife Eileen, Baroness Paisley.

I thought this odd. A quick scan showed the other party leaders standing around the back, and Gerry Adams not yet in the room at all.

Later that evening I asked a government spokesman about this seating arrangement, and was told Dr Paisley needed to be close to the platform because he was rushing to the airport immediately after making his own statement about the talks. And it was true Dr Paisley and his wife were heading back to a family party to celebrate their fiftieth wedding anniversary.

Even so. A seat in the second row would hardly have made any difference. And the impression lingered, that the Big Man looked not only merely comfortable but as if his presence alongside British and Irish ministers was a statement in itself.

This week, and with the deal done, a senior British source was more forthcoming as we revisited the St Andrews scene. 'There is no doubt in my mind that that was the moment he [Paisley] crossed over to being First Minister designate,' he told me.

Months of negotiations and March 2007 elections to a new Assembly still lay ahead. But this impression certainly informed the tone of my reports on the morning after St Andrews: 'The DUP leader, the Rev. Ian Paisley, and Sinn Féin's Martin McGuinness appear to be facing into an agreement which could see them jointly lead a new power-sharing in Northern Ireland by next March ... For all the natural disposition to resist hype and spin, what was unmistakable last night was a professed belief – again shared by the DUP and the British government – that what had taken place in the last few days might just prove "bigger than the Belfast Agreement".'

As *The Irish Times* had foretold, Paisley had staked-out a position on policing which the Americans supported and from which the British and Irish governments could not expect him to resile. The final pieces in the necessary choreography were falling into place and on 30 December 2006 the newspaper signed-off on the old in anticipation of a very happy new year for the peoples of Northern Ireland: 'What was implicit in signing up to the Belfast Agreement almost nine years ago would seem now to have come to pass. The árd comhairle of Sinn Féin supported the recommendation of its president, Gerry Adams, yesterday to hold an árd fheis next month to support policing in Northern Ireland. This is indeed a seismic development. Once republicans cross the policing Rubicon, there really can be no turning back.' After 'a lifetime of playing opposition politics' and denouncing all compromise, the editorial continued, it was not difficult to understand the nervousness of many in the DUP: 'For all their protestations to the contrary, they are following a similar path to the Ulster Unionists under David Trimble in seeking to secure the future of Northern Ireland within the United Kingdom while at the same time ensuring that the constitutional alternative, a united Ireland, is pursued by purely peaceful means.' All that said, the clinching argument, as canvassed previously in the paper, was that 'in staking his position on the policing issue, Dr Paisley has raised the prospect of a prize that eluded Mr Trimble.'

Before taking office Dr Paisley would have to junk a load of his own preconditions. Yet this proved no problem to the new, pragmatic Paisley who decided that – leaving aside the question of IRA disbandment altogether – republican acceptance of the police did finally amount to acceptance of the legitimacy of the British state in Northern Ireland. On 18 January 2007 I suggested the question of devolution was no longer a question of 'if' for Dr Paisley, simply 'when': 'The widespread perception within the republican community may be that, in real terms, the Adams leadership has already gone through the pain barrier. Taoiseach Ahern, like Mr Blair, certainly appears to anticipate that changes in attitude to the PSNI will follow swiftly on foot of the Árd Fheis.' The analysis continued: 'Indeed, Mr Blair's insistence that full support for the police can still facilitate devolution by March 26th might seem to suggest – contrary to the árd fheis motion – that Martin McGuinness will be able to take the pledge of office promising to uphold the rule of law and support the PSNI by that date. If he cannot (whether because of Sinn Féin's conditions – or because in such circumstances they choose to interpret the pledge itself as conditional) that will not be a problem for Dr Paisley, though it would certainly torpedo Mr Blair's March deadline.'

The unrelenting good news for Mr Blair was that nothing, really, was now going to be allowed to become a problem: 'Even if interrupted by temporary breakdown on March 26th, the Prime Minister can calculate that Mr Adams has nowhere else to go and that for Dr Paisley – for whom, unlike Mr Adams, devolution is actually a strategic goal – the question is probably no longer "if", but "when".' In that context, too, it was instructive to note a new DUP calculation 'that they might, on balance, fare better under Mr Blair than Mr [Gordon] Brown – and that Mr Blair seems intent on staying in office at least until June'.

Some in the DUP had thought to deny the then departing Mr Blair his Northern Irish 'legacy'. But Dr Paisley, too, proved a man in a hurry, his eye also on the history books.

'WE'RE ON A ROAD, AND WE'RE NOT TURNING BACK'

On Tuesday, history will be made when Dr Ian Paisley assumes the leadership of a power-sharing Northern Executive with Sinn Féin as his principal partner. It will work – so long as people don't expect too much at the start, he tells Frank Millar.

FROM *THE IRISH TIMES*, 5 MAY 2007

If it's any consolation to Martin McGuinness, the Rev. Ian Paisley won't observe the niceties with me either on this occasion. 'I'm not getting into all that hand-shaking business,' he bellows in greeting at the House of Commons. We will return to this, for the personal and human dimensions would seem crucial in any genuine process of peacemaking. And a settled peace is what the DUP leader believes will result from next Tuesday's unprecedented events at Stormont.

That famous 'hand of history' will sweep across Lord Carson's statue at the Parliament Buildings again as the Big Man – watched by British Prime Minister Tony Blair and Taoiseach Bertie Ahern –

assumes the leadership of a compulsory power-sharing Executive with Sinn Féin as his principal partner. It is not as he would have devised it. Respected commentators also suggest the Good Friday model might serve better as an instrument of conflict resolution than of good government. Despite such reservations, can people be confident it will work? 'I think they can be confident it can and will work if they don't expect too much from it at the beginning,' Dr Paisley replies: 'I mean, with this hype in the country – and there is a hype, which everybody acknowledges – they might think this thing was going to work miracles. We will get back to our debates and a lot of divisions. But – with everybody saying "we must make it work, we're going to get nothing else from the British government at the moment" – I think the tools we have, while they may not be the best, are tools that could do the job, with goodwill and energy.'

And is he satisfied that all parties in the new government are fully signed up to exclusively peaceful and democratic means, and to the principle of consent? 'I believe they are,' he affirms. 'I also believe they realise it will not be like the last time, and that if any person doesn't keep to the [ministerial] pledge of office, they will forfeit the right to be there. I think they see now that the British government will say that the people that kept their pledges will carry on, the people who have not kept their pledge will leave.'

Can he really be confident of that? 'I am. I believe that's what would happen. I think everybody that's in it realises that's what would happen. There are [exclusion] mechanisms that could be used, and I think would be used, because I don't think the people of Northern Ireland would tolerate that. I think the degree of tolerance they've given in the past is over. And irrespective of what their previous actions may have been ... I think the people now expect a new day, new platform, new faith, and "you'd better keep to it".'

When did he decide he could trust Sinn Féin on this? And how important was its decision to endorse the Police Service of Northern Ireland (PSNI)? The unionist leader confirms this was a crucial test. 'Having been brought up in Northern Ireland, I understand republicanism,' he says. 'Republicanism believes that Britain is an intruder in a country they've no right to be in. Therefore, they believe the police, representing the British government, British laws and the British court jurisdiction, are their enemy. They looked at the police as a legitimate target to be killed and murdered and blown up. Now that has changed, and will be changed by solemn resolution by everybody who takes part. They will have to declare they are going to support the Northern Ireland police.'

So, endorsing the police is acceptance of defeat for republicanism? 'It is, certainly. It's more than that. It's a change in the overall republican thinking. Before, they never would – it would be like selling their birthright to say "yes, I acknowledge that man is a policeman, he's entitled to be here and he's entitled to get me to keep the law".' Does endorsing the PSNI render the IRA redundant, in his view? Or is the continued existence of its army council still a problem? 'I think they know that the army council has to go. To a degree, the army council has gone out of activity. I think it's fair to say the army council is not acting as a militant operation at the moment, and never will ... As I have said, if they want to have an old boys' club, they can have it. But they can't have an army directed by an army council in Northern Ireland.'

Sinn Féin's motion made support for the PSNI conditional on a timetable for the devolution of policing and justice powers. Does Dr Paisley think that was mere pre-election rhetoric? Or does he see devolution of these powers happening? 'Oh it [support for the police] has happened,' Dr Paisley asserts. 'When they take that pledge, they're not going to be pledging it in those words. The pledge is to the rule of law, and they will lend their aid to the rule of law as it is carried out by the PSNI, without condition.'

That said, the First Minister-designate would like to see the day when the people could assent to the transfer of policing and justice powers, possibly even on his watch. And he is confident the IRA will not prove an obstacle to that: 'I don't think the IRA/Sinn Féin or whatever you like to call them feel there is any other road for them. There's nothing to go back to. And we've said we don't want to go back to living in a defence fortress all the days of our life.'

When did Dr Paisley finally decide he could trust the peace process, and that republicans were for real? His, he says, was a strategy 'to deal with the things that were evident', one of which being that republicans did not support the police. 'How can you have any form of self-rule except [by supporting] the police? So I started a campaign that said the attitude to the police must be repudiated and a new attitude to the police must come about.' He would claim victory through 'constant reiteration', although he says Blair and Ahern didn't support him at the outset and were reluctant to force the issue.

Now that his decision is made, and given the current all-round spirit of generosity, would Dr Paisley accept that he owes something to those who went before, such as David Trimble? Not a bit of it. 'I took the line that it was a terrible pity for unionism that unionists ever agreed to share power with people who were still terrorists. I was consistent all through on this matter.'

So he no longer regards Gerry Adams and Martin McGuinness as terrorists, and accepts republicans have turned over a new leaf? 'To a degree that we have seen, yes. But I would like to see the army council come to an end and there are some other things I would like to see. But we're on a road, and we're not going to turn back, that's what I feel about it.'

In the same search for generosity, McGuinness says we would never have reached this point without Blair. Does he agree? 'Oh, I think he worked hard at it, he did. But if he had adopted sooner what he had to adopt in the end … He tried to have forms of words that suited everybody, and I could not accept them.'

In his other ministry, Dr Paisley will have spoken of the house divided against itself being unable to stand. Can devolution offer Northern Ireland a settlement, when the DUP thinks to use it to consolidate the union with Britain, while Sinn Féin sees it as transitional to Irish unity? Isn't the reality that republicans will use the institutions to pull the North ever closer to the Republic? 'Not while I'm around,' he declares contentedly.

Nor is he embarrassed to be pushing for corporation tax levels similar to those in the Republic, despite my suggestion that this is fundamentally an anti-unionist position. 'No, it's not because we have suffered as a result of what has happened, and we are entitled to everything we can get so that we can be competitors of the southern part of our island.'

It's reported that Dr Paisley has taken to calling McGuinness 'the Deputy'. If not embarrassed, is he in denial about the fact that the Sinn Féin nominee is in fact co-equal to him as First Minister? He tells me I have this wrong too. 'He's the Deputy First Minister. He's not co-equal,' Dr Paisley insists, before acknowledging that 'there is jointery' to the Office of First and Deputy First Minister and that the system can work only by agreement. 'There is jointery, though it's not what people think,' he concedes, before adding: 'But I think it will work out … There are places that he would not go, and there are places that I would not go.' Where would he not go as First Minister? 'Well there are things I wouldn't go to. Say the pope came, I wouldn't go to a mass service.' But shouldn't he be First Minister for all the people of Northern Ireland? 'Well I might be. But that doesn't mean I have to throw away my religious beliefs.' So where would he go, then, to spare McGuinness's blushes? 'I said to the Deputy, "there's places you wouldn't go" – I wouldn't expect him to go to Buckingham Palace. He's a Member of this House of Commons and he won't even sit in it.'

How did he feel when he first met Adams and McGuinness? 'I didn't feel too good. I said that. I said I'd have to swallow my spittle.

Let's be absolutely clear, these things do not go away in a moment.' I'm pressing because, apparently, there will be no handshake to seal the deal. Doesn't a peace process at some point require exactly such a basic, human gesture? Dr Paisley is insistent: 'I think that is nonsense. We've had handshakes over deals before and it's been theatrical folly.' I observe that he's right up there with the best political actors, as he hints of what might yet pass: 'All things being equal, I wouldn't be holding back. But I believe I have to show that we must get to the end of this path. We're not at the end of the path but we're on our way.'

Given the decisions he has had to make, would Dr Paisley have any difficulty if Bertie Ahern were to invite Sinn Féin into government after the general election this month? 'No I wouldn't,' he replies laughing. 'I taunted him with that before. I said, "why not bring them into your government?" But now [the Taoiseach] says he doesn't like the theology of their politics.' But it wouldn't worry him? 'Oh, if they bring them in, I would probably mock them and say "we showed a good example".'

Given the price he's had to pay for devolution and staying within the United Kingdom, would he not have been better to have taken his strength and negotiated directly with Dublin? Would a united Ireland really be that much worse? He may have changed somewhat, but Dr Paisley won't be tempted down that path: 'I think the union runs into the core of the Ulster people. As republicanism is part of theirs ... I think you have to realise there are things embedded in you by birth, by religion, it's probably in our genes.' But he also wants to repeat what he said on his recent trip to Dublin, 'that we do not need to build hedges between us, that we can be friendly neighbours'. And while in Northern Ireland that means unionists and republicans acknowledging their political and religious differences, he predicts, 'we can also show as genuine and honourable people that we can live together.'

15

Ireland at Peace – Bertie Ahern 2008

The former Taoiseach is emphatic that the constitutional position of Northern Ireland is now 'settled'. If it is so, many will feel it is surely down to him as much as to any other politician. When Tony Blair introduced the honoured guest to address the joint houses of parliament at Westminster in May 2007 he told the assembled peers and MPs he certainly could not have secured the peace without his good friend Bertie. For once at least there was no suspicion of New Labour 'spin'.

For ten years as Taoiseach, Bertie Ahern had impressed people on all sides with his extraordinary commitment to finding a just and balanced settlement in that troubled place. So it was appropriate that he would spend his last day in office alongside also departing First Minister Ian Paisley at a commemoration event on the banks of the Boyne.

Like his opposite number in Number 10 Downing Street, nothing could have prepared Ahern for the demands the ancient quarrel would make upon his time and office. Yet he met them with a consistent display of public good grace despite a widespread perception that the North's political class could try the patience of a saint.

I travelled to Dublin just a few weeks after he left office in May 2008, and first of all asked him about this. The tenth anniversary of the Belfast Agreement had triggered a fair amount of – some would feel too much – celebration. Of course we knew everybody had done good and deserved prizes. Yet at least one senior member of the British cabinet had confided his view that the Northern Ireland parties had been grossly over-indulged. Freed of the constraints of office, perhaps the former Taoiseach would like to confirm that he, too, found them a pain?

But he was having none of it, speaking instead, instinctively, with empathy, for those of his trade who had laboured through abnormal times and a bitter conflict. 'Well, they weren't. The way I looked at it from the years when I started dealing with Northern Ireland, which was really in the late '80s when I started meeting delegations and deputations, when I was a minister first, 21 years ago ... they had been in conflict practically all their lives and every group you met, every family you met, had been affected directly or indirectly through the troubles. So the fact that they were under stress and tension was not surprising.'

The young Ahern naturally took a keen interest in the North's politics 'after the riots of '68, the civil rights marches on 5th October '68, the Apprentice Boys' march in Derry, 12th August '69'. And what he recalls is that Northern Ireland produced 'good politicians' in abundance: 'I mean they had always good politicians. They always had good speakers. They always had people who were well able to do the chat shows and so on. But inevitably in a conflict situation – and this is no different to anywhere in the world, now that I've read more and more about other places in the world – they were always talking at each other and against each other.' In reality, he says, it was not until the 1990s that people started looking for common ground and a way forward. 'All of the '70s and '80s were about conflict,' he reminds before dismissing the idea that, when it eventually came to it, creating a solution was really just about building on what had been attempted before.

Seamus Mallon's famous expression about the Belfast Agreement as 'Sunningdale for slow learners' comes to mind as Mr Ahern explains: 'The reality is that there was no consensus or no agreement in '74. I mean Sunningdale hadn't got a hope. We didn't have a hope. It was negotiation in a vacuum without people being involved.' Likewise with the Anglo-Irish Agreement of 1985: 'It hadn't got a hope because everybody was in different positions and, in any negotiations, there's no point in sitting down negotiating between a group of people and ignoring all the others and then saying "we have agreement". It doesn't happen. It doesn't happen in a sweet shop if there's a conflict between the management and the staff.' This, from the Ahern perspective, was the difficulty with all that had gone before: 'So it wasn't until the '90s that there was a genuine attempt, in my view, to try to start pulling people together. And it was only when you got a collective position that you could make any advance.'

So Bertie Ahern came to the task with natural sympathy for the politicians, and the sense of exclusion they carried and represented on behalf of their communities. Yet we are told by Alistair Campbell, Tony Blair's former communications director, that at one point during the negotiation in the final week before the Good Friday the Taoiseach came close to punching David Trimble. Many might imagine that could all too easily be true. But the man who made his reputation negotiating deals with trades unions will admit to nothing he hadn't seen before: 'I mean, listen. The reality of any negotiation is you have to soak up a fair amount of pressure and people have to say their bit and blow off the things that are on their mind. Anyone who's a negotiator can accept that regardless of what it is that it's not easy. If you're dealing with an industrial dispute you're going to have to listen to the rancour of the workers and the management, why everybody is wrong and they're right. So the fact that David Trimble and probably everybody else at times were blowing their head off – and naturally enough I would have got it from the Unionists or the DUP more than from the other side – that never fazed me to be honest.'

Still on that point, Mr Ahern might want to be discreet but I'm also told the language was sometimes pretty rough between himself and Seamus Mallon, and also at times particularly so between himself and Gerry Adams. All he will admit is that the discussions at practically every point were tough. 'Weston Park was very tough. The last one in Scotland, in St Andrews, was very tough. But I don't remember any easy ones. And, always, I used to look at this to see, "can you make a bit of progress and can you move it on?" What I tried to do, I won't say successfully all the time, was just to see … at least if we left it in a position, even if it was a difficult night or a difficult day or a difficult session and we were going nowhere, at least try and leave it no worse than we started it. There was no point in falling out with these people. If you're ultimately going to get a success you have to try and keep the thing on the boil.'

People would naturally focus on tensions that would be expected between Bertie Ahern and the unionists. Yet there was surely a very real tension in his relationship with Adams and with Sinn Féin. First, perhaps, because Sinn Féin was an electoral competitor. Second, and more importantly, I suggest, because of the potential conflict between a Taoiseach's desire to bring former terrorists in from the cold and his role as Taoiseach as defender of democratic standards?

With a reminder of the commitment of successive governments to the project, Mr Ahern fairly convincingly deals with the first question: 'I think we managed all the time to be able to say the right thing to get militant republicans into the peace process and bring them forward. If we ever had to consider that there would be an electoral loss to Fianna Fáil we never would have done that. So I can genuinely say that was never an issue.' But that didn't mean there were no tensions: 'There were definitely difficult times on that, for we really believed there should be more pressure put on the militants to pull things forward. But in all of that I had great admiration for both Martin and Gerry. It always was a bit slower than we wanted, always a bit more difficult than we wanted. But all the way from 2000 on I think we were making progress. Every time was always a bit less than you wanted. But we were making improvements and, in fairness, I had to deal with Gerry in '97. When I took over, which is sometimes forgotten now, there wasn't a peace process, there wasn't a ceasefire.'

Despite that fact, some close observers would suggest that Ahern had the easy part and that, from the Irish point of view, the real 'heavy lifting' was done by his predecessor, Albert Reynolds. Mr Ahern says he doesn't bother 'correcting any of these things'. But he clearly notes them. Recalling the shooting of two RUC men just days before he assumed office, the aftermath of bombs in Manchester and London and several incidents along the border, he records: 'That's where I took it up from. I didn't take it up from the ceasefire. In fact the ceasefire position had really soured since January '96 and the relationship with the Irish government had soured from 1996, maybe before it.'

I wonder if one of the reasons he gave the republican leadership more leg room than others would have thought appropriate was because he knew from early on that the end result would be such a distance from what they had set out promising their own people?

Mr Ahern replies: 'Yeah, and you know that all had to evolve. It was incremental all the way. Say if the DUP, the UUP and Sinn Féin or SDLP were to set down exactly what their stall was in 1994 and '95, you know it probably never would have worked. All the time it had to be "we'll move to the next bit." The fact that the Good Friday Agreement in '98 took on aspects of what had been there for maybe 10, 20 or 30 years, that was kind of irrelevant. We weren't just taking the bit up. The fact is they were never implemented. In fact there was never even a good shot at implementing them. Sunningdale ended within days of the Ulster Workers' strike, so it was irrelevant that they [those proposals] were documented before. They could have been documented in 1690, it made no difference. The fact was, now we had an international agreement. Now we nearly had everyone on board and now we had to go about implementing it. And as George Mitchell said on that famous Friday, which didn't surprise me one bit, we now had the template to move forward but our job here was going to be the implementation of it. And I mean every little bit of the period from Easter '98 on, was about the implementation phase. I never believed we were going to get up in the morning after 10 April 1998 and get an easy pass, and then move straight into decommissioning and all the other issues that were torturously difficult to deal with.'

The 'big benefit' says Ahern looking back was 'the change between dealing with Blair and dealing with the Tories before Blair'. He recalls

Sir Patrick Mayhew raising the so-called 'Washington Three' decommissioning requirement and his own criticism then from the opposition benches in the Dáil: 'I was very critical because it was, in the eyes of republicans, being seen as "surrender". I remember some very senior Tory politicians saying "surely, Bertie, you can get them to say they're giving a bullet, just for the symbolism?" And of course that was the very point the Tories didn't understand. In the end the IRA gave in tons of arms. But it was the symbolism that equalled surrender, which is what the Tories wanted, which had created the circumstances along with the atmosphere not being very good here [in Dublin] in '95 and '96 that brought down the ceasefire. And what changed the situation, which I don't think Blair gets credit for, is how he changed that dynamic.'

Blair changed the dynamic and the two of them got us through to 1998. Still, I wonder, did they always get the balance right? Mr Ahern has explained how decommissioning wasn't going to happen in the 'surrender' terms sought by the Tories. Yet it was a requirement of the Irish state as well, wasn't it? Dick Spring when Tánaiste under Albert Reynolds had raised the issue of the 'giving up of arms' very early on. Does Mr Ahern think that he and Blair could have done more earlier to require the decommissioning, and that they might have saved David Trimble and the Ulster Unionist Party in the process?

'Yes, well you see it was the fact that it wasn't going to work the way people were talking about prior to 1998. Decommissioning was not a clause of the Good Friday Agreement. To set up an international body to examine the issue of decommissioning was what was in the Agreement of 1998. So what we had to do then was set about a way that would become meaningful and that hopefully would see the issue resolve itself. OK, it's done that now, except for the loyalists – that bit is still outstanding. Would it have been better if it had happened quicker? I did try to get Sinn Féin, after the Omagh bombing, to make that quick move and just go for it then because it was a very good circumstance. And I do think that window of opportunity was there. And I think if Trimble had done things just after that, and if Sinn Féin had done things after that, we certainly would have shortened the circuit and built more confidence. And it would have helped David Trimble, there's no doubt about that.'

Yet in autumn 2003, after the aborted negotiation that led to the debacle at Hillsborough, I remind Mr Ahern he later told the Dáil he'd had a sick feeling in his stomach and hadn't thought it a good idea at all to travel that day.

The former Taoiseach readily confirms: 'No, no and it wasn't. I knew that day wasn't going to work.' He knew there wasn't enough there for Trimble, or to carry Trimble through the ensuing election? 'No, what was wrong was that we had attempted to choreograph that particular negotiation and that particular day as we had done many times before but it didn't work – because the IRA had de Chastelain the night before, and he didn't get free until the following morning and there wasn't the time then for us to be very clear about what was decommissioned, what the benefit of that was, how we could sell that in a meaningful way. The whole thing had to be rushed, shoehorned into a very short space of time, which was never going to happen.'

With Trimble's fate hanging in the balance, why then didn't Taoiseach Ahern stop Blair in his tracks? 'I tried that morning,' he tells me. 'I tried to convince him that morning not to go, that we would just abort the day. But they [Downing Street] were adamant that we should go ahead. And I mean I knew from the fact that we hadn't had the contact with de Chastelain the previous evening. I waited here in this room. We were here till 2 o'clock in the morning. I'd said to Brian Cowen that we shouldn't travel at all that day. Tony was adamant we should. But I knew it wasn't working. It wasn't that there wasn't a sizeable amount of arms decommissioned. There was. But it was the fact that you were just trying to push it and raise it. It didn't give David a chance to talk to his Assembly Party, to sell the thing right and it was never going to work. And of course de Chastelain was tired.'

I want to come back to the consequence of that day but, first, to fast-forward then to 2006. Again, here he was, the Taoiseach, the keeper of the democratic state in Ireland. Never mind the British and whatever they were up to with the republican movement. Taoiseach Ahern had obligations to his own state. Did he never worry, particularly after the murder of Robert McCartney and after the Northern Bank robbery, that maybe he was being taken for a ride? That maybe the two governments were just too indulgent of the republican leadership, and that they would always come in short?

The speed of his answer suggests that Mr Ahern perhaps dwelt on such questions quite a lot. 'I was the one who went out and blew the whistle that time,' he says, in reference to what was then the biggest bank robbery in these islands: 'Everybody else was taking it nice and calm. The Northern Bank raid was on 19th December 2005. I was the one who went out on the Taoiseach's interview, on 'This Week' on the following Sunday, and spelled out precisely that this wasn't acceptable, that this was in fact the way for the DUP not having to do anything after the previous 8th December talks.' Mr Ahern also believes his intervention had the effect of changing the dynamic. 'Now I was mainly on about the Northern Bank raid at that stage. Robert McCartney came on 30th January, after the '72 commemoration of Bloody Sunday. So it was very clear on the Northern Bank raid where I stated my belief that it was the IRA. Now that created a lot of anxiety between me and Sinn Féin, as you know, for some considerable time. But that was my call, and it was a call I made. The British government had said nothing and incidentally none of the parties in the North had said anything either. And when I blew that, of course, when the Robert McCartney murder happened everybody was at it then because it was open season.'

This is fascinating terrain. Does Bertie Ahern think the British actually just would have preferred not to know? 'Well, I don't know,' he replies, seeming to confirm that very suspicion. 'But I decided to make that call for the very reasons that you outlined, that I wasn't going to be able to let that go. It's a call that I was glad I made because even though it created ferocious tension and ferocious suspicion on all sides for a while, it was better to get it out of the way because, in my view, and I don't think this can be argued … the fact that I took a very tough line on that created its own dynamic.'

I seem to remember, even as the Taoiseach was pointing the finger at the Provos, there were some unattributable British briefings suggesting that if it was the IRA it might prove a good thing because the money was probably going to pay the pensions of the IRA volunteers soon to be stood down. Nor is there anything faulty with Mr Ahern's powers of recall: 'That's stuff that was being clearly said at the time.'

So this was the kind of nonsense that was going on. And yet right up to St Andrews 2006, the Minister for Foreign Affairs and the Northern Ireland Secretary of State – even as Ahern and Blair were chasing the ultimate deal with Paisley – were still resisting the idea that Sinn Féin signing up to support the police was obviously going to be a condition of the deal?

The former Taoiseach casts his mind much further back to explain something of the difficulty of this issue: 'The Patten thing started in '98. I kept very close to Patten. At that time when he was doing the public meetings we followed him very carefully, and it was clear from the Patten Report that it could only be done by getting the reform of the RUC on the one side and, at the same time, us trying to convince all the nationalist parties that they had to play a real role in this. That was difficult. We spent hours on end in Weston Park bringing the Shinners through it. Hours. I recall one incident for Brian Cowen. I put Brian into a meeting with [Sinn Féin's] Gerry Kelly and the guys for hours, and he drove them mad. Brian's is not exactly my temperament, but he was going through line by line with Kelly for hours. And, of course, everything was an argument, everything was an issue and at the end of it they wouldn't agree to anything. But I was very happy. Weston Park wasn't the greatest success in 2001 but I was very happy that we were at least engaging with them on the substance of Patten.'

Maybe. But five years later in 2006, they were almost at a deal with Paisley, and the two governments look as if they're still scared to say to the Shinners, 'You've got to sign up and support the police. There's no ambiguity about it.' Incredibly, even after the bank robbery and the murder of Mr McCartney, Irish and British ministers were still saying policing couldn't be 'a precondition' for a deal?

Mr Ahern knows where this is headed and determines to stay true to diplomatic form: 'Whatever people were saying publicly it was being spelt out very, very clearly to them that they had to sign up to it. And I know that for poor old Trimble years earlier, if it had been at that stage, it would have been a big difference. I know that. But the point is, remember, from the republican side, they were trying to take guys with them who'd spent their lifetime in an armed struggle, trying to take them to support reformed policing. It was a huge, huge decision. Could it have been done quicker? We were trying to get them to do it from Weston Park, and we didn't get there until St Andrews. But all the time it was getting that bit better. Even before St Andrews there was good communication happening around parades between the Shinners and the police, so it wasn't that nothing was happening.'

And of course this was so difficult for Sinn Féin because endorsing the police was the final acceptance of the legitimacy of the British state? Mr Ahern has no doubt: 'Paisley could never have made the move he made unless there was an acceptance that policing was going to work. And the Shinners could never have made the decision unless there was an acceptance of the devolution of policing. That was the quid pro quo, which is hugely important.' With that issue left for new First Minister Peter Robinson and Deputy First Minister Martin McGuinness to resolve, Mr Ahern wants to emphasise the point about a prior understanding between the two sides. 'Just remember on that point, because I did that bit of the negotiations myself with Ian and with Gerry Adams, and it was the quid pro quo,' he confirms. 'Historically, one would not have happened without the other.'

Going back to 2003 when Tony Blair decided to go ahead and have the election, and trust to Trimble's luck holding one more time: Seamus Mallon has since claimed that it became a matter of British policy and Irish policy at certain levels in London and Dublin to deliberately lose the centre parties and facilitate the ascendancy of the DUP and Sinn Féin.

Mr Ahern is adamant: 'No, no that's not correct. It was the will of the people that the centre parties got squeezed. From our point of view both governments would have hoped that the SDLP and the UUP still would have done well. We would have hoped that both of them did well in that election, and we were concerned from what we were picking up – and particularly what the British government had from polls – that the centre was being squeezed. But we weren't going round relishing the idea of having to start dealing with Gerry Adams in a very strong position and Ian Paisley likewise. Perhaps there was a bit of inevitability but it didn't seem to us very easy, that we were going to be able to pick this up on the other side of the election ...'

If it hadn't come good in the end between Sinn Féin and the DUP, that presumably would have fundamentally been Blair's fault because Blair had made the key decision in the autumn of 2003 to proceed?

'Well, it was their call to proceed. In fact at times we wanted to go earlier, and other times we wanted to go later. We were trying to get the perfect time. That was October 2003, with the election in November 2003. My natural instinct was I would never go for a winter election. To be honest with you I was watching the SDLP's back more than I was watching anyone else's back. I just thought this was very difficult for the SDLP to go out on a winter election and be able to get the resources and the manpower to be able to equal the effort that I knew the Shinners would put in.'

Bertie Ahern I think understands why I'm dwelling on this. Like him I see no point second-guessing the free choice of the electorate. Yet it seems to many people that the big question, now that we have these two power blocks, is whether they can actually work. Because there is something in the temper and the character of both these parties which, I put it directly, Bertie Ahern himself would not much like. They each have a controlling nature. They represent very narrow sectional interests. Isn't there is a real question as to whether these two parties can take the situation forward and be the agents of change and reconciliation on the ground in Northern Ireland.

'Well, that's the challenge,' Bertie Ahern agrees, before adding that it need not present a problem for some time yet. 'When will that become a big issue? I don't think it has to happen for some years yet,' he says: 'The reality is that if the Agreement has worked as negotiated, and if the Assembly continues to be a very robust political debating house, and if the Executive are determined to work together, they'll have their political arguments, they'll have their tensions as any government has ... single party governments have tensions. The cross-party, cross-community, cross-religious divide is enormous. But if they keep their minds focused on what they're trying to achieve and to get away from the past and the violence of the past I don't see why it can't work.'

At the same time Mr Ahern anticipates an eventual demand to move away from the obligatory-coalition model at Stormont: 'There will come a time ... it's not going to be in the next four or five years in my view ... but there will come a time when that system will suffer because there is no natural opposition. That'll be the time. But that doesn't have to happen until we well put the violence behind.' So the system remains for the short to medium term more an instrument of conflict resolution than, necessarily, of good government? 'Exactly. People are working together. I mean it's a bit like what's happening in Germany at the moment. I mean – is the way the German government is at the moment, with all the big parties being together, is that the best form for German democracy? I'd say not. But it is what the people drew up. The only way of respecting the peoples' wills for peace and tranquillity and sustaining the future in Northern Ireland was to throw up that [1998] formulation. So there will come a time where people will say "you need an opposition, you need us and them". But there's no rush for that.'

He says there's no rush, and people who have invested much hope in the process will doubtless find reassurance here. Yet I recall the partnership proved difficult enough when David Trimble and Seamus Mallon were running it from the centre. How much more troublesome might it be for the DUP operating alongside Sinn Féin? Many in the DUP were discomfited by the "Chuckle Brothers" routine that came to characterise Dr Paisley's surprisingly warm relationship with Martin McGuinness. I suggest they were discomfited because many in the DUP still define themselves in terms of 'smashing Sinn Féin', or at least keeping republicans 'in their place' – while Sinn Féin insists the whole arrangement is but a transition on the way to Irish unity. Isn't it likely that this wholly unnatural structure will implode with those two parties driving it?

'I don't see why it will implode with Sinn Féin and the DUP because it's important for their own political credibility now to be able to show the people that they can work together. Have their differences, no problem about that. Arguing about education or exams or whatever, that's everyday politics. But I think their credibility as political parties has to be that they can manage and run Northern Ireland. And that's not to manage and run Northern Ireland, if you're a serious politician, just for your own party. I mean as Fianna Fáil were reminded longways back, you can't be Fianna Fáil running the Republic for Fianna Fáil. You have to be able to win support, to be able to go out to a middle ground or to pick up as much as you can of some extremes, otherwise you get nowhere. I think that's going to be the same for these two parties,' says Mr Ahern.

Yet in the here and now, next generations of Protestants and Catholics are being reared behind sectarian 'peace walls' in Belfast. The apartheid-state of living – with generations growing up never knowing anybody on the other side of the divide – that's all still going on. It's always seemed to me the next phase of this has to be reconciliation on the ground between those communities. You've got political structures, and politicians can agree certain things. Yet 'hearts and minds' on the ground are of a different order again. Surely Northern Ireland still needs reconciliation. And what I'm really wondering – given that Bertie Ahern really would not fancy the DUP in a month of Sundays, and that he's generally understood to detest Sinn Féin – is whether he really believes those parties can be the instruments of reconciliation?

'Well, the reconciliation has already happened,' he assures, citing various events and happenings attracting huge support particularly from younger people from both communities, and across the border in both directions. 'Now, a lot more has to happen, and a lot has to happen in the education system, trying to get people to participate a bit more in sports together and that. But I think that's happening and I don't see a difficulty quite frankly with either the DUP or the UUP along with the SDLP and the Shinners being able to make these changes. I think they're up for it. I mean listen, some people will be more reluctant, there's no doubt about that. But you would be a very brave politician in Northern Ireland in the coming years to stand up and say you're not in favour of this project going on, you want to go the reverse trend. I don't think that anyone will want to do that. They'll argue for their cause, and they'll argue whatever the issue is. But I think that there's an irreversible road of cooperation and of community involvement. Now will it happen without people working at it? Will it happen if the political establishment decide they want nothing to do with it? No it won't. But I think they would not be doing service to their mandates and to the people if they don't genuinely activate themselves in trying to make progress. I think they will. There's a few of them I'd be a bit sceptical of more than others. But will Peter Robinson and Martin McGuinness and the others push forward? I think they will.'

For all Mr Ahern's confidence, I wonder actually if Peter Robinson will be able to square the circle. He's got to face the 'Traditional Unionist Voice' challenge from former colleague Jim Allister, for example. Many unionists seemed willing to rally to the anti-agreement outsider despite Dr Paisley's strong influence. Might they not be more tempted to do so now faced perhaps with a less commanding Robinson leadership? Mr Ahern doesn't think so: 'Maybe, but I don't think so. I think it beholds all of us who care about the process to make sure that there's support for the people who are expressing a constructive, futuristic, modern, democratic role and not to give way to people who are trying to go back to extremes. It's extremes got us where we all were. So if you want to be a politician in Northern Ireland now you're going to have to be fair and open minded. Of course stand up for what you believe in and stand to your causes but you're going to have to do it in a way that has not been done for the last half century.'

There is always nervousness around change, and maybe, too, an unhelpful tendency to flex muscles. Might Sinn Féin be tempted to test Mr Robinson too early over things like devolution of policing and justice powers? Mr Ahern thinks not, while repeating that Sinn Féin 'had a cast iron guarantee that 1st May was the deadline' for achieving it. Cast iron? 'It was absolutely crystal clear from the British government and from everybody else.' But from the DUP? 'Everybody that would move. I mean there's no doubt May was the date.' Yet the DUP has consistently said it never signed up for the May 2008? 'Yeah well, I mean, listen,' says Mr Ahern, clearly unimpressed with any protestations to the contrary now. 'The devolution of policing from May was part of the deal in my view. OK, you can say that the governments didn't extract that from everyone in writing. We extracted nothing from them in writing but it was what the two governments agreed and everybody else agreed. But did Sinn Féin in any way ruffle that? No they didn't. I think they've been highly responsible. I think they've not created problems for either Paisley or Peter in this. They know that the changeover has to happen and they know that the negotiation process which is going on has to happen. So I think they've been very, very responsible. And I think they have to be given credit for that.'

Looking to the future, what risks does the former Taoiseach foresee? 'The risk is anybody trying to go backwards or breaking what was in the Good Friday Agreement or the St Andrews Agreement,' he says unsurprisingly. 'Maybe the tolerance of the first year won't hold as good. Maybe there'll be arguments around issues but once those arguments are on policies, once they're on issues, once people work together to try and get the quid pro quo ... and once people are tolerant of each other, I think they can continue to make progress.' Of more pressing concern to the former Taoiseach is the state of the global economy: 'Now, there's a big issue around the economy. I would rather see the world economy being kind of five years back to help Northern Ireland at this stage. I think economic risks will create maybe more tension. I think things are going to be much tighter and more difficult but that won't last too long. My advice to the politicians in the North, and I said this when I was last up there, is 'OK, this is a downturn maybe, 2008/2009, but it'll come back again. And Northern Ireland is going through a great period at the moment. I walked Belfast the other week for 40 minutes and I passed 19 different construction sites. So it's on an up. If they get over this bump, I think the work that's going on now will nearly bring them over the bump, then it needs more investment. It needs more renewal and they need more help on that. So I think the risk is on the economic side and we need to be constructive about helping them to get investment in because if you get investment in, you get jobs in. If you get jobs in you get people wanting homes, and if people want homes they'll settle down. And that's the thing it needs, an economic plus.'

In the light of all he has said it might seem absurd to ask. But elections, like changes of personnel, can also cause difficulty. In 2007 Sinn Féin suffered a massive setback in the Irish general election at Bertie Ahern's hands. Sinn Féin had harboured high ambitions and were left nowhere by the Irish electorate. Yet circumstances change. Bertie Ahern has just been talking about the effects of a global downturn. Who knows what circumstances Taoiseach Brian Cowen might face when it comes next to an Irish election. Isn't there always going to be a danger with Fianna Fáil/republican politics that, for all the antipathy and hostility, there could come a moment where the mutual interest and advantage of Fianna Fáil and Sinn Féin in the South would play to the detriment of the new dispensation in the North?

Bertie Ahern doesn't think so: 'I don't think there's any danger of that. I hope I've created this situation, where we've brought it to a position where everybody knows where we're going and nobody is going to go back to that. I hope I have brought the tolerance and respect of understanding very fully and fruitfully to the Unionist tradition. The things I've done on the Somme and the reconciliation of the Boyne, Articles 2 and 3, all of these things, there's huge support for this, and I don't think anyone's going to break away from that. You know, once the basis of consent is there ... and the line that Paisley was always happy with was when I said the constitutional issue was settled.'

How true is it to say that it's settled? 'It is settled. It's settled on the basis that the only way it can change is on the basis of consent. I mean if the people of the Republic of Ireland vote that the flag of green, white and gold is going to be pink, orange and red, you'd change it. You change things by democratic vote.'

In interviews given immediately after he left office Mr Ahern had seemed to be saying to people in both parts of this island, 'You know what folks, forget about the unity issue, this arrangement, this sharing of the island, this is the way it's going to be.' Did I get that right? 'This is the way it's going to go and ultimately other issues will come up again but it has to be done by personal persuasion. That's what Paisley said. It's movement by persuaders,' he affirms. So is it even worth anybody's while thinking about Irish unity? 'Oh yes, there'll be talk about it. It's still Article 1 in the Fianna Fáil Constitution,' he reminds me. But would 50 per cent plus one be a basis on which to achieve it? 'No, no,' he replies, clearly dismissive of the idea that unity could be accomplished on a simple sectarian headcount: 'Fifty plus one is not the way to do it. The only way it can be done is if there's a sizeable amount of people on the island of Ireland, north and south, believe this was the way forward. Fifty per cent plus one is not the way to do it. That would be a divisive thing to do. And there's no point in having votes that find out that you're 1 per cent short or 1 per cent over. That's not the way to do it.'

The evolution of Irish policy on Bertie Ahern's watch has been remarkable. Some involved in the earlier stages of the peace process had expected the easy part would fall to Ahern and Blair. Against that, one admirer insisted that Ahern inherited a pan-nationalist front and had to convert it into 'a pluralist peace process'. One predecessor as Taoiseach, Garret FitzGerald, also characterised the change in Irish policy as the recognition, driven in part by IRA violence, 'that the security interests of the Irish state required a stabilisation of the Northern Irish polity within the United Kingdom'. At the end of the day, wasn't that the ultimate achievement?

Bertie Ahern isn't going to answer for any of his predecessors: 'I just knew what my motivation was. One of the things that struck me being Lord Mayor of Dublin was that I was representing everybody in Dublin, and I had a dream time. I can say it now, 20 years back I was genuinely respected by everybody, it didn't matter who or what they were. I was invited to everything, I spoke at everything. I got huge press. I launched things as Lord Mayor that you wouldn't maybe otherwise have been asked to do. But it brought home to me, and I was relatively young then, that if you want to get things done you have to appeal out to a broader set. I worked after that at my own political philosophy to broaden Fianna Fáil's base, to stop the thing about single party government, to stop the thing about not looking for transfers [of votes from other parties], to stop thinking about not holding out the hand of friendship to Northern Ireland people. I went to university debates with Jeffrey Donaldson and others, way back before anything was happening, and I knew then it was a slow, slow process of actually building up contacts and friendships ... I realised there was another way of doing this and now I'm convinced that was the way to do it.'

But as the son of a republican and as an Irish republican himself, reared on unity and Articles 2 and 3 and all of that, did it cause him any pain? 'Oh it did. I mean there was a big risk. The biggest risk I took, undoubtedly, was convincing the party to go with me on Articles 2 and 3.' My understanding was that Taoiseach Ahern faced a lot of opposition on that? 'There was opposition,' he confirms. 'It was never huge but there was opposition and I had to spend hours on end in small groups convincing and persuading people. But in fairness to the party, I think that's why they trusted me afterwards, when they went with me on that. After I sat down with them and I went down the country with them, and I moved around with them and I talked to those who were waverers and I carried them with me, they stuck by it. The hardest thing to do was convince them that if we did this, we could make this work and that everyone would move with it.'

Finally, in terms of future risks – in his address to both houses of parliament in May 2007 the Taoiseach warned that this prize of peace would require continuing highest priority by the British as well as the Irish government. Isn't there a risk – because administrations get bogged down in current issues and crises – that the British might turn their attention away? 'I think that marker has to be put down, Frank, and people have to keep on saying that. You don't get a problem solved that's gone on for hundreds of years and then you close the file and say "that's fine now".'

Epilogue
Tony Blair's Irish peace

FROM *BLAIR'S BRITAIN*, EDITED BY ANTHONY SELDON,
(© CAMBRIDGE UNIVERSITY PRESS, 2007)

When he entered Downing Street on 2 May 1997, Tony Blair would not have believed the extent to which two conflicts – one ancient, one modern – would shape his premiership and inform his legacy. Nor that it would be a deal with the octogenarian Reverend Ian Paisley – sealed in his last days in Number 10 – that would enable the Prime Minister to set seemingly stable peace in Northern Ireland against the violent uncertainty to which he would have to leave Iraq.

It might not have been quite what the author of the famous email had in mind months before, advising on the orchestration of Blair's farewell tour, urging him to depart the stage leaving the crowds cheering for more. Cheering crowds would have been too much to expect in Belfast, where the antagonisms and scars of bitter division and brutal conflict would not be quickly excised. Indeed some on both sides had watched in disbelief as their tribal chieftains inched toward accommodation, convinced, hoping, praying ... that their leaders might still be engaged in an ever more elaborate version of the all-too-familiar 'blame game'.

Yet it was truly a remarkable moment at Stormont on 8 May 2007 when Blair, accompanied by Irish Taoiseach Bertie Ahern, watched Paisley and Sinn Féin's Martin McGuinness assume their joint office as First and Deputy First Ministers in Northern Ireland's new power-sharing Executive. And it would certainly be one for Blair to savour in the post-Downing Street years.

A HELPING HAND

But Blair could hardly have failed in Northern Ireland, could he? For had nationalist Ireland not already done much of the 'heavy lifting' by the time he arrived in power? Specifically, had the IRA not ensured politics would eventually triumph after concluding that republicans could not hope to force British withdrawal and Irish unification by means of 'the long war'?

The Conservatives would insist any assessment of the Blair government's conduct of the British economy should begin with its 'inheritance'. In Northern Ireland, too, the new Prime Minister owed much to those who had gone before. It would be right in any circumstances to acknowledge the cast of characters which contributed to the promising prospect that greeted Blair on his first visit to the province within weeks of taking office. It is also necessary to chart the evolution of the peace process to appreciate and contextualise the extraordinary developments that would occur on Blair's watch, and his contribution to them.

The Provisional IRA's original ceasefire of 31 August 1994 might have exploded with the bomb that killed two British civilians at Canary Wharf on 9 February 1996. However, the consensus remained – not least within the Northern Ireland Office (NIO) – that the bombing as much as anything reflected republican impatience with an exhausted Major government, perceived by then to be dependent on Ulster Unionist votes in the House of Commons. Unionists inevitably saw the bomb in the City of London as proof that the IRA's 'cessation' of operations was tactical and predicated on a guaranteed – united Ireland – outcome. Those British civil servants with access to the hard intelligence instead saw a republican leadership effectively marking time pending the commencement of fresh negotiations with an incoming Labour administration. When those negotiations finally got under way, moreover, the parties would discover that the essential framework of a political settlement – including dual referendums as the means of 'self-determination' by the peoples of Ireland – had been defined by visionary SDLP leader John Hume as far back as 1990.[1]

Soon after Margaret Thatcher and then Taoiseach Garret FitzGerald signed the 1985 Anglo-Irish Agreement, Hume had engaged in a personally and politically perilous attempt to persuade Sinn Féin president Gerry Adams that IRA violence was not only immoral but counterproductive. Hume's thesis was that the Thatcher/FitzGerald deal established for the first time British 'neutrality' on the question of the union of Great Britain and Northern Ireland. He was mistaken. Edward Heath's government had signalled it would have no desire to impede the realisation of Irish unity, should a majority seek it.[2] And the belief that Britain was 'neutral' on the constitutional issue certainly informed unionist fears through the long years of the ensuing 'troubles'. Perhaps it did not matter in the great scheme of unfolding events because republicans had not believed it until this point. Sceptics would counter that such matters of fact were too lightly discarded as the republicans searched for a new narrative with which, ultimately, to justify the end of their terrorist campaign. In any event, Hume's argument appeared to be given added validity in November 1990 when Margaret Thatcher's then Secretary of State, Peter Brooke, found utility in declaring that Britain had 'no selfish strategic or economic interest' in remaining in Northern Ireland. In fairness, Brooke's words were also apparently intended to signal an emotional allegiance to the union that only a majority for Irish unity could displace. However, and inevitably perhaps, the focus remained on the argument that it was primarily republican violence that gave the British reason to stay – and that London would present no obstacle if only nationalists and republicans could persuade unionists that their future lay outside the United Kingdom in some form of 'new' and 'agreed' Ireland.

It later emerged that from at least 1982 Adams had also been engaged in secret diplomacy with Redemptorist priest Fr Alec Reid, a largely unsung inspiration of what was known in the first instance as the 'Irish' peace process. Adams had also opened indirect contact the previous year with Charles Haughey, as the then Taoiseach sought to negotiate a resolution of the 1981 IRA hunger strikes with Prime Minister Thatcher. In August 1986, some months before Haughey was again elected Taoiseach, Fr Reid travelled to see him at his Georgian estate at Kinsealy outside Dublin. According to one authoritative account, this crucial discussion resulted in the first offer of an IRA ceasefire just nine months later and the subsequent creation of the strategy that would see the end of the IRA's long war against the British state in Northern Ireland.[3]

Others, too, helped shape and direct it, not least Irish diplomat Seán O hUiginn, regarded by many as the single most formidable exponent of Irish nationalism. Much attention focused for a time on proposals thought to have resulted from the famous 'Hume/Adams' dialogue. But O hUiginn was the intellectual driving force in the Irish Department of Foreign Affairs where Labour leader Dick Spring served as Foreign Minister in the 1992/94 Fianna Fáil/Labour coalition led by Taoiseach Albert Reynolds.

It is also necessary to record that the much-vaunted 'pan-nationalist front' in this period was hardly a seamless robe. The effort to bring the IRA and Sinn Féin into politics saw profound pressures brought to bear within the SDLP and upon successive coalition governments in Dublin. It could hardly have been otherwise as the 'constitutional' parties debated how far they would be prepared to go to accommodate republicans who continued to kill and bomb, and purported to do so 'in the name of the Irish people'.

This internal nationalist debate was graphically illustrated at one point when Spring disagreed with a proposal by Reynolds to present, as the Irish government's own, a draft joint declaration sent to it by the Provisional IRA. The draft was in fact a response to one that had originated from Reynolds' own emissary, the influential Martin Mansergh. At the core of this disagreement appears to have been Reynolds' plan to present the proposal to Major as a fait accompli. And it illuminated fundamental questions which – while illustrating the significant advance already made in republican thinking – also revealed the extent to which they would still have to travel if ever there was to be a successful engagement with unionists. On the one hand, the republican draft indicated acceptance that 'self-determination by the people of Ireland' would have to be achieved 'with the agreement and consent of the people of Northern Ireland'. Against that, the republican expectation seemed to be that, in return, London would have to accept that this act of self-determination would result in 'agreed independent structures for the whole island within an agreed time-frame'.[4]

It was precisely such ambiguities that unionists detected in the Joint Declaration for Peace issued by Reynolds and Major in December 1993 and the Joint Framework Documents concluded by Major and then Taoiseach John Bruton in February 1995. The need for the 'consent' of the people of Northern Ireland for constitutional change was there. So too, however, were proposals for new North/South institutions with 'executive, harmonising and consultative functions over a range of designated matters to be agreed'. Unionists regarded this as code for an embryonic all-Ireland parliament. Nor could it be said they were wrong, after Irish Foreign Minister David Andrews would declare the Irish intention was to see cross-border bodies operating with powers 'not unlike a government'.

Reynolds undoubtedly inspired his own officials and commanded the respect of Sinn Féin leaders. However, his apparent certainty about republican bona fides and his unshakeable 'can do' approach made life difficult for the Conservatives, not least by so discomfiting the unionists. Indeed, when Reynolds once famously asked 'Who's afraid of peace?' many unionists saw it as something of a threat.

Then Ulster Unionist leader James (Lord) Molyneaux would be widely ridiculed for suggesting that the emerging process had the capacity to 'destabilise' Northern Ireland. The point was not that unionists did not want peace – rather they feared 'the price' at which it was being offered and that might be paid for it. Nationalists and republicans might have warmed to the spectacle of President Clinton overriding British concerns in granting Adams a visa to visit the US at a crucial juncture. And Clinton, along with leading figures in 'Irish America', would fairly claim their share of the credit for the events leading to the negotiation of the Belfast Agreement in 1998 and the DUP/Sinn Féin settlement subsequently brokered by Blair and Taoiseach Ahern in 2007. Back in 1995, however, unionists were easily psyched by a 'pan-nationalist consensus' stretching all the way from the office of the Taoiseach to the Clinton White House, and by the expectations it fostered.

The surprise was that unionists reacted as calmly as they did to the revelation of the Major government's own secret 'back channel' to the IRA. And some of them – including loyalist paramilitary spokesmen like Gusty Spence, Gary McMichael and the late David Ervine – attempted to make fairly sophisticated assessments of their own about the IRA's intentions. Major's Secretary of State, Sir Patrick Mayhew, and his deputy, Michael Ancram, also provided protection for unionists in the three-stranded talks process that would be the basis for the negotiation of the Belfast Agreement, and, above all, with the so-called 'triple lock' requiring that any outcome be acceptable to the parties and people of Northern Ireland and parliament at Westminster. However, it would be some time before it became clear that there was no 'secret deal' on an agreed outcome between the British and the Provisionals. Moreover, the Conservatives had 'form', most recently in the shape of the 1985 Anglo-Irish Agreement. It was perhaps not totally surprising then that Molyneaux's successor, David (Lord) Trimble, decided he could get a better deal from Blair – notwithstanding Labour's traditional policy of seeking Irish unity by consent.

NEW LABOUR, NEW POLICY

In one particularly memorable interview during the Iraq war, Blair defended his policy in respect of 'liberal interventionism' and the American alliance, suggesting the situation was worse than the Labour left suspected – that he actually believed in these things.

As with Iraq, so in Northern Ireland people would frequently ask whether the Prime Minister believed in anything much at all and, more to the point, whether anything he said was to be trusted. The read-across from the international crisis – and the recurring question of 'trust' – would certainly inform thinking and reinforce prejudices across the Northern Ireland divide. For nationalists and republicans, evidence that the Blair government and its security services manipulated the intelligence about Saddam Hussein's alleged weapons of mass destruction would be taken as proof of the unchanging character and nature of 'perfidious Albion'. Despite the support of their MPs for the war, meanwhile, many unionists were reminded of past American support for the IRA and thought Blair guilty of double standards – tough on terrorism abroad while accommodating its perpetrators and apologists at home.

Unacknowledged for the most part was what for some was the biggest paradox of all: the insistence of Anglo-Irish policy that Sinn Féin be included as of right in an Executive in Belfast, while the Ahern government maintained the party had not satisfied the democratic test, and therefore remained unfit for ministerial office in the Republic.

Blair finally addressed this issue in a speech in October 2002, admitting: 'To this blunt question: "how come the Irish government won't allow Sinn Féin to be in government in the South until the IRA ceases its activity, but unionists must have them in government in the North?", there are many sophisticated answers. But no answer as simple, telling and direct as the question.'

Blair was speaking during the crisis sparked by the discovery of an alleged republican 'spy ring' at the heart of the Stormont administration, warning that he could not continue 'with the IRA half in, half out of the process'. Yet he obviously never thought to transform the situation by answering the 'blunt question' himself, and telling Dublin that he would no longer tolerate the paradox and that the question of devolution for the North would be put on hold until the South resolved its own republican problem.

In posing the question, the Prime Minister at least acknowledged its effect on unionist opinion. But did he actually share their sense of grievance? What was the merit in identifying a problem while doing nothing to seek its resolution? Was this not evidence rather of Blair's willingness to say what seemed to be required at any particular moment in time? As described above, much of the big thinking, and structural and administrative preparation, had preceded him. Did he have any strong views of his own about what would constitute a legitimate settlement in Northern Ireland? Or was the search for peace there simply one of those 'eye-catching initiatives' with which (courtesy of another embarrassing leaked email) we knew he liked to be associated?

Those irreconcilables who damn Blair and all his works would doubtless have him denied even his Irish peace prize and cheerfully answer this last question in the affirmative. However, the answer – at least in the 'big picture' terms that Blair himself liked to speak – must surely be 'no'.

Blair could certainly be inconsistent. His short-termism and lack of attention to detail would infuriate many. And he was indisputably capable of saying different things to different people. In this, however, he appeared to share a particular prime ministerial skill with his predecessor. On many occasions journalists had listened open-mouthed outside Number 10 as Northern Ireland's politicians left meetings with Major absolutely convinced that the Prime Minister was on their side. Downing Street seemed to have that effect on players from all sides.

However, from his earliest days as Opposition leader, Blair was telling anyone who would listen that he would be firmly on the side of those seeking an accommodation and an end to the conflict. Rather like in that Iraq interview, he also gave notice that he would be in it for the long haul. And, vitally, he made the policy adjustment that would give him the prospect of succeeding where so many others had failed.

Few were paying much attention in September 1995 when Blair told *The Irish Times* he expected Northern Ireland would prove 'as important an issue' as any that would confront him in British politics.[5] On the eve of a trip to Dublin, Londonderry and Belfast he was hardly going to admit that the British public were monumentally bored with the subject – or that he would have 'bigger fish to fry' as an incoming Prime Minister following Labour's eighteen years in opposition.

Yet that had been precisely the fear harboured in Dublin. Mo Mowlam, the Opposition spokesperson who would become his first Secretary of State for Northern Ireland, performed an important role in maintaining Irish faith. During one encounter in the Travellers Club in London Blair likewise assured senior NIO officials that he would be 'free to act' on Northern Ireland and would not be 'tied by party issues' of the kind perceived to have inhibited Major.

This might have appeared to be a reference to the 'High Tory Unionist' tradition that found expression from time to time through people like Viscount (Robert) Cranborne, then Conservative leader in the House of Lords. It did not, however, portend a Labour lurch in an anti-unionist direction. On the contrary, while Mowlam schmoozed nationalists and republicans – and set the scene for the restoration of the IRA ceasefire and Sinn Féin's speedy admission to talks – Blair had already embarked on his own charm offensive with the unionists.

Not yet reconciled to the principle of 'consent' – and thus Northern Ireland's right to say 'No' – republicans wanted Blair to assume the role Major had declined, and act as a 'persuader' for Irish unity. In his *Irish Times* interview Blair made clear he would be doing nothing of the sort. Confirming his change in Labour's 'unity by consent' policy, Blair said: 'I believe the most sensible role for us is to be facilitators, not persuaders in this, not trying to pressure or push people towards a particular objective.' Declaring himself 'easy either way' as to whether Northern Ireland stayed in the United Kingdom or joined a united Ireland, he replied: 'What I personally want to see is the wishes of the people there adhered to ... If it is their consent that matters, and their wishes that are uppermost, then that is what I want to see implemented.' He was also clear: 'If I was to sit here and say "well, I want to give effect to the wishes of the people of Northern Ireland but I'm going to be in there trying to tell them they've got to unite with the South", the only result of that would be to incapacitate my government from playing a proper role.'

This was painful for supporters of Labour's traditional Irish policy. But, as with Iraq, so in respect of Northern Ireland it might prove even worse than they thought. Some may have comforted themselves that Blair's policy shift was about presentation, the compulsion to tack to the Tory position, the desperate need not to be seen or cast as 'soft on terrorism'. Others doubtless hoped there was 'New Labour' artifice here, designed to lure unionists into negotiations in which they would inevitably lose ground. In fact, Blair had set Labour on a path beyond ostensible 'neutrality' on Northern Ireland's constitutional position to one of effective support for maintaining the union.

In observing this, it is not necessary to contend that Blair started out from a position of high principle, or with a carefully considered plan. He never planned his relationship with President George W. Bush, and obviously could not have known how the events of 9/11 would recast his entire foreign policy. But few would doubt that he became a believer. In one respect, indeed, it is possible that Blair's war experiences reinforced his sense of 'the United Kingdom'. Even if for purely pragmatic and presentational reasons, Blair would also be able to argue that Northern Ireland could not exclude itself from his government's UK-wide devolution project. And by the time the rising nationalist tide overwhelmed Labour in Scotland in 2007, Blair, like Gordon Brown, was ever more insistent that the Kingdom was greater than the sum of its parts.

Whatever his original motivation, Blair made Belfast the port of call for his first official trip outside London following the 1997 general election. Fresh from electoral triumph, and plainly feeling anything but incapacitated, he assured his audience this was no accident: 'I said before the election that Northern Ireland was every bit as important to me as for my predecessor. I will honour that pledge in full.' Their destination was clear, said Blair: 'To see a fair political settlement in

Northern Ireland – one that lasts, because it is based on the will and consent of the people here.' But so too was the context. Assuring them that his agenda was 'not a united Ireland', the young Prime Minister ventured to say that none in his audience were likely to see it in their lifetime. Then he declared: 'Northern Ireland is part of the United Kingdom, alongside England, Scotland and Wales. The union binds the four parts of the United Kingdom together. I believe in the United Kingdom. I value the union.'

This was music to the ears of Trimble, who had already decided Blair was a man with whom he would do business. However, their subsequent successful enterprise would rely heavily on a third 'moderniser'. In June 1997 Bertie Ahern became Taoiseach for the first time. And it would be Ahern's ground-breaking engagement with Trimble – and, in particular, his subsequent willingness to withdraw the Irish constitutional claim to Northern Ireland in face of fierce resistance within the Irish system – that would finally enable Blair to put the union on a secure footing.

It would be a very different union, with compulsory power-sharing between unionists and nationalists and republicans, an effective dual premiership at Stormont, checks, balances and mutual vetoes in an unprecedented system of devolved government bound to the principles of equality and 'parity of esteem', and tied to an over-arching North/South and East/West British–Irish framework. In strict constitutional terms, however, Blair's eventual bequest would give unionism the best deal available from any British Prime Minister in fifty years.

As the original civil rights crisis erupted in the late 1960s, Prime Minister Harold Wilson actively pursued a fifteen-year plan for Irish unification. Heath's government was seen as instinctively anti-unionist and abolished the discredited Stormont parliament in 1972. And the 'most unionist' of them all, Thatcher, had excluded unionists from the process leading to the 1985 Anglo-Irish Agreement that for the first time formally recognised Dublin's interest in, and right to be consulted about, Northern Ireland.

The subsequent Belfast Agreement secured by Blair and Ahern on Good Friday, 10 April 1998 would trigger the biggest crisis within unionism since the early 1970s, and eventually see Paisley's Democratic Unionists supplant the once hegemonic Ulster Unionist Party. Yet by May 2007 DUP ministers in Belfast would be echoing Trimble, loudly trumpeting that Northern Ireland's constitutional position was secure, and likely to grow even more so following the restoration of devolved government (though this would seem at least questionable).

Perhaps British policy would have naturally evolved in this way after the IRA abandoned its violent campaign. Ironically, too, the IRA's violence had forced a fundamental Irish rethink of what Garret FitzGerald describes as 'the counterproductive and provocative anti-partition policy' to which the parties in the Republic had committed themselves between 1949 and 1969: 'It also forced a recognition that the security interests of the Irish state required a stabilisation of the Northern Irish polity within the UK.'[6] The fact, however, is that it only finally happened on Blair's watch.

THE HAND OF HISTORY

The Prime Minister would be mocked mercilessly after first feeling the 'hand of history' during an emergency dash to the province in April 1998. His task then was to save the inter-party talks chaired by former US Senator George Mitchell. With only days left to what would prove the first of many British–Irish 'deadlines', the Ulster Unionists and the moderate Alliance Party had reacted angrily to the first draft of an agreement presented by the independent international chairman. 'If Tony Blair wants an agreement he'd better get over here fast' was the terse message from then Alliance leader John (Lord) Alderdice. Trimble's private communication to Blair's chief of staff Jonathan Powell, meanwhile, ensured the Downing Street cavalry were already on their way. And of course Powell himself was a vital member of the elite troop. Acting as Blair's 'shock absorber' and 'early warning system', as well as 'interface' for Blair's Northern Ireland strategy across other departments of government, this unusual 'civil servant' would also at times be expected to go to places and talk to people when and where prevailing political conditions decreed that a Prime Minister or Secretary of State could not.

Ironically, given what was to pass in 2007, a crowd of Paisleyites were on hand to jeer Blair's arrival at Hillsborough Castle and, they hoped, to witness his failure. There was seemingly no guarantee that he would succeed.

Senator Mitchell would later suggest that Paisley's decision to boycott the original inter-party talks actually cut Trimble the necessary slack with which to make the first landmark Agreement from which all else would subsequently flow. However, there was little sign of it on 7 April as Mowlam welcomed her Prime Minister to the Queen's official residence in Northern Ireland. Blair was pessimistic, his communications director Alastair Campbell apparently even more so.[7] Yet in an episode that might have made even the legendary spin-doctor blush, Blair appeared to experience one of his 'Princess Diana' moments. Just in time for the early evening news and with no hint of embarrassment, the Prime Minister solemnly declared: 'Now is not the time for sound bites, we can leave those at home. I feel the hand of history upon our shoulders.'

This was classic Blair, oblivious to ridicule, commanding attention to that 'big picture'. And 'history' would indeed be made just three days later, and less than twenty-four hours beyond the original dead-line. A full quarter of a century after the then Ulster Unionist and SDLP leaders Brian Faulkner and Gerry Fitt had attempted it in the Sunningdale Agreement, here was a power-sharing settlement to be driven by the constitutional 'centre parties' in what Seamus Mallon – Hume's subsequent nominee for Deputy First Minister in the first Executive – would characterise as 'Sunningdale for slow learners'.

In spite of Hume's pre-eminence – and that he and Trimble would subsequently share the Nobel Peace Prize – Mallon was the acclaimed SDLP star of this negotiation. Like many others he wept tears of joy on the final morning after what he described as 'the greatest night' in a long political career.

The tears were, of course, fuelled in part by the sheer exhaustion of some of the principals. The conflicting briefings of the rival parties also pointed to what Adams correctly predicted would be 'trench war-fare' still to come. Yes, it was possible that day to anticipate the light after Northern Ireland's long darkness. Yet, as a triumphant and final-ly vindicated Hume reminded, this was not so much the end, or even the beginning of the end, more the end of the beginning.

From the outset controversy attached to a 'side-bar letter' given by Blair to Trimble even as Mitchell prepared to unveil the final Agreement. In it the Prime Minister assured the UUP leader that if the Agreement's provisions for excluding ministers who failed to honour the commit-ment to exclusively peaceful means proved ineffective, he (Blair) would change them. This spoke directly to continuing unionist concerns about the 'conditional' nature of the republican movement's participation in the political process and, of course, to the issue of republican weapons that had dogged the process since the first IRA ceasefire.

It would become a commonplace that the question of 'decommis-sioning' had been a particularly unhelpful invention by the Major government. In fact, Tánaiste Spring had been among the first to sug-gest that ceasefires would have to be followed by 'a handing up of arms'. Echoing this, Major and Mayhew argued that disarmament was rendered necessary by the IRA's refusal to confirm that its cessa-tion was 'permanent' and intended to hold in all circumstances.

In what would become a familiar theme explaining many subsequent controversies from the republican perspective, Adams and McGuinness characterised the decommissioning demand as evidence of an agenda devised by British 'securocrats' (MI5 and other servants of the secret state) intent on republican humiliation and defeat. However, the response from Sir John Chilcot, former permanent secretary at the NIO, is compelling and accords with the objective political realities. According to him, decommissioning was 'the snake coiled at the heart of the peace process' and 'an inescapable physical and political problem which had to be addressed in the full knowledge of all the republican history, sentiment and resistance surrounding it'. For Trimble, certainly, it became the litmus test of the republican commitment to the Mitchell Principles of exclusively peaceful and democratic means.[8] This translated into a UUP policy proclaiming the simple message: 'no guns, no government'.

Unfortunately for Trimble, it would never be so simple. Secretary of State Mowlam eventually finessed the issue, declaring IRA and loyalist paramilitary disarmament 'an obligation' under the Agreement. However, she and Blair sided with Sinn Féin, the SDLP and the Irish against Trimble – upholding their view that the Agreement did not stipulate decommissioning as a 'precondition' for Sinn Féin's entry into government.

They were right, and the seeds were sown of Trimble's eventual downfall. The Agreement placed an obligation on the parties to use such influence as they had to secure decommissioning by May 2000. And Mallon at one point – in an initiative conspicuously not taken up by the rest of his party or the Irish government – expressed a willingness to see Sinn Féin ministers expelled from office if the IRA did not meet the May 2000 target date. Trimble, moreover, would contend that he never abandoned the 'no guns, no government' policy – continuing his effort to disarm the IRA through the suspensions of the Executive forced by him in 2000 and 2002.

However, his failure to make it a condition of the Agreement foretold the scenario in November 1999 when he was finally forced to 'jump first' into government with Sinn Féin, albeit with a post-dated letter of resignation that would oblige Mowlam's successor Peter Mandelson to impose the first suspension just six weeks later.

In taking the power to do so, Mandelson faced stern opposition from Sinn Féin and the SDLP, as well as the Irish government and the Clinton administration. They viewed this exercise of British sovereign power as a clear breach of the international treaty that was the Belfast Agreement. The calculation in Downing Street and the NIO, however, was that they had no choice, since there was no guarantee that Trimble, if allowed to resign, would secure a unionist majority in the Assembly for his re-election as First Minister.

The Belfast Agreement had won a spectacularly fair wind by way of popular endorsement in the dual referendums held simultaneously in May 1998 in Northern Ireland and the Republic. Private polling ordered by Tom Kelly – then Mowlam's communications director, later to become Blair's official spokesman and a significant player in relation to Northern Ireland policy – suggested the vote in Northern Ireland could be lost. Senior SDLP and Irish figures would complain bitterly that Blair took terrible liberties with the Agreement in order to assuage unionist doubts about decommissioning and the proposed release of paramilitary prisoners. But they would at least acknowledge that it was Blair's campaigning zeal – and the solemn 'pledges' written in his own hand, albeit broken at great cost to Trimble – that saved the day.

Blair, however, could not return to the fray for the 'internal' Northern Ireland elections to the new Assembly the following month. And it was at this point – beset by critics in his own party led by MP Jeffrey Donaldson – that Trimble fell short of a secure majority and found himself effectively 'holed below the water line'.

True to form, Paisley, then still the minority unionist leader, had characterised the Agreement as another 'sell out' on the road to a united Ireland. In this, and his subsequently successful effort to destroy Trimble's majority leadership, he would be greatly assisted by Adams' repeated assertion that the Agreement provided for a 'transition' to Irish unity.

Trimble's counter-argument was that the IRA and Sinn Féin had in fact been fought to a standstill by the British state and brought to accept a 'partitionist' settlement. To his mind, Adams' talk of transition to unity was strictly for the birds – necessary rhetoric to keep the republican troops on board as the republican movement made the all-important 'transition' from terror to democracy. In this, crucially, Trimble was bolstered by the acceptance of the principle of 'consent' for any future change in the constitutional position – and Ahern's final amendment of Articles 2 and 3 of the Irish Constitution withdrawing the Republic's formal claim to the territory of Northern Ireland.

After the high-water mark of the referendums, however, unionists showed an increasing tendency to believe Adams and Paisley over any assurance by Trimble and Blair. First Minister Trimble would also be further undone both by the explicit provisions of the Agreement and – more corrosive still – by his failure to have secured on decommissioning that which he said was necessary to sustain unionist confidence.

The release of loyalist and republican prisoners and the reform of the Royal Ulster Constabulary – complete with the removal of its royal title – strengthened and emboldened Trimble's internal enemies and DUP rivals. To which might be added that Trimble himself often appeared conflicted about the Agreement he had signed. Something of the intense pressure on the man was certainly reflected by his initial welcome for the legislation effecting the prisoner releases, and his subsequent decision to vote against it in the Commons. Policing reform was likewise always going to be neuralgic from the unionist perspective. Yet Trimble and his party appeared in denial about the really quite predictable proposals of the international commission led by former Conservative Party chairman Chris (Lord) Patten.

The Patten Commission was specifically tasked to advise on the culture and ethos of the policing service, and it was widely expected, at minimum, that Patten would propose the removal of titles and emblems exclusively identifying the police with the symbolism of the British state. Long after it was credible to do so, Ulster Unionists maintained that since Northern Ireland's constitutional position had been accepted, the symbols of its Britishness could hardly be in dispute. Nationalists and republicans countered that they had not made the Agreement in order themselves to become unionists, and that the Agreement established their right to regard themselves as Irish while promising 'parity of esteem' for their tradition. For all the furore, critics of Trimble's handling of this issue would also note that, while denouncing Patten, his party (and Paisley's DUP) took their positions on the new Policing Board and cooperated enthusiastically with the new dispensation. Indeed Trimble would subsequently venture that its ultimate success would see the recruitment of officers to the 'new' Police Service of Northern Ireland (PSNI) from within the republican community.[9]

In the final event, however, it was the admitted opacity[10] over decommissioning – and the inevitable requirement that Trimble 'jump first' into government with Sinn Féin, having said that he would not – that marked the beginning of the loss of trust that would contribute to Paisley's triumph in the second Assembly elections held in November 2003.

Trimble refuses to concede that he might have been 'suckered' by Blair and suggests that – even as it was being hailed around the world – he regarded the Belfast Agreement as a work-in-progress. 'I knew there were battles still to come, that there was going to be a battle over putting the IRA out of business,' he would say later. 'But for me on 10 April 1998 having an agreement – yes, with that battle still to fight – was much better than having no agreement, and the world blaming me for there not being one.'[11]

The price of international approbation, however, was disillusionment and increasing vulnerability on the home front. In failing to resolve the issue with Blair in the week of the Good Friday negotiation, Trimble left an enormous hostage to Paisley's subsequent electoral good fortune. Unbelievably, too, in neglecting to stipulate republican support for the PSNI as the price of participation in government, Trimble also left Paisley a trump card to play in the 2006 St Andrews negotiations leading to the 2007 settlement between the DUP and Sinn Féin.

Reg Empey, who succeeded Trimble after the party's rout in the 2005 general election, would frequently complain that they had done all the 'heavy lifting', making the task easier in turn for Paisley's DUP. And as the so-called 'extremes' themselves began converging on the centre ground, some veterans of the process would reflect that there had perhaps been something almost inevitable about the eclipse of the moderate Ulster Unionists and the SDLP.

However, Blair could see no inevitably happy outcome in November 2003 when he realised, too late, that he had trusted to Trimble's luck holding once too often. Trimble would subsequently admit that 'hubris' led him to think he could negotiate a better deal with Adams in the late summer of 2003 than Blair and Ahern had managed.[12] And he would compound his internal difficulties with an extraordinarily ill-considered attempt to expel Donaldson and two other dissident MPs from his parliamentary party. In such circumstances the UUP leader did astoundingly well to trail Paisley's DUP by just three seats when the 2003 Assembly election count was completed. However, Donaldson's prompt defection to the DUP along with two colleagues instantly transformed Paisley's margin of advantage – one that would see the DUP take nine Westminster seats in the ensuing general election while Trimble lost his own and saw his party reduced to one seat in the new House of Commons.

Blair was downcast, and took time to convince that there was the remotest possibility of rebuilding the essential architecture of the Belfast Agreement during Paisley's reign as undisputed leader of Ulster's unionists. In invoking 'history', the Prime Minister had risked its cruel rebuke. After all, equally great if not greater men and women than him had sought to end centuries of conflict in and about Ireland.

It would also be entirely in character that Paisley – the self-styled 'Dr No' of unionist politics – might think to see Blair off, as he had done Wilson, Heath, Callaghan, Thatcher and Major before him.

'History', its hand and its challenge, would be invoked again and again through the tortuous and interminable negotiations that followed in Downing Street, Lancaster House and Leeds Castle. However, when the putative 'Comprehensive Agreement' failed in December 2004 – again on the issue of verifiable IRA decommissioning, and after Paisley demanded republicans wear 'sackcloth and ashes' in token of their repentance – that call to history came to be regarded as devalued currency in a process that began to look like an end in itself. Within days of that attempt, police in both states were blaming the IRA for the £26.5 million Northern Bank robbery. And by the time President Bush snubbed Adams in favour of the sisters of murdered Belfast man Robert McCartney at the annual St Patrick's Day festivities in Washington the following March, the wheels looked finally to have come off the peace train.

Amazingly, though, Blair's own luck was to hold, and suddenly it seemed he would not be denied the prize after all. It would not be until January 2007 that it became clear that Paisley had overruled the strong instinct of some of his closest colleagues to deny Blair and 'wait for Gordon' (Brown) before concluding a settlement. By that stage, however, a most unlikely relationship had developed between the two men. There would be suggestions that they liked to discuss theology, although – with Blair reportedly contemplating conversion to Rome – it would seem likely that speculation along these lines was overheated. Yet the famous Blair 'empathy' was undoubtedly once more in play. And the Prime Minister grew convinced that Paisley sensed the time right for a settlement provided Sinn Féin met his terms on decommissioning and, crucially, agreed to 'cross the Rubicon' and finally accept the legitimacy of the Northern Ireland state by fully endorsing the police. Blair was lucky also in that, while fast approaching his own 'sell by' date, he found himself dealing with an ageing DUP leader also in something of a hurry to secure a more satisfactory 'legacy'.

So the world watched in disbelief as television beamed the remarkable images of Paisley and Adams sitting down together at Stormont on 26 March 2007 to seal their very own DUP/Sinn Féin agreement. And there would be tears again too, this time in the Republic a week later, as Dr Paisley shook hands with Taoiseach Ahern and declared a new era in relations between Northern Ireland and the Republic.

Thus Blair's Irish 'legacy' was secured at the last gasp. And many of those who played their part along the way would testify to the Prime Minister's heroic role, time and again citing his extraordinary tenacity and commitment. Yet, about a man never knowingly undersold by the Downing Street spin-doctors, such descriptions themselves suddenly appeared to err on the side of historic understatement.

Introducing the honoured guest to address both houses of parliament in the Royal Gallery at Westminster on 15 May 2007, Blair was equally clear that he could not have done it without Taoiseach Ahern. And rightly so. Various 'solutions' had been tried before, each assuring unionists that the principle of 'consent' was sacrosanct, and all of them invalidated in unionist eyes by the Republic's territorial claim to Northern Ireland. Had Ahern not amended Articles 2 and 3 of his country's Constitution, there would have been no engagement with Trimble, no Belfast Agreement, and certainly no Paisley goodwill trip to Dublin.

During the final stages of the 2007 negotiations, Peter Hain, who had succeeded John Reid at the Northern Ireland Office, specifically warned the DUP they could not count on anything like the same level of commitment or interest from any alternative Labour Prime Minister. With Blair's departure and Labour's leadership election hovering into view, the specific message was that Prime Minister Gordon Brown would have more compelling priorities before attempting to win a fourth term in office. Some close to Paisley suspected an element of bluff. Interestingly, however, they decided not to call it, and they were probably wise. Of course, Brown would not have rejected a peace deal early on his watch. However, the ever present risk, frequently cited by Ahern in particular, was of 'events' – whether planned by 'dissident' republicans or others – that might see the process derailed. Mandelson might strike a chord when he complained that for Blair at times the 'process' was indeed everything, its maintenance if not forward movement necessary if only to ensure things did not slip back.[13] Yet after the extraordinary events of May 2007, who would say that Blair had been wrong?

RIGHT AND WRONG

Was there a moral dimension to making peace? And did Blair – 'a guy with a moral dimension to everything' – observe it? The Prime Minister would retire to worldwide acclaim for bringing people and parties not always famed for being on the side of 'good' to a new, common and peaceful purpose. So many would find it surprising that, by this writing, former Deputy First Minister Mallon should have emerged as

Blair's sharpest critic – openly suggesting that the Prime Minister was 'amoral' in his political dealings and 'didn't know the meaning of the word "honesty".[14]

Downing Street was dismissive when Mandelson accused Blair of at times 'conceding and capitulating' to republicans. But they were surely stung when Mallon, in the same newspaper series, described Blair as a man who would 'buy' and 'sell' anyone, while accusing London and Dublin of deliberately disposing of the 'centre parties' in favour of 'the extremes' represented by the DUP and Sinn Féin. 'It was strategy,' Mallon would insist. 'You had people like Jonathan Powell and others in Dublin who had decided that to make this work you had to dispense with middle unionism and middle nationalism. I think it was as calculated as that.'

The inevitable retort would be 'sour grapes' on the part of Mallon, who had failed, after all, along with First Minister Trimble, to 'make it work' and thus preserve the moderate centre. While admitting the question also in his own mind, the impact of Mallon's charge would be lessened by Trimble's belief that 'Blair was probably the last one to buy into the NIO view that this [DUP/Sinn Féin ascendancy] had to happen'.[15]

Mallon's contention is that Blair betrayed Trimble by allowing the fateful 2003 Assembly election to proceed despite the failure of General John de Chastelain, head of the Independent International Commission on Decommissioning, to report on IRA disarmament with the detail and transparency demanded by Trimble and deemed necessary for his political survival.

In fairness to Blair, Trimble recalls that SDLP leader Mark Durkan was with the Irish and the Americans in pressing Blair that the election, already twice postponed by London, must proceed. Trimble's natural temptation to conclude that perhaps he was 'sold short' by Blair is also tempered by his experience that – on the issue of decommissioning – the SDLP had invariably sided with Sinn Féin against him.

That said, Trimble would share the underlying concern reflected by Mallon, and by Durkan, before the 2007 Assembly elections, when he asked: 'Can the parties that gave us the worst of our past [Sinn Féin and the DUP] give us the best of our future?'

Admirers of 'realpolitik' would rightly dismiss complaints about the verdict ultimately delivered by the electorate. And they would draw comforting signs from the early days of the new Stormont administration that the DUP and Sinn Féin might actually make a better job of working the partnership arrangement than the Ulster

Unionists and the SDLP had managed.

However, the Durkan question would find a resonance among many people who genuinely wished to see the new power-sharing venture succeed. It would be attended by continuing and legitimate questioning as to whether it had been necessary for Blair to lose the two parties – the UUP and SDLP – seen to protect and defend politics through more than thirty years of assault by republican violence and DUP sectarianism and intransigence. Many close observers would remain convinced that Sinn Féin had played a deliberately 'long peace' in pursuit of its goal to supplant the SDLP in preparation for a bid for power in the Irish Republic, which failed badly in the May 2007 Irish election. Had Prime Minister Blair been too indulgent of a republican leadership plainly seeking a way out of violence while maximising its leverage through continual internal 'management' problems? And specifically – following the 9/11 outrages in America, said by Blair and Bush to have changed the global climate in relation to terrorism and its toleration – should Blair have demanded better, tougher terms, and earlier, from a republican leadership for whom there really was now no going 'back to war'?

Looking forward rather than back, there will be uneasy, still-to-be answered questions too about the 'character' of Northern Ireland's new political elite. Having seized power, will the DUP and Sinn Féin prove capable of genuinely 'sharing' it for the common good? Can commitments to justice and equality have meaning without a shared commitment to reconciliation between communities still living a segregated, 'apartheid' existence behind the so-called 'peace walls'? Will declared republican support for the police be reflected in the cultivation of a culture of lawfulness and the breaking of paramilitary control on both sides? Crucially, will devolution provide a settlement finally permitting the development – never before experienced – of a common commitment to a place called 'Northern Ireland'? And, while plainly desired by unionists, how would that sit with Sinn Féin's insistence set on 'process' and 'transition' leading to Irish unity?

Questions. Blair's great promise to the people of Northern Ireland was that, henceforth, such questions would be explored and addressed in conditions of peace and with a commitment on all sides to purely peaceful and democratic means. In delivering that transformation, this British Prime Minister really did make history in Ireland. Even he, of course, could not have thought to end it.

NOTES

1. John Hume interview, *The Irish Times*, 13 January 1989.
2. British Green Paper, 1972, IFB no. 117004987.
3. E. Moloney, *A Secret History of the IRA* (Harmondsworth: Penguin/Allen Lane, 2002), pp.261–2.
4. F. Finlay, *Snakes and Ladders* (Dublin: New Island Books, 1998), pp.188–9.
5. Tony Blair interview, *The Irish Times*, 4 September 1995.
6. Garret FitzGerald article, *The Irish Times*, 19 May 2007.
7. A. Rawnsley, *Servants of the People* (Harmondsworth: Penguin, 2000), p.131.
8. Senator Mitchell was originally asked to head an international body to report on the decommissioning issue. On 22 January 1996 it said that prior decommissioning would not happen but suggested that decommissioning could take place in parallel with political negotiations. It also set out a list of anti-violence statements – the 'Mitchell Principles' – that parties in the negotiations should accept.
9. F. Millar, *David Trimble: The Price of Peace* (Dublin: Liffey Press, 2004), pp.101–4.
10. Ibid., Chapter 3, 'Guns and Government'.
11. Ibid., p.76.
12. Ibid., p.172
13. Peter Mandelson interview, *The Guardian*, 13 March 2007.
14. Seamus Mallon interview, *The Guardian*, 14 March 2007.
15. David Trimble, interview by author, 22 May 2007.

Index